"The faculty of Mount St. Mary's Seminary & School of Theology has produced an outstanding collection of essays in honor of Archbishop Dennis Schnurr on the occasion of the fiftieth anniversary of his priestly ordination. While many theologians reflect on the diaconate and priesthood, these scholars offer useful insights into the identity of the bishop and importance of episcopal ministry in the life of the diocese. Archbishop Schnurr's commitment to the seminary, priestly vocations, governance and stewardship, building on the legacy of his predecessors, will have a lasting impact on the mission of evangelization for generations to come."

—Bishop Earl Fernandes,
Diocese of Columbus

"In its multifaceted, interdisciplinary study, the Athenaeum of Ohio's theological faculty rightly honors Archbishop Dennis Schnurr and his twenty-three years of episcopal ministry begun in the Diocese of Duluth and continued in the Archdiocese of Cincinnati. Every bishop should read this book. The Catholic faithful—both clergy and laity alike—will also do well to study it in order to appreciate all the more the bishops who in imitation of Christ crucified have laid down their lives in service."

—Joseph Carola, SJ,
Professor of Patristic Theology, Pontifical Gregorian University

"The recovery of a robustly episcopal focus at the heart of Catholic ecclesiology was one of the major contributions of twentieth century *ressourcement*, codified at Vatican II. In continuity with this important development, the present volume offers a highly pertinent reflection on the bishop's office at a significant moment in the theological and pastoral life of the post-conciliar Church. The quality and originality of this collection of nine essays makes a genuine contribution of doctrinal service to the universal Catholic communion and manifests the theological vitality of the local Church of Cincinnati, under the guidance of Archbishop Dennis Schnurr."

—Anthony Giambrone, OP,
Professor of New Testament, École biblique et archéologique française de Jérusalem

Antistite nostro: The Episcopal Ministry in the Life of the Local Church

Archbishop Dennis M. Schnurr

Antistite nostro: The Episcopal Ministry in the Life of the Local Church

Festschrift in Honor of Dennis M. Schnurr, Archbishop of Cincinnati

Edited by
RYAN T. RUIZ and DAVID J. ENDRES

Foreword by Timothy P. Broglio

WIPF & STOCK • Eugene, Oregon

ANTISTITE NOSTRO: THE EPISCOPAL MINISTRY IN THE LIFE OF THE LOCAL CHURCH
Festschrift in Honor of Dennis M. Schnurr, Archbishop of Cincinnati

Wipf & Stock
An Imprint of Wipf and Stock Publishers
199 W. 8th Ave., Suite 3
Eugene, OR 97401

www.wipfandstock.com

PAPERBACK ISBN: 979-8-3852-1768-7
HARDCOVER ISBN: 979-8-3852-1769-4
EBOOK ISBN: 979-8-3852-1770-0

VERSION NUMBER 072324

Portrait by artist Tim Langenderfer.

Contents

Contributors

All contributors are faculty members of the Athenaeum of Ohio/ Mount St. Mary's Seminary & School of Theology, Cincinnati, Ohio.

Anthony R. Brausch is president of the Athenaeum of Ohio and rector of Mount St. Mary's Seminary. He is a priest of the Archdiocese of Cincinnati and earned both a licentiate and doctorate in philosophy from the Pontifical Gregorian University in Rome. He serves as a consultor to the Holy See's Dicastery for the Clergy.

David J. Endres serves as academic dean of the Athenaeum of Ohio and professor of church history and historical theology. A priest of the Archdiocese of Cincinnati, he holds a doctoral degree from the Catholic University of America and is editor of the scholarly quarterly *U.S. Catholic Historian*.

Matthew C. Genung is associate professor and the Ruth J. and Robert A. Conway Foundation Chair in Biblical Studies. He holds a doctorate and licentiate in Sacred Scripture from the Pontifical Biblical Institute in Rome.

Tracy W. Jamison, an ordained deacon of the Archdiocese of Cincinnati, is professor of philosophy. He earned master's and doctoral degrees in philosophy from the University of Cincinnati.

Samuel B. Johnson is assistant professor of biblical studies. He earned both a master's of theological studies and a doctorate of philosophy from the University of Notre Dame.

Andrew J. Moss, a priest of the Diocese of Columbus, Ohio, is an instructor of canon law. He holds a licentiate in canon law from St. Paul University, Ottawa, Ontario.

Alan D. Mostrom, an assistant professor of systematic theology, earned a doctoral degree in theology from the University of Dayton.

Ryan T. Ruiz, a priest of the Archdiocese of Cincinnati, is dean of the School of Theology and associate professor of liturgy and sacraments. He received a doctorate in sacred liturgy from the Pontifical Liturgical Institute of Saint Anselm in Rome and serves as a consultant for the US bishops' Committee on Divine Worship.

Anthony J. Stoeppel, a priest of the Diocese of Tyler, Texas, is associate professor of pastoral theology. He earned both a doctorate and licentiate in sacred theology from the Pontifical University of the Holy Cross in Rome.

Foreword

The publication of a Festschrift marking the Most Reverend Dennis Schnurr's golden jubilee of priestly ordination strikes me as a singularly appropriate way to laud the ministry of this pastor. I am delighted to participate in the project by contributing this foreword.

Fifty-one years ago, as a new man at the North American College, I met Archbishop Schnurr, then a fourth-year student, a transitional deacon, known already for his acumen in temporal affairs. Our paths crossed again when he served at the apostolic nunciature in Washington, DC, while I was in direct service to the Holy See in Africa. I witnessed from afar his monumental work as general secretary of the National Conference of Catholic Bishops (now, the United States Conference of Catholic Bishops) to ensure that the conference staff was clearly at the service of the pastors of the church. Now, of course, we are brother bishops and he is the metropolitan of the ecclesiastical province in which is found my home diocese of Cleveland.

In these pages you will find a scholarly examination of the three *munera* that constitute the mission of a successor of the apostles in his diocese. It is an appropriate way to honor the twenty-three years that Archbishop Schnurr has exercised episcopal ministry, first in Duluth and now in Cincinnati. What better way to celebrate an anniversary than to deepen our understanding of the church and the service that must characterize it? What more appropriate way to honor a devoted archbishop than by considering at a high level episcopal ministry as it is exercised locally, regionally, and nationally?

In 2001 when he and I were ordained bishops, the conciliar vision of episcopal office was certainly well defined and lived in a certain way. However, much has evolved in those years, and we find ourselves still as shepherds but also attentive to the advice of the legal profession, sensitive to the new opportunities to preach the Gospel, eager to heal wounds from the past, and ever more conscious of an increasingly global society. It seems to me that the authors of this tribute have taken to heart the importance of a strong biblical and patristic foundation for episcopal ministry along with an awareness of its lived experience in our times. Theologians and scholars offer their contributions to enriching our appreciation for the role of the bishop, and the whole church can rejoice in this unique gift.

It is a weighty role to serve as the vicar of Christ for a portion of the people of God.[1] The bishop must be concerned first and foremost about the salvation of those entrusted to his care. He must foster vocations, which the Archdiocese of Cincinnati has done very successfully and to which the excellent seminary Mount St. Mary's of the West contributes, assuring the formation of candidates for the archdiocese, but also for many other dioceses that avail themselves of the program.

In the United States, the bishop is also charged with the management of the temporal affairs of the diocese. He is tasked to ensure that the patrimony continues to advance the mission of preaching the Gospel, providing the sacraments, caring for the aged and infirm, and meeting a host of other social needs so pressing in these times. It is the bishop who ensures the care of the poor, called by St. Lawrence, deacon and martyr of Rome, the true treasures of the Church.[2]

The fathers of the Second Vatican Council wrote about how the contributions of one bishop enrich the whole church: "It is true that by governing well their own Church as a portion of the universal Church, they themselves are effectively contributing to the welfare of the whole Mystical Body, which is also the body of the Churches."[3]

There are many more facets to this ecclesial service. One that also comes to mind, because it is now one of my pressing concerns, is participation in the activity of the national conference of bishops. Archbishop Schnurr has served the conference in many ways, first as associate and then general secretary. Later, as a bishop, he chaired a number of committees and is considered a resource for so many practical questions that the US bishops must face. I have often treasured his counsel and his memory of the recent history of the conference.

He took to heart the teaching of *Apostolos Suos*, the document on the nature of the episcopal conference, published in 1998. There the importance and necessity of the body was emphasized, but its nature and relationship with the individual bishop was also specified. Those distinctions are always important and help in effective governance.

1. Second Vatican Council, *Lumen Gentium*, sec. 27.
2. Guéranger, *Liturgical Year*, 302.
3. Second Vatican Council, *Lumen Gentium*, sec. 23.

Allow me to add my voice of heartfelt congratulations to my brother Dennis as he marks the golden jubilee of his sacerdotal ministry. *Ad multos Annos!*

The Most Reverend Timothy P. Broglio, JCD
Archbishop for the Military Services, USA
President of the United States Conference of Catholic Bishops

BIBLIOGRAPHY

Guéranger, Prosper. *The Liturgical Year: Time after Pentecost, Book IV*. Translated by the Benedictines of Stanbrook Abbey. Fitzwilliam, NH: Loreto, 2000.

Second Vatican Council. *Lumen Gentium*. The Holy See, Nov 21, 1964. https://www.vatican.va/archive/hist_councils/ii_vatican_council/documents/vat-ii_const_19641121_lumen-gentium_en.html.

Preface

In a sermon delivered on the anniversary of his episcopal ordination, St. Augustine offered the following reflection:

> The day I became a bishop, a burden was laid on my shoulders for which it will be no easy task to render an account. The honors I receive are for me an ever present cause of uneasiness. Indeed, it terrifies me to think that I could take more pleasure in the honor attached to my office, which is where its danger lies, than in your salvation, which ought to be its fruit. This is why being set above you fills me with alarm, whereas being with you gives me comfort. Danger lies in the first; salvation in the second.[1]

Although stark and sober, these comments highlight a beautiful reality about the episcopal office, namely, that the bishop ideally stands as a man willing to sacrifice everything—even the greater security of his own salvation—for the spiritual and temporal welfare of his flock. With his pastoral staff in hand, the bishop, like the watchman spoken of in Ezek 33:1–7, stands "on a height for all his life to help" his flock,[2] either pulling the sheep with the crook of his staff from the dangers lurking around them or prodding them with the end of his staff to safe pastures. The bishop does this not to satisfy mere contractual obligation, but to fulfill the full force of charity, directly imitating the Good Shepherd who nourishes his flock with his very self in the Sacrament of Charity, the Eucharist.

The impact that the bishop has on the life of his diocese is direct and immediate. Following the reflections of St. Cyprian, the third-century bishop of Carthage, we are reminded of the fact that "the bishop is in the Church, and the Church is in the bishop; and those who are not with the bishop are

1. Augustine, "Sermo CCCXL," 1414.
2. Gregory the Great, "Homilia XI," 1365.

not in the Church."[3] The reason for this is that the bishop contains within himself the fullness of the three *munera*—or offices—of Christ. The bishop is the first and principal *sacerdos* of his diocese: "When the bishop is present, it is he who celebrates the eucharist; the priests concelebrate with him. It is he also who presides at the rites of initiation."[4] The bishop is also the primary teacher of his local church, instructing his people as any successor of the apostles should. Thus, "just as there is only one altar so there is only one *cathedra*," representing the teaching office of the *episcopus*.[5] Finally, the bishop is the chief shepherd, or ruler, of the flock: "He lives very close to his people, consults his presbyters on important matters, and even seeks the consensus of the people. But he is dependent on no one. He is the head of the community."[6] Thus, the priestly, prophetic, and kingly offices of Christ are manifested in one man who stands as a bridge builder—*pontifex*—for the clergy and people of his diocese. The purpose of this Festschrift, then, is to honor a bishop whose priestly, prophetic, and kingly approaches to his episcopal office have borne great fruit for the churches entrusted to his pastoral care for over twenty-three years of ministry as bishop and archbishop.

Dennis Marion Schnurr was born on June 21, 1948, in Sheldon, Iowa, the son of Edward and Eleanor Schnurr. Having grown up in Hospers, Iowa, Dennis Schnurr discerned his priestly vocation in that small, tight-knit rural community, and was subsequently ordained a priest for the Diocese of Sioux City on July 20, 1974. Following his first pastoral assignment in his diocese, Father Schnurr was then sent for further studies at the Catholic University of America. After earning his doctorate in canon law, Father Schnurr returned to the Diocese of Sioux City to begin service as chancellor and in other key roles, before being assigned to serve at the apostolic nunciature in Washington, DC.

In 1989 Father Schnurr was appointed associate general secretary of the then National Conference of Catholic Bishops (now, the United States Conference of Catholic Bishops) and succeeded as general secretary of the conference in 1994. After successfully organizing the events surrounding the 1993 World Youth Day in Denver, Colorado, Father Schnurr was named a prelate of honor by Pope St. John Paul II. Monsignor Schnurr was then appointed the eighth bishop of Duluth, Minnesota, on January 18, 2001, and was ordained on April 2 of that year. On October 11, 2008, Pope Benedict

3. Cyprian: "Unde scire debes episcopum in ecclesia esse et ecclesiam in episcopo; et si qui cum episcopo non sint, in ecclesia non esse," quoted in Botte, "Collegiate Character," 78.

4. Botte, "Collegiate Character," 79–80.

5. Botte, "Collegiate Character," 80.

6. Botte, "Collegiate Character," 83.

XVI named Bishop Schnurr coadjutor archbishop of Cincinnati. Upon Pope Benedict's acceptance of Archbishop Daniel Pilarczyk's resignation on December 21, 2009, Archbishop Schnurr succeeded as the tenth bishop and ninth archbishop of Cincinnati.

In all his varied assignments, first as priest and then as bishop, Archbishop Schnurr has amplified the ecclesiological richness of the Catholic Church, forging stronger bonds of communion between the universal and local church. This, to be clear, is the duty of any diocesan bishop. While the ultimate point of reference for ecclesial communion is the supreme pontiff, the ministry of the local bishop—the *antistite*, or high priest, as he is entitled in the Roman Canon—is meant to afford the clergy and faithful of a particular locale the surety of knowing that they are grafted onto the whole. In an interview given after his reception of the pallium—the small, woolen-banded vestment given by the pope to metropolitan archbishops to mark their jurisdiction and their communion with the Petrine See—Archbishop Schnurr noted that "no matter how effective the bishop may be in his diocese, he can't lose sight of the fact that it's part of the universal church. Being part of the universal church is not just part of the truth of the church, it's the way our living out of the gospel is accomplished. It can't be accomplished in any other way."[7]

This Festschrift is the fruit of an expressed desire on the part of the contributors—all of whom have benefited from the episcopal ministry of this particular *antistite*—to thank Archbishop Schnurr for having taken up the burden of the apostolic office for so many years. However, the aim of the Festschrift is not so much to offer a panegyric for the present holder of the office, but to praise the office in general. The collected essays approach the question of the episcopal ministry from the perspective of the church's rich theological tradition, and aim to enlighten both clergy and laity alike about the ministry of their respective bishops, as well as to encourage bishops themselves in the exercise of their own sacred office. The structure of this collection follows the three *munera* of the episcopal—and, by extension, presbyteral—office: the *munus sanctificandi*, the office of sanctifying; the *munus docendi*, the office of teaching; and the *munus regendi*, the office of ruling.

The present work would not have come to fruition without the support of Father Anthony R. Brausch, the rector and president of Mount St. Mary's Seminary & School of Theology (the Athenaeum of Ohio), who had the initial inspiration to produce this Festschrift. As such, it is quite appropriate that the introductory essay be furnished by him. Father Brausch's

7. Schnurr, "Interview with Archbishop Dennis Schnurr," para. 8.

essay takes a unique approach to the episcopal *munera* through the lens of both the Johannine corpus and modern and contemporary philosophy. In particular, he examines the opposition or "hate" faced by those consecrated by Christ to continue his mission in the world. The biblical opposition faced by the first apostles, and the philosophical strain of opposition faced by the current successors to the apostles, finds resolution in the *Logos*, so long as the world (*kosmos*) allows itself to be relativized in its light.

The first section of this Festschrift leads us in a reflection on the *munus sanctificandi*, or the priestly office of the bishop. Father Ryan Ruiz's contribution to this study examines the ecclesiological significance of the bishop's name as it is articulated in the eucharistic prayer of the Mass. This ancient practice of inserting the names of the church's chief shepherds in the midst of the great prayer of the liturgy provides an opportunity to reflect on the essential marks that make the church "one, holy, catholic, and apostolic." The contribution of Father Andrew Moss, analyzing the bishop's role as the regulator of concelebration in his own diocese, is a timely treatment of a liturgical practice that arose with renewed vigor after the promulgation of *Sacrosanctum Concilium* but that has also been a source of ongoing debate—and some tension—in some dioceses since then. His essay, thus, encourages the bishop to be vigilant regarding his role according to the norm of law to regulate concelebration in his local church.

The treatment of the teaching office of the bishop—the *munus docendi*—begins with Alan Mostrom's essay that brings systematic theology in dialogue with its biblical and patristic interlocutors. This essay aims to recover the typological connection between the Levitical priesthood and the Catholic priesthood, which, in turn, provides insights into the teaching office of the hierarchic order. From the ambit of philosophy, Deacon Tracy Jamison approaches the topic of the bishop's role as teacher of the supernatural deposit of faith from the perspective of the dialectical model of Aristotle. His essay makes clear the pivotal role played by the bishop as the primary participant in the teaching ministry of the Lord in the local church. Samuel Johnson's essay returns focus to our scriptural inheritance. He uses the biblical image of the throne—evoking an inference to its liturgical corollary, the *cathedra*—to reflect on how the early church, much like her Jewish ancestors, understood her corporate identity through individual figures who embodied an entire people. Thus, the classic "one and the many" dichotomy leads the reader to reflect on the paschal mystery of Christ and the church's participation in that mystery.

The final section of this Festschrift, dealing with the *munus regendi*, provides the reader a sense of the historical, practical, canonical, and biblical. Father David Endres's treatment of Archbishop William Henry

Elder—Archbishop Schnurr's predecessor by over a hundred years, whose tenure as archbishop of Cincinnati sought to restore trust in the local church following a catastrophic financial scandal—provides a sketch of an indefatigable "watchman" whose perseverance through a particularly trying time ultimately set that diocese on firmer foundations. Father Anthony Stoeppel's practically-minded essay on the diocesan bishop's role as administrator of, and collaborator with, his flock, will resonate with bishops and, by analogy, parish priests, who might see the "burden" of pastoral ministry most often found in their attempts to lead their people in a shared vision of the church's mission. This section also presents a biblically inspired reflection by Matthew Genung on the bishop's role in forming the ethos of a people and building the kingdom of God here on earth. His essay analyzes Luke 22:29–30, the pericope where the Lord installs the apostles on thrones to judge the twelve tribes of Israel. However, he contextualizes this authority by way of the hermeneutic of *diakonia*, and specifically that of the table fellowship established in the Lord's own passion, death, and resurrection.

Since the art of teaching, studying, writing, and learning is not done in a vacuum, we hope that the work represented here exemplifies the excellence found in the entire faculty, staff, and student body of Mount St. Mary's Seminary & School of Theology, an institution that aims to provide bishops throughout the country with the collaborators needed to fulfill the mission of Christ in their dioceses. This collection of essays reflects the gratitude of one group of scholars for the local bishop who has provided them the resources needed to do the important work of forming individuals in the splendor of truth.

Many other individuals have helped with this project and provided invaluable assistance in preparing the manuscript for publication. A special note of gratitude goes to Melanie Suer, who helped proofread the document and provided invaluable assistance in preparing the manuscript for publication. Also, we are indebted to our peers in the academy who generously reviewed these essays and provided important insights and suggestions to help make them strong contributions to this collection. Finally, we are grateful to Archbishop Timothy P. Broglio for his willingness to provide the foreword. Archbishop Broglio has exercised his own priestly and episcopal ministry in an exemplary way throughout the world, first in service to the Holy See as diplomat and apostolic nuncio, and now to our armed service personnel as archbishop for military services and to our national church as president of the United States Conference of Catholic Bishops. Thus, if anyone could provide a keen insight into the reality of local churches across the globe, and the bishops who are called to lead them, it would be Archbishop Broglio.

As St. Augustine reflected, the bishop carries a heavy burden. However, this burden is made lighter by the fact that the one who carries it does so in charity for the salvation of those entrusted to his care. May the reader reflect well on the life and ministry of his or her own bishop, and be drawn more deeply into the mystery of Christ's Mystical Body, where all have an important part to play, but ultimately find guidance in the visible head of the local body that leads us to greater communion with the invisible and supreme head of the body—our Lord and Savior, Jesus Christ.

Ryan T. Ruiz and David J. Endres
Coeditors

BIBLIOGRAPHY

Augustine. "Sermo CCCXL, in die ordinationis suæ." In *Liturgy of the Hours: Ordinary Time Weeks 18–34*, translated by the International Commission on English in the Liturgy, 4:1414–25. Office of Readings, September 19. New York: Catholic Book Publishing, 1975.

Botte, Bernard. "Collegiate Character of the Presbyterate and Episcopate." In *The Sacrament of Holy Orders: Some Papers and Discussions Concerning Holy Orders at a Session of the Centre de Pastorale Liturgique, 1955*, 75–97. Collegeville, MN: Liturgical, 1962.

Gregory the Great. "Homilia XI." In *Liturgy of the Hours: Ordinary Time Weeks 18–34*, translated by the International Commission on English in the Liturgy, 4:1365-66. Office of Readings, September 3. New York: Catholic Book Publishing, 1975.

Schnurr, Dennis M. "Interview with Archbishop Dennis Schnurr." Interview by John L. Allen Jr. *National Catholic Reporter*, Jun 29, 2010. https://www.ncronline.org/blogs/ncr-today/interview-archbishop-dennis-schnurr.

Introduction: The *Episcopus*

Witness to the *Logos* and the Ordering of Reality

—Anthony R. Brausch

The exercise of episcopal ministry has never been easy. If we include Jesus within this lineage as its source and principle, the difficulties begin with his own preaching and mission. And it is probably safe to assume that the growing sense of anxiety in the hearts of the apostles was not lessened when Jesus informed them on the night before his passion, "If the world [*kosmos*] hates you, realize that it hated me first. If you belonged to the world, the world would love its own; but because you do not belong to the world, and I have chosen you out of the world, the world hates you" (John 15:18–19).[1] If they were not aware of it before, the apostles now had every reason to suspect that whatever the Lord was calling them to share in would not be easy.

Early Christianity, especially the lives of the Twelve and St. Paul, gives ample testimony to the difficulties and dangers associated with preaching the Gospel and professing Jesus as Christ and Savior. Practically all the New Testament Epistles provide insight into anticipated difficulties: oppositions from outside the church provoked by preaching the Gospel and criticism and divisions within occasioned by that same preaching and the exercise of authority (shepherding). However, also consistent throughout the canonical Epistles is the witness to a confidence and joy in the midst of exercising the apostolic *diakonia* (service). A possible source for these consolations (besides the outpouring of the Spirit itself) is to be found in the risen Lord's rehabilitation of Peter for his ministry: the thrice repeated question, "do you

1. Greek text is from Nestle-Aland, *Greek-English New Testament*.

love me?" and the threefold missioning of Peter, "feed my lambs," "tend my sheep," "feed my sheep" (John 21:15–17).

Distinct from the indwelling of the Spirit, but related to it, is the confidence grounded in being called and sent: that is, the surety that the mission and the work are not of one's own inspiration and creation, nor motivated by self-promotion and personal gain. The joy also is not simply the individual's, but the Lord's and, by extension and participation, that of the church. It is the experience of seeing life in the Spirit grow in the Lord's flock through the ministry of the church. As grave as the difficulties and challenges may be, it is not the Lord's intention that his disciples be miserable. Weighed down perhaps, but not joyless.

The opposition, the hate, spoken of by Jesus to the apostles, raises, at a minimum, the question as to why this is so. According to the Lord, being chosen "out of the world" and identified with him as his friend is the necessary and sufficient condition to becoming the object of the "world's" hate and rejection. What is the content of this "hate," and what is it about being chosen "out of the world" that provokes it so? If some light can be shed on this, then perhaps the shape and content of the joy within the exercise of the apostolic ministry will also be seen more clearly.

This analysis of the *episcopus* (bishop) as one who identifies with the Lord and not the world and, therefore, suffers the world's rejection, will move along these lines: First, the antagonistic structure between Christ and the world (*kosmos*) entails deep ontological and epistemological commitments. Because each—Jesus and the *kosmos*—makes claims on the totality of what is, taking a stance on one side or the other necessarily entails implicitly professing a structure of being itself. Second, ontological and epistemological commitments reveal themselves or are enacted *ontically*, in practical, historical phenomena. Third, in order to understand the world's hate, it is necessary to deduce from some phenomena the ontic presentation and its underlying ontological structure.

To do this, we will first view the ontic presentation of the oppositional structure in relation to the *munera* of the episcopal office. The justification for this is that the world's "hate" is not provoked simply because of what the apostles profess, but what they do: the active carrying out of the mission into which the Lord consecrated them. In this light, it is the act of teaching, the work of sanctifying, and the organization of the nascent kingdom of God into a visible society that is the provocation itself. This, in turn, provides an indication as to the possible structure of the *ontic* or practical manifestation of its opposition. The ontological form, or the universal structure, is embedded in John's Gospel and will be explored through a few key terms used in the Johannine pericope. It will then be possible to take a look at the ontological commitments motivating the practical forms of the world's hate in opposition to the *munera*. This will be done by highlighting the philosophical currents from which the practical forms take their substance. These currents will help make clear what is at stake and how they work to undermine not simply the exercise of the *munera* but the very grounds upon which their intelligibility is founded.

THE "WORLD" PROVOKED

As witnessed to by the early church, "feeding" and "tending" is at once a practical, spiritual, and theological undertaking. All three *munera* are likewise practical, spiritual, and theological in their exercise. Many bishops would attest that it is the practical side of the exercise of the *munus regendi* that occupies the bulk of their time and accounts for most of their experienced difficulties and worries. The *munus sanctificandi* and the *munus docendi*, on the other hand, are the chief source of their joy and consolation. Although the language of the *triplex munera* is a recent development in the church's reflection on the ordained ministry,[2] there is a parallelism here between the threefold charge to Peter and this contemporary articulation of the office. The "feeding" and "tending" that is to shape the life of the bishop today is readily recognized in the activities of teaching, sanctifying, and governing.

But the exercise of the *munera*, as practiced in the church, would not seem sufficient to provoke, let alone account for, the world's "hate" as attested to by Jesus. Certainly, it is more comprehensible as a feature of those times when belief in the influence of worship on the actions of the gods was widely accepted and the political and national interests were understood as being closely tied to the favor or disfavor of the deities. This is the understanding of reality that prompted attacks against the Christian faith in its earliest centuries and, in answer to those attacks, motivated St. Augustine's reasoned response in his *City of God*.

But things should be different today. One would expect that in an era such as ours where there is absolutely no temptation to think, either outside or inside the church, that serious consequences follow from approaching the divine in the wrong way, there would be few who would object to the exercise of the episcopal ministry.[3] In the contemporary perspective, the church and her bishops operate as a flawed—perhaps seriously

2. See Nichols, *Holy Order*, 126–30.

3. This is not a question as to *how* the ministry is exercised, for which there is no lack of critics either outside or inside the church. Rather, it is an objection based on *that* it is exercised at all.

misguided—nongovernmental organization (NGO) whose time is past and whose influence cannot be reduced quickly enough to a historical footnote. Objectively speaking, it would seem there are no longer any real grounds for this "hate," but this is not what is experienced. For even if the *munera* are exercised in such a way as to make clear the church's intention not to overstep the limits imposed upon her, culturally or legally, the world seems to remain interested in and intent on opposing what the church teaches and defends, even within the circumscribed area of her recognized and accepted competence. For all that the church has to say about promoting the good of humanity and society, the "world" still seems to resent the church's voice, even in the midst of a secular, diversity-celebrating public square. What is the reason for this? And, if so, is it simply the ancient challenges in contemporary guise? Or is there something new at work, something that requires the chief shepherds' vigilance and response?

There is, in fact, something new afoot. While, as will be seen, the same antagonism between the *kosmos* and Christ remains, it has not simply taken on a new guise. Rather, it has picked up new instruments highly adapted to undermining the very understanding of reality necessary for the reception of the Gospel message and the ministrations of the church. These new instruments are the result of the present confluence of three related, pretheological—that is, philosophical and cultural—developments: the deconstruction of language, the relativization of history, and the totalization of personal agency. Individually, each is powerful enough in its own right. Taken together, they are something entirely new within the context of human culture and understanding, for they are embraced as the means through which the full emancipation of humanity from its past forms of consciousness and naturalistic determinisms can be affected. As such, they may very well constitute the *nihilism* of which Nietzsche warned (or perhaps welcomed?).[4]

To give these new instruments a practical form, another parallel may be suggested, one that works on the side of the Gospel's rejection and gives shape to the world's "hate" for the church's witness. Whereas the parallel between Jesus's threefold charge to Peter—a charge touching profoundly on his threefold denial—may be seen to be reflected in the tripartite ministry shaping the apostolic mission, its opposing parallel touches profoundly on the denial of the very ontological/epistemological grounds upon which that ministry is exercised.

The structure of the parallel, then, looks like this: (a) *Munus docendi*, the deconstruction of language as the absurdity of the transcendent; (b)

4. Cf. Nietzsche, *Will to Power*, 12–15.

Munus sanctificandi, the absolute historical contingency of the sign as the banality of the sacramental; and (c) *Munus regendi*, the power of personal agency as ground of subjectivity and community.

The parallel is not simply a convenient way to organize the current challenges to the church's ministry but rather the three *munera*, individually and taken together, reflect commitments on an ontologically and epistemologically deep level, deep enough, in fact, to determine the shape of humanity's understanding of itself within Being as well as the possibility of meaning on an existential level. They are *ontic*—phenomenal expressions, including the reality of "making present in truth"—of *ontological* realities—structures of being and meaning within which humanity is conscious of itself as existing. If the challenge to the *munera* is also directed at this same level of fundamentality, then the rejection by the world of the commitments sustaining the intelligibility of the exercise of the *munera* necessarily entails commitments to a structure of reality and knowledge equally as deep and all-determining.

In order to place the challenges within their proper context, that is, in the light of Jesus's articulation of the antagonism between himself and the world, it is necessary for a clearer understanding of the structure of this antagonism. This will be found within its Johannine framework.

THE JOHANNINE FRAMEWORK

A very serviceable framework for considering the present challenges is readily discernible in the Johannine literature. The Word enters creation and history in a finite, human form: "For God so loved the world [τον κόσμον] that he gave his only Son" (John 3:16). The "world's" response is rejection and "hate." The Word made flesh, now resurrected, missions the apostles to make his life present to the whole world in the Spirit through word and sacrament, which takes concrete form in the *munera* of the office into which they have been called and consecrated. The "world's" opposition takes its concrete shape in direct response to the *munera* themselves.

While there are a number of ways in which the present challenges to the ministry may be approached and an adequate background provided, the Johannine literature has the advantage of being very clear as to both the existence of the opposition and the language by which it is described. This allows us to set the stage with just three key terms from the Fourth Gospel: μισεῖν (*misein*, hate), κόσμος (*kosmos*, world/universe), and λόγος (*logos*, word). Filling out the concept of *misein* will ensure that we are not inflating its content and overextending its significance. The background to *kosmos* will help clarify in what sense it can be considered as the actor or subject of this stance of "hating." And exploring, albeit only partially, the theological weight of the term *logos* will allow an appreciation for what the term carries into the Johannine usage as to its uniqueness as well as its possible ontological/epistemological implications.

Μισεῖν (*Misein*, Hate): The World's Hate

The term used in John 15:18 is *misein*. In the Septuagint (LXX),[5] the term is used in reference to several relational structures: hate between brothers, God's hatred of idolatry and evil, the hatred of God and the righteous by the ungodly, and the hatred of the righteous for the ungodly. The content of *misein* is both relational and theological; the "hate" of the ungodly for the righteous and the righteous for the ungodly is not "primarily a passion of the human heart."[6] On one hand, it is the "passionate disowning in faith of the evil or the evil person who God Himself has rejected," and on the other, it is "a sign of the rejection and obduracy" of the one who consciously transgresses the commandments and ignores the divine will.[7] In both cases, it is a matter of will and deed resulting in rejection and separation from the other. This distancing makes concrete the intention or stance vis-à-vis the other of not being identified with or complicit in the objective form of existing chosen by the other. And so, on the part of the righteous, it serves so as to remove one from the possibility of contamination. On the part of the ungodly, it serves to remove oneself from the context of judgment, either explicitly expressed or implicit in the presence of the righteous, or the presence of the divine.

In both cases, the "hate" which is expressed is nested within an overall structure of value and meaning whose content is determined by its relation to the divine will. So, while it is certainly a personal stance vis-à-vis the divine, invoked within that stance is the acceptance or rejection of the divine will and, implicitly, the structure of reality as decreed in that will. In the Old Testament, however, there is not a sense of the world itself or the *kosmos* as a whole being at odds with its divine author. Despite its disordered nature and the presence of sin, the full picture of the oppositional structure only

5. References to the Septuagint (hereafter LXX) are from Rahlfs and Hanhart, *Septuaginta*.

6. Michel, "μισέω," 4:683–94.

7. "One hates God by consciously transgressing His commandments, ignoring His will, and mocking and persecuting the righteous. Hatred of God is thus a sign of rejection and obduracy." Michel, "μισέω," 4:687.

comes to light in the New Testament, specifically in the Pauline and Johannine literature.

Put to use in both John's Gospel and his Epistles, *misein* is a primary carrier of the weight of the sustained Johannine thematic of the present time as *krisis*,[8] i.e., judgment; a judgment inaugurated with the incarnation of the Word.[9] Never far from the mind of the evangelist is the absolute and necessary division and tension between one's acceptance of Jesus as the revelation of God and one's rejection of him. The rejection of the person of Jesus and his truth is made clear through the polarities of love and hate, truth and falsehood, light and darkness—themes that structure the whole of John's presentation from the very beginning.[10] J. Painter offers that this reflects an overall comprehensive view of reality. One in which

> the understanding of God as creator of all things is held in tension with a recognition of the reality of the power of evil that is opposed to God and seeks to frustrate God's purpose. Human life is lived between God and evil, light and darkness, truth and falsehood, love and hate/murder. Although the present world is God's creation it is dominated by the power of evil. However, it will not remain, because God has ordained an end to evil.[11]

For the evangelist, rejecting Christ is to love one's own works, which are evil, and to prefer the darkness (John 3:19). Far from the evangelist's mind is any hint that the decision is one of merely subjective, private appropriation—in a modern sense—of self-affirmed aspects of the relationality to truth, nor is there any type of gradualism that would allow for a half-hearted or "lukewarm" stance vis-à-vis the incarnate Word (cf. 1 John

8. Büchsel, "κρίνω," 933–54, esp. 941: "In Jn. *krisis* is the world judgment of Christ, originally future, 5:28f and 1 Jn. 4:17, but also present already, 3:18–21; 5:24f., 30; 12:31; 16:11."

9. See Painter, *1, 2, and 3 John*, 64–74, for a discussion of common authorship and current scholarly consensus. For our purposes here, it is not necessary to take into account whether the author of the Gospel and Epistles is common or several since the language and themes are recognized as being closely aligned. See also Brown, *Epistles of John*, 19–35, esp. 20. Although Brown works from the hypothesis that there is a common author for the Epistles and argues to a different author for the Gospel, he begins his exposition by accepting the position of B. H. Skeeter, namely, "the three Epistles and the Gospel of John are so closely allied in diction, style, and general outlook that the burden of proof lies with the person who would deny their common authorship."

10. Painter offers, "One of the most striking shared perspectives between the Gospel and the Epistles is summed up by the term 'dualism'—between light and darkness, truth and error/falsehood, God and devil, love and hate. These polarities determine the view of reality expressed in the writings." Painter, *1, 2, and 3 John*, 61.

11. Painter, *1, 2, and 3 John*, 61–74.

4:2–6). Rather, throughout the Gospel, the Epistles, and into Revelation, the intensification of the antagonism is so striking and energized that it is more readily understood as an all-encompassing either/or. In terms of the Gospel, Otto Michel sums this up succinctly:

> The contrast between ἀγαπᾶν/μισεῖν reaches a climax in Johannine thinking. The divine movement of love (ἀγάπη) here too comes into conflict with the cosmic movement of hate (μῖσος). Both are so exclusive and comprehensive that they disclose the nature of God and the world. In its hate of the world for God, for Christ, for the disciples, and for the community, lies true sin and murder. Light is here differentiated from darkness.[12]

And for 1 John:

> To hate the brethren is to live in the sphere of darkness rather than the light (1 Jn 2:9, 11; 3:15; 4:20). The epistle does not show how this hatred finds expression. What is meant, however, is that a power of darkness determines the relation to the brethren. Hate becomes a demonic metaphysical power.[13]

From this quick exploration of John's appreciation for the world's "hate," it is possible to obtain a first sounding of its depths. It is not an emotional or passion-based rejection on the part of the individual nonbeliever, but a fundamental stance in the face of the reality that is revealed and should be recognized in Christ. In touching on the demonic and metaphysical, the biblical sense of this "hate" points also toward the possibility of an ordered or organized resistance to the divine will, a resistance for which the individual person is not only a primary subject or agent but also for which he or she is a participant, either willingly or unwittingly.[14]

Κόσμος (*Kosmos*, World/Universe)

The earliest definitions attached to the term *kosmos* carry the meaning of order and structure.[15] For instance, when Homer describes what the Greeks have built in order to deceive the defenders of Troy, it is in *hippou kosmon*, the structure of a horse. But *kosmos* is also used in reference to various

12. Michel, "μισέω," 4:691.

13. Michel, "μισέω," 4:691.

14. Both the Old Testament and New Testament give ample evidence of these two possibilities—from the Levitical treatment of sins committed unknowingly to Christ's naming of Peter as Satan.

15. The following is taken mainly from Sasse, "κόσμος," 3:868–98.

types of orderings of groups of men as well as communal life overall. For the Greeks, however, that which is well-ordered or well-structured carries with it also the significance of beauty or comeliness. And so at the same time, also in Homer, it is used to signify "adornment." In this sense, its reference is to women, the adornment of temples and other structures, as well as to cultic actions. The ideas of order and adornment merge then and find expression in conceptions of "world," "cosmic order," "universe," and "heaven"[16]—all collections or entities ordered on the most expansive scale.

Hermann Sasse summarizes the term's origins:

> The κόσμος—sometimes διάκοσμος . . . is in the first instance the order whereby the sum of individual things is gathered into a totality. In other words, it is the cosmic system in the sense of the cosmic order. Only later does κόσμος come to denote the totality which is held together by this order, i.e., the world in a spatial sense, the cosmic system in the sense of the universe.[17]

The attributes that come to characterize the idea of *kosmos* are those of unity, integration, and beauty. Another attribute that comes to be associated with the notion is that of the harmony between the various levels of *kosmoi*. Although the pre-Socratics understand the interactions of the levels of the various orders in different ways, "in each and every case we find the same underlying conviction that there is a deep natural relation between the cosmos of the world, the cosmos of human society, and the cosmos of man."[18]

As the term is taken up in the LXX, it is employed in both senses—adornment and order—but, at first, is not used in the sense of "the all" or "universe" or "world." The "heavens and the earth" (Gen 1:1) is the typical Hebraic expression that comes directly into the Greek. It is with Hellenistic writers, under the influence of common Greek usage, that *kosmos* comes to be employed in the sense of "world" (cf. Wis 9:9 and 2 Macc 8:18). Sasse offers, "In the history of the word κόσμος there is no more incisive event than its adoption into the vocabulary of the LXX. From this point on we have to reckon with a biblical as well as a philosophical concept."[19]

In the New Testament, the use of *kosmos* shows a decisive and near-total suppression of the term in the sense of order and adornment. In only one instance does it mean adornment (1 Pet 3:3).[20] There are none in the

16. Sasse, "κόσμος," 3:869.
17. Sasse, "κόσμος," 3:870.
18. Sasse, "κόσμος," 3:874.
19. Sasse, "κόσμος," 3:880.
20. First Peter 3:3: "Your adornment [*kosmos*] should not be an external one: braiding the hair, wearing gold jewelry, or dressing in fine clothes."

sense of order or ordering. All other instances of *kosmos* carry the significance of "world" in some sense. In the whole of the New Testament, more than half of its uses are found in the Johannine literature.[21]

Within the New Testament usage, it is possible to see a developing sense of the term while still retaining its basic structure of meaning. Literally, it is employed for the universe and the sum of all created being. But, brought into the light of the Christ event, it is now understood, definitively, as transitory and passing away. Sasse tells us that "the linguistic sense of the early Church does not allow it to use this term for the eternal world of eschatological hope" precisely because the present time and *kosmos* are transitory.[22] Although transitory by nature, the *kosmos* is still the area of God's activity and is still inhabited by a humanity in need of God's saving action and presence. Under the influence of early Christianity's concern for understanding and participating in God's saving work, *kosmos* takes on the shade of meaning related to this overall scope. Thus, "When the term no longer denotes merely the dwelling-place of man or the theatre of human history, but the setting of God's saving work then it takes on a new significance which is distinctive in the NT and for which there are not parallels either in the Greek world or in the Jewish."[23]

The appreciation that the *kosmos* is antagonistic to God's saving work comes into focus for the New Testament precisely because of the revelation of God's saving work in Jesus:

> Through the cross of Christ, says Paul in Gl. 6:14, the world is crucified to me and I to the world. Hence there arises the distinctive nuance which has ever after clung to the word κόσμος in the NT and the Church. The world is the epitome of unredeemed creation. It has become the enemy of God. It is the great obstacle to the Christian life.[24]

This is the background of the Johannine use of *kosmos*, the subject whose hate is directed toward the Christ and his disciples. John's usage is easily placed beside that of Paul's insistence that believers are not contending against "flesh and blood but with the principalities, with the powers, with the world rulers (*kosmo-kratoras*) of this present darkness, with the evil spirits in the heavens" (Eph 6:12). The reality of the *kosmos* then, only comes into full view when the light of Christ, the Word Incarnate, shines from

21. Sasse, "κόσμος," 3:883.

22. Sasse, "κόσμος," 3:885.

23. Sasse, "κόσμος," 3:889.

24. Sasse, "κόσμος," 3:893.

within it. It is only then that the depths of its fallenness, and all that that entails, is able to be perceived. This is important. There is no neutral place from within the *kosmos* from which to evaluate its truth. For John, there is no possibility of the "neutral observer."

Just as in the case of *misein*, for John there is the presence of a personified yet structural/universal rejection of the Christ. The focus for the "world's hate" is also of the nature of a personal and, at the same time, universal reality: the *Logos* made flesh.

Λόγος (*Logos*, Word)

Consideration of this term is strictly with its use in the Prologue. It will be seen how this specific instance can be reconciled with its prior uses as well as its deployment in the rest of the New Testament; however, it is important to note that the evangelist's employment of *logos* in John 1:1 is absolutely unique. At the same time, its uniqueness does not inhibit it from drawing other meanings to itself.

The earliest meanings that attach to the term developed alongside its verb form *legein*, "to say." In Homer, the verb has the meaning "to gather," "to collect," and then by extension, "to select" and "to enumerate." From here, the verb developed in the direction of also taking on the sense of a listing or narration of what has been gathered, as well as "to take account of." From these, "there arises the sense of 'consideration,' 'review,' 'evaluation,' [and] 'value.'" Along these lines then, "it is an easy step to the meanings 'reflection,' 'ground,' 'condition,' which became important in everyday use and in philosophy."[25]

Logos is used much more widely and in a great number of varied senses following the age of the great epics. In common usage, it supplants both the term that had been used to denote "spoken utterance" (*epos*) as well as the term for "meaningful statement" (*mythos*). *Logos* comes to be used for any given "word" as well as "rationally established and constructed speech," while *mythos* comes to denote "history."[26] Thus, while it takes on a more nuanced philosophical usage, it also comes to be more widely used for all types of speech. Hermann Kleinknecht points out that even as the word develops to cover a wide range of meanings and employments, "it should not be overlooked, however, that for the Greeks λόγος is very different from an address or a word of creative power. No matter how we construe it as

25. Debrunner, "Words λέγω, λόγος," 4:74.

26. Debrunner, "Words λέγω, λόγος," 4:74.

used by the Greeks, it stands in contrast to the 'Word' of the OT and NT."[27] To make clear the distinction, *logos* is not used to command or proclaim but is used in reference to something that is "displayed, clarified, recognized, and understood."[28] It is in this vein that it takes on the sense of an order and law within the cosmos and the world, an order that is intelligible. It is understood in the sense of a universal and not that of a particular moment or instance of speech. For Heraclitus,

> the same λόγος constitutes the being of both the cosmos and man, it is the connecting principle which forms the bridge and possibility of understanding 1. between man and world, and also between men, 2. between man and God, and finally in later antiquity 3. between this world and the world to come.[29]

In the philosophical and speculative domain of terms and meanings, *logos* is identified with intelligibility, rational power, nature, being, and norm. In one sense, it may be said to be the placeholder for all the concepts that circle around the structure, agency, and mystery of intelligibility and understanding, in both its bounded, contingent articulation in the human mind, as well as the eternal, necessary structure and movement of the celestial realms.

In the LXX, *logos* is used in a number of ways, but its most basic employment is to translate the Hebrew *dabar* ("word"). Interestingly, the root *dabar* and its etymology show a connection to the concepts related to "background," or "having a background" or "basis." The sense of this background is both conceptual as well as historical. Everything is known from its background, its history, and meaning. In this way, it is not limited in its meaning to the purely conceptual but to the conceptual as embedded in the narrative (history) of its relations, what is "behind" it as it is present now.

Theologically, *dabar* shows two related aspects, one which is dianoetic, related to *nous* (thought), and the other dynamic, related to power or energy. In its dianoetic aspect, *dabar* captures the relationship between the thing known and the knower inasmuch as the relationship is present in the word itself. "By its *dabar* a thing is known and becomes subject to thought."[30]

The dynamic aspect, though less evident, is more interesting since it brings to the fore the uniquely Hebraic sense of *logos*. Otto Procksch offers that, for the Hebraic understanding,

27. Kleinknecht, "Logos," 4:79.
28. Kleinknecht, "Logos," 4:80.
29. Kleinknecht, "Logos," 4:81.
30. Procksch, "Word of God," 4:92.

> every *dabar* is filled with power which can be manifested in the most diverse energies. This power is felt by the one who receives the word and takes it to himself. But it is present independently of this reception in the objective effects which the word has in history. The two elements, the dianoetic and the dynamic, may be seen most forcefully in the Word of God, and the prophets had a profound grasp of this from both sides, so that in this respect they are the teachers of all theology.[31]

This is much different from the Greek sense of the term, for "only in the Heb. *dabar* is the material concept with its energy felt so vitally in the verbal concept that the word appears as a material force which is always present and at work, which runs and has the power to make alive."[32] From this develops the moral sense of *dabar* (*logos*) inasmuch as the correspondence of the word to the thing or reality, fidelity to the background or history of the relation into which the word is now spoken, and that which is spoken into being with the word now spoken (with the power to shape the future) are all concentrated in the reality of "truth." "In every spoken word there should be a relation of truth between word and thing, and a relation of fidelity between the one who speaks and the one who hears. Hence the word belongs to the moral sphere, in which it must be a witness to something for the two persons concerned."[33]

There is one final aspect of the Septuagintal use of *logos* to mention before turning to John's Gospel. Throughout Ps 119, *nomos* (law) and *logos* (word) are used practically interchangeably. The Word of God is the Torah. It is both legal covenant and promise, and therefore carries the power and efficacy of God's relation with Israel (vv. 57, 58). The Word stands in heaven (v. 89) and its sum is truth (v. 160).[34] There is the explicit idea of the preexistence of the Torah and it being the source of life. The precepts, commandments, and word of the Lord are the source and summit of comfort and accompaniment. Meditation on them makes one wise (v. 98) and gives greater understanding than have the teachers or the aged (v. 99). Examples could be multiplied, but the *logos* is clearly a relational reality; it is an existential—*the* existential—structure of the life of the righteous man because it is the ground of reality and true understanding of the real.

31. Procksch, "Word of God," 4:92.

32. Procksch, "Word of God," 4:93.

33. Procksch, "Word of God," 4:93.

34. Cf. Procksch, "Word of God," 4:100. Verse 89 reads, "Εἰς τὸν αἰῶνα, κύριε, ὁ λόγος σου διαμένει ἐν τῷ οὐρανῷ." And verse 160, "ἀρχὴ τῶν λόγων σου ἀλήθεια."

It is well known that John's Gospel begins with a deliberate restating of the beginning of Genesis. What might not be as familiar is that the Prologue is the only time in the Gospels in which the construction ὁ λόγος (the Word) is used without an accompanying qualifier. Coupled with the imperfect of the verb "to be" ("In the beginning *was* the Word . . ."), this construction is distinguished from all other typical uses.

The familiar phrase "the word of the Lord" can be found in the Epistles (e.g., 1 Thess 4:15; 2 Thess 3:1), in Acts of the Apostles (e.g., 15:36), and in other pericopes. It is clear, however, that in these instances "the word of the Lord" references the saving message and actions of Jesus. Gerhard Kittel points out that at no point is there a temptation to incline toward the Old Testament dynamic in which the word of the Lord is spoken through the prophet as a message from outside the prophet for which he is now responsible.[35] Only Mark 2:2 betrays some of the possibly earliest thinking inasmuch as it relates that "he [Jesus] was preaching the word to them." But, as Kittel observes, "There is an unmistakable material tendency to regard Jesus Himself as the One who gives and is this Word, not only in His addresses, but in His whole earthly manifestation."[36] John 1:1 brings this tendency to both its material and theological culmination insofar as both are concretized, that is, made present in a finite, history-bound reality in this man, Jesus, the man John knows, follows, and loves.

It is at this point that the more speculative or philosophical overtones of the term *logos* are said to come into play, though in reality, they are not needed. Granted, John's use of the term in the Prologue does not absolutely exclude these overtones, and in the history of Christian theology, they are a rich source of reflection. But what John accomplishes is much more fundamental in its overall effects, theologically and ontologically.

First, John places the Word in the very place occupied by the Law. He does this by a threefold transposition: the summation of the Law and Prophets is the commandment to love God and neighbor; love is not an attribute of God, for God *is* love (1 John 4:8); and the Word of God "became flesh and dwelt among us." Through his use of *logos* in the Prologue, John picks up all the salvific content, power, and efficacy of the Torah, the Word of God in the LXX, and transfers it to the Word made flesh. "For the law was given through Moses; grace and truth through Jesus Christ" (John 1:17).

Second, it is to be emphasized that this is not the culmination of a growing realization in John followed by a conceptual universalization of the identity of Jesus with *logos*. We do not see here a theological process

35. Kittel, "Word and Speech," 4:113.

36. Kittel, "Word and Speech," 4:129.

resulting in either the personification of a concept (*logos*) nor the universalization of an individual. There will always be the temptation to read it in this vein, but that is to set aside John's firsthand, tactile experience and testimony to "what was from the beginning, what we have heard, what we have seen with our eyes, what we looked upon and touched with our hands, concerns the Word of life" (1 John 1:1). There is nothing speculative or philosophical about this for John. It is not a relationship to a concept but to a person. But that relationship is one of truth only from within the standpoint of love, a love to which one has surrendered oneself and is now all defining, in terms of his whole understanding and relation to the "world" and to "hate": "Do not love the world or the things of the world" (1 John 2:15) and if one hates his brother he necessarily still walks in darkness (1 John 2:8–9).

Third, although there is no reason to bring into our understanding of John's use of *logos* the metaphysical and speculative content of the Greeks, it is legitimate to see within John's use of the term a powerful conceptual field to draw to itself all previous positive uses and meanings. This is not because John's use is drawn from them but because John has posited the Word Incarnate as the principle of reality and relationality, whether material, conceptual, historical, or supra-historical. As such, the Word Incarnate is the absolutely unique form within the realm of intellectual and cultural history. However much previous myths and incarnational narratives played on similar themes, and to whatever extent philosophical insight and reason lay claim to illuminating the truth of humanity, empirical reality, and history, Jesus's claims and the scriptural witness insist they are all relativized in relation to him. Hans Urs von Balthasar states:

> This form (the Christ-form), to summarize, does not appear as something relatively unique, as might be said of the creations of the other great founders. Qualitatively set apart from them the Christ-form appears absolutely unique; but, on the basis of its own particular form the Christ-form relates to itself as the ultimate centre the relative uniqueness of all other forms and images of the world, whatever the realm they derive from. This relatedness of all myths and religious conceptions, indeed of everything in the world of man which can be and is an authentic revelation of God, to the centre of God's Incarnation necessarily has two sides: it is fulfilment through judgment.[37]

37. Balthasar, *Glory of the Lord*, 507.

JOHANNINE RESULTS

"Fulfilment through judgment" captures well the thrust of John's language. In this context, fulfillment does not simply mean something that was partial is now brought to completion. Rather, all understandings, concepts, relations, all structures and content through which man's life is lived, especially his history and future, are now seen as partial (judgment) and, at the same time, brought into relation—as partial and limited—to the whole in and through the *Logos* made flesh. In this, each of the terms plays its role well. *Kosmos* and *misein* show themselves capable of carrying more than the conceptual weight of their natural "material" meanings, for in the light of the *Logos*, they are now seen to be capable of true ontological significance. To employ a Heideggerian expression, they are now seen to be *existential* structures of being itself, though in its fallen condition.[38] As such, *kosmos* is all within created reality that refuses to be "relativized"—judged—by the light of the *Logos*. *Misein* is the commitment to that refusal.

And here we come to the crux of the matter: the *kosmos*, taken in its natural sense as "universe" or "totality," the whole of all that is, is the sphere in which all created beings find their place. It is the arena of time and space, of all that has been and will be and nothing lies outside of *its* relativizing power. Included in this are also the created, immaterial angelic spirits which also, inasmuch as they are not God, must choose whether to hand themselves over and thus allow themselves to be "relativized" in the light of the *Logos*. It is either this or they lay claim to a freedom and expression of being strictly their own and hold all other things relative to themselves. This is the structure of the great lie, spoken *en arche* (in the beginning) by the father of lies, "You will be like God . . ." (Gen 3:5).

The shape and content of the world's "hate" is its refusal to acknowledge the *fact* of a finite, contingent, historical event, that relativizes all else. The birth, life, and death of this individual, Jesus, as placed within the vast sweep of time and space along with an infinite sea of possible causal sequences that is the present of human freedom, meaning, and consciousness, cannot be accepted as the one fixed point and reality from which all else is and is true. The "world" is more than willing to love its own, that is, all partial truths, all relativized values, all that claim the truth as "mine." These know their place. The world even loves Jesus, as long as he is stripped of this one claim: "*I am* the way and the truth and the life. No one comes to the Father except through me" (John 14:6; emphasis added).[39]

38. Heidegger, *Being and Time*, 33.

39. The declaration *Dominus Iesus* by the Congregation for the Doctrine of the Faith is in direct reply to those positions within the church proposing to relativize this

PHILOSOPHICAL CURRENTS SHAPING THE PRACTICAL FORMS OF THE WORLD'S HATE

The practical forms of the world's "hate" given above can now be approached with a sense of what is at stake. But these practical forms will only rise to the level of something new, and perhaps unprecedented, if their particular challenges seek to impact ontology itself—that is, on the level of the structure of being—and the result undermines or directly opposes the structure of being and reality within which the exercise of the *munera* is intelligible.

Given in the order they will be treated, the practical forms are the absolute historical contingency of the sign as the banality of the sacramental; the power of personal agency as ground of subjectivity and community; and the deconstruction of language as the absurdity of the transcendent.

We will approach these forms from within the philosophical/cultural path marked out by Georg Wilhelm Friedrich Hegel and Karl Marx, Friedrich Nietzsche, Martin Heidegger, and Jacques Derrida.[40] In order not to get tangled in details of their systems, we will highlight just two features each philosopher shares: the importance of the negative, negation, or the "nothing" within their thinking, and the projected capacity of each to relativize the whole of human experience within their systems. All of them make clear the necessity for casting off the anthropological/cultural constructs built from within the Judeo-Christian *logos* tradition.

The Absolute Historical Contingency of the Sign

Thomas Stark, in his essay "The Historicity of Truth: On the Premises and Foundations of Walter Kasper's Theology," clearly lays out what the consequences are for Catholic theology if it entrusts itself to Hegel.[41] Kasper's early theology embraces aspects of the Hegelian understanding of history, but Kasper also recognizes that Hegel is the father of modern atheism.[42] What Hegel brings onto the scene is the all-encompassing dialectical pattern by which all development takes place, including reality-as-a-whole's

---

claim in light of some more universal principle.

40. An argument for direct causality from individual philosopher to cultural impact is not being made here. The influence of each of these thinkers is widely recognized, and their ideas are consequential. But the very fact that a way of thinking about the world and society comes to be recognized, disseminated, and then becomes influential already clouds the picture as to whether the philosopher (or theologian) is being descriptive, proscriptive, or prophetic as they express their thoughts publicly.

41. Stark, "Historicity of Truth," 69–100.

42. Kasper, *Jesus the Christ*, 182–85; Kasper, *God of Jesus Christ*, 28.

consciousness of itself as real, which it does through the growing consciousnesses of finite humanity. The emergence of human consciousness as both the microcosm of consciousness itself and its ever-greater universality (*Geist*) through the progression of dialectically structured transitory "moments" reveals the pattern for the whole. It is an ontology that sacrifices all ontic realities to its future, for at the heart of this famous dialectical pattern is the notion of the negative or negation.[43] Hegel's own organic example of this (which is also his most accessible) is that of the bud that gives way to the blossom and the blossom to the fruit. Along the developmental path, or progressive realization of the truth of the plant, each stage already carries within itself its self-negation.[44] Bud, blossom, and fruit are only "moments" along the progressive unfolding of the truth of the plant. None of the moments through which the progression moves are in themselves true. They are transitory moments making present the *phenomenon* of the whole. The "whole is the truth,"[45] and the "whole" is the process and the progress. On a practical level, this necessitates that progress must negate what came before; this negation, which is a type of "violence,"[46] motivates the movement of Being and its truth through its historically contingent expressions.

Within this framework, it is not possible for there to be any concrete, historical sign that does not come under this rubric. Thus, all "historical" events lose their significance inasmuch as they are relativized by the "now." No historical event can lay claim to establishing for subsequent generations truths or values that necessarily remain normative. Their "truth" is only known in their transitory relevance as the present perceives that truth to be.

The "violence" and negation Marx espoused takes a more material, practical form. He appropriates Hegel's dialectic and drops the sense of the transcendent from his understanding of reality. This liberates humanity from the tutelage of the universal and allows for materiality and *praxis* to be determinate for history and the structure of values. Material reality (expressed in basic material needs and desires) joins with *praxis* (the work and instruments through which those needs are actively met) and gives rise to the universal (the "truth" of what it means to be human at that moment in

43. Hegel, *Phenomenology of the Spirit*, 10.

44. The "self-negation" is on two levels, conceptually and ontically. Conceptually, the bud is only a bud *of* a blossom, meaning, by definition the idea of "bud" is found in what it is not, the plant (to which it belongs) and the blossom (toward which its existence as a bud is directed). Ontically, the bud ceases to exist or is negated by the emergence of the blossom.

45. "Das Wahre is das Ganze." German text as found in Hegel, *Fenomenologia dello Spirito*, 69.

46. Hegel, *Phenomenology of the Spirit*, 51.

history). A change in *praxis* or *materiality* necessarily produces a change in what is accepted as true. This applies to all aspects of human experience (e.g., family, politics, societal relations, morality). The ultimate universal toward which the whole process is driven is the emancipation of the human person from material need and want. The future, then, is a produced reality. The movement of this material dialectic is first through the slow development of labor, its instruments and its concomitant economic systems. But then, as the proletariat comes on the scene and becomes conscious of itself as the proletariat, the future will be consciously produced through revolution.[47]

The upshot of the Hegelian/Marxist reading of ontology and history is the deep conviction that only the active overturning of present structures—economic, societal, and cultural—is in accord with reason and in service to human freedom. Holding on to past forms, values, and signs is not simply meaningless, it is an active allegiance to structures of oppression and violence against the future.

The Power of Personal Agency as Ground of Subjectivity and Community

For the power of personal agency to serve as the ground for both subjectivity and community, two things are necessary. The first is the legitimation of the relocation of values to the person courageous enough to claim the power to create values. This Nietzsche supplies. And the second is an ontology that affirms the mystery of the "I" as embedded within the "we," while at the same time untethering it (the mystery) from any grounding other than being itself. This, Heidegger provides.

Nietzsche is well known as the prophet of the advent of the *übermensch* (the "overman"). The one who is a self-referential creator of values. The heralding of the *übermensch* is found in his celebrated *Thus Spake Zarathustra.*[48] Nietzsche sees the specter of true *nihilism* on the horizon, due almost entirely to the fact that the culture lacks the courage to face reality, the reality that humanity has always been the creator of its values and needs to be so now. To conceal or anesthetize oneself from this fact by professing a value structure it does not make operative in its actions and life is to court

47. The most accessible form of Marx's program is found in the *Manifesto of the Communist Party*, which Karl Marx and Friedrich Engels coauthored in 1848.

48. Nietzsche, *Thus Spake Zarathustra*, 35: "And Zarathustra spoke this to the people: 'I teach you the *overman*. Humankind is something that must be surpassed. What have you done to surpass humankind? . . . The *overman* is the meaning of the earth. Let your will say: the overman *shall be* the meaning of the earth."

nihilism and commit suicide.[49] For Nietzsche, it is apparent that the real life has gone out of the whole of the Judeo-Christian value structure and culture. But it lingers on and so invites meaninglessness. The *übermensch* is looked for, but its time is not yet. What is needed first, to clear the way, is the courage and will of the lion, the one with strength to reject and to say "no" to the whole construct.[50] Instead of saying "yes" to the will of God, now cast by Nietzsche as the "great dragon," the "spirit of the lion says, '*I* will.'"[51] Nietzsche's understanding of the transvaluing of values is as an exercise of the will, of human agency, an agency free enough to do so with no regard or thought for—positively or negatively—that which came before. The capacity for carrying out this revaluation of all values, which will be for humanity an opening of freedom and life, is within the "will to power" of humanity and only waits for those or the one strong enough to exercise it rightly.

Martin Heidegger's contribution to this trend goes well beyond his stated project in *Being and Time* (1927) of addressing the question of the meaning of being. For, in working up a completely new understanding of being's ontological structure and a lexicon for describing it, Heidegger succeeds in producing a compelling picture for how meaning, being, and time are structured for *Dasein* (existence). Yet, he does so while failing to provide any grounding for it.[52] Within his analytic of *Dasein*, Heidegger works through the various equiprimordial structures though which the being of *Dasein* has its being as *Dasein*. The descriptive language employed provides for great insight into how *Dasein* is structured dynamically by and for meaning. However, in the end, *Dasein* is completely dependent on its own resources for the purposefulness of its being. *Dasein* as "being-there"

49. Nietzsche, *Will to Power*, 45. Nietzsche's notes for a planned first book of the four-volume *The Will to Power* begins with, "What is dawning is the opposition of the world we revere and the world we live and are. So we can abolish either our reverence or ourselves. The latter constitutes nihilism."

50. Nietzsche, *Thus Spake Zarathustra*, 52: "To create new values—that even the lion cannot yet accomplish: but to create itself freedom for new creating—that can the might of the lion do. To create itself freedom and give a holy No even to duty: for that, my brothers, there is need of the lion." This is, of course, in contrast to the Lion of Judah, the Christ, who says, "Your will be done."

51. Nietzsche, *Thus Spake Zarathustra*, 52 (emphasis added). "Its last Lord it here seeks: hostile will it be to him, and to its last God: it will struggle with the great dragon for victory. What is the great dragon which the spirit is no longer inclined to call Lord and God? 'You will,' is the great dragon called. But the spirit of the lion says, 'I will.'"

52. Part of the reason for this is that the project, of which *Being in Time* was the first half, was never completed. Heidegger never really specified why he left it unfinished, but there is reason to believe it was because he became concerned that temporality was not sufficiently fundamental for the necessary grounding. Freedom seems to displace temporality. See Kisiel, "Drafts of 'Time and Being,'" 149–74.

is "thrown" into existence, but "from where" it is thrown is a mystery. It has its way of being as "being-toward-death," and that "toward which" is also mystery. But as the "being for whom being is a question,"[53] what opens up for *Dasein* in the center of its existence is its existence as possibility and as exposed to the abyss. From a later reflection of this, we can sense that being and thinking about being (philosophy) are in the uncanny position of being suspended over "no-thing" and perhaps the absolute void:

> What then is philosophy supposed to offer us? Immediately, nothing at all. We satisfy it well enough if we cast aside that misinterpretation and thereby surmise the abyssal character of beyng [sic] in beings—and we are prepared for philosophy if a mission of creativity, always remaining in the domain of creativity, strikes us.[54]

In straightforward terms, Heidegger provides a sophisticated ontology placing human freedom and creativity as the "happening" or "event-ing" of being and meaning.

The popularity and influence of both Nietzsche and Heidegger pushes into the circles of academia and the cultural intelligentsia an understanding that culture, value, human nature, and meaning are meant to be creatively emergent from humanity's own purposiveness, which comes from nowhere except its own agency. While they were not thinking on the level of the personal, subjective individual per se, the possibility, if not the necessity, of the absolutizing of subjectivity is already present. Because one's subjective being is, and is created, in one's own freedom and purposiveness, the only modality in which the voice or will of the "other" can be taken up is if this "other" is already predisposed to being folded into the subjective purposiveness of the one. Here there is no possibility of real *dia-logos*. The problematics opened up with this approach to being were soon recognized, and the philosophical efforts to both ground the existentiality of the subject as well as bridge the chasm between subjects shaped a great deal of mid-twentieth-century continental philosophy.[55]

53. Heidegger, *Being and Time*, 32.

54. Heidegger, *Ponderings*, 310.

55. Sartre, *Being and Nothingness*. Consider, for instance, the work Sartre does in *Being and Nothingness* to work through the structure of this bifurcation, especially the sections dealing with the existence of others and the body.

The Deconstruction of Language as the Absurdity of the Transcendent

The figure of Jacques Derrida stands in here as representative for the whole of a multifaceted, philosophically diverse, social, and cultural phenomenon often labeled "postmodernity." It has close ties with the structuralist movement, which sought to bypass the whole problem of the subject being at the center of the "world" by "decentering" the subject and seeing both subjectivity and meaning as derivatives of the structures that constitute the "world," i.e., structures of language, social, symbolic phenomena. Subsequently, "On this model, meaning was not the creation of the transparent intentions of an autonomous subject; the subject itself was constituted by its relations within language, so that subjectivity was seen as a social and linguistic construct."[56] Derrida stands in the line of the post-structuralist critics who agree with the decentering of subjectivity. But they believe a more radical reading and critique of Western metaphysics and language is needed if the binary structures of Western values and its social/political theory are to be *de-constructed*.[57] Ultimately, all these structures are language: written, verbal, sign or symbol, physical or psychical. Language constructs the "lifeworld" of consciousness, and *writing* (the total complex of sign and symbol) constructs the public space and the unconsciousness of the culture; the *written* is its articulation of value and meaning, and so it is to language that Derrida turns his efforts.

Derrida, under the tutelage of Nietzsche and Heidegger, recognizes the decay of the whole body of what is "Western," i.e., that which has been brought into presence through "technics and logocentric metaphysics for nearly three millennia."[58] The sign of this decay is "really its own *exhaustion*," and one of the symptoms betraying this exhaustion is the inflation of "language." Derrida has a specific, technical sense of what this means, but he also sees everyday cultural phenomena that confirm him in his diagnosis. The frantic manner in which society produces language and sign, and yet so quickly discards it, is not a sign of health and vigor but the indication that it is dying.[59]

Language now, instead of carrying significance and meaning, is the tool of political speech, propaganda, and marketing. It no longer has the

56. Best and Kellner, *Postmodern Theory*, 19.

57. Best and Kellner, *Postmodern Theory*, 22. The work of Nietzsche and Heidegger are foundational in this effort, "in particular, Nietzsche's attack on Western philosophy, combined with Heidegger's critique of metaphysics, led many philosophers to question the very framework and deep assumptions of philosophy and social theory."

58. Derrida, *Of Grammatology*, 8.

59. Derrida, *Of Grammatology*, 8.

ability to carry the transcendent and so is both used and heard almost exclusively as manipulation. It is "inflationary" in the strictest economic sense of being devalued from its own proliferation and from within its own value structure: "This inflation of the sign 'language' is the inflation of the sign itself, absolute inflation, inflation itself."[60] For Derrida, the *logos*-centric structure of the Western cultural heritage no longer has the structural stability to sustain itself. It is not the case that the transcendent or the *logos* was removed or no longer believed by *us*. This would be to still posit a type of substance-as-presence ontology and the distinction between signifier-signified. No, what Derrida maintains is that language itself, as structure and as moving through time (also structured by language), is what sustained the *logos*, and not the other way around.

Derrida acknowledges that we are caught within the structure of Western metaphysical language and you cannot invent a new language. It is the language we have to use. But its "historical *closure*" is discernible.[61] By being attentive and deconstructing the language from the inside, we are emancipated from the existing structures in the realization that underlying it all there is *nothing*. Humanity's efforts to wrap itself and its reality in language, sign, and culture are simply our own efforts to provide ourselves a habitable environment. Nothing more. And that environment—Western culture as whole with all its *logos-centric*, metaphysical baggage—is almost entirely formed by structures of dominance, violence, racism, and patriarchy. The deconstruction of language then, in the eyes of its practitioners, is the deconstruction of these structures.

CONCLUSION

We began by considering what could be the motive, content, and practical form of the world's "hate" about which Jesus forewarned his apostles, with the hope of gaining some insight into what places itself in opposition to the exercise of the episcopal ministry. The exploration of the three key terms from John—*misein*, *kosmos*, and *logos*—brought out into the open that professing Jesus as the Word Incarnate is, at the same time, to accept him as the center point of reality. Everything that is, is in relation to him and the historical fact of his existence. The antagonism then, waged throughout history in various forms, is between a *kosmos* that demands to relativize everything from within itself and the invitation of the Christ that all be seen in his light.

60. Derrida, *Of Grammatology*, 6.

61. Derrida, *Of Grammatology*, 14 (emphasis original).

It was then possible to consider the present forms this antagonism takes by drawing on three contemporary philosophical/cultural currents and placing them opposite the threefold *munera* of the episcopal office. The survey of these philosophical/cultural currents—the absoluteness of historical contingency, the primacy of personal agency, and the deconstruction of language—shows that all three prophesy and promote a complete rereading and undermining of the structure of being and discourse that shapes the Judeo-Christian heritage. Each in its own way recognizes and acknowledges that the Christ event is at the center of this cultural heritage. And each makes clear that they do not see a *logos*-centered future for humanity as a possibility. History is moving on, and progress is not on the side of the *logos*. But, even more, for those who take up this critique, *logoscentrism* carries within it—quite literally—all of the baggage and forms of violence and oppression associated with this history. Adherence to any form of it opposes freedom. From this perspective, it becomes a moral imperative to withstand it, to the point that it could be considered the highest form of moral responsibility to undermine and deconstruct its foundations: socially, theologically, and philosophically.

This, finally, brings us around to our original questions and allows us to perhaps understand, beyond its literal sense, another verse from John's Gospel, spoken by Jesus: "They will expel you from the synagogues; in fact, the hour is coming when everyone who kills you will think he is offering worship to God. They will do this because they have not known either the Father or me" (John 16:2–3). *The* issue—the true point of contention upon which all else rests—is the Word made flesh. Believing in the Divine *Logos* made flesh in the humanity of the historical person of Jesus is to place at the center of all being and meaning an immovable source, grounding, and end: the unique, noncontingent concrete hermeneutical principle of Being. "I am the way and the truth and the life" (John 14:6) holds not simply for certain domains of being (e.g., the spiritual) but for all of it, in particular and universally. And as the layers of that reality are explored and the mysteries plumbed, it is not the voiceless abyss of *nothingness* that is encountered but the personal address of love.

The *episcopus* is not simply the witness to a particular confessional commitment in the midst of the world and its history but a witness to the *logos* as the ordering principle of all that is, including each human person's personal experience of that reality and the structure of meaning within it. This is no easy thing and is fraught with danger. There is always the risk of inadvertently picking up the instruments of the *kosmos* and using them in the midst of the ministry and thereby providing a countersign. In that case, the Lord will ask the same question as he did of Peter: "Do you love me?"

And if the answer is the same as Peter's, then the Lord will respond, "Feed my sheep."

BIBLIOGRAPHY

Balthasar, Hans Urs von. *The Glory of the Lord: A Theological Aesthetics*. Vol. 1, *Seeing the Form*. San Francisco: Ignatius, 1989.

Best, Steven, and Douglas Kellner. *Postmodern Theory*. New York: Guilford, 1991.

Brown, Raymond E. *The Epistles of John*. The Anchor Bible Series 30. Garden City, NY: Doubleday, 1982.

Büchsel, Friedrich. "κρίνω." In *Theological Dictionary of the New Testament*, edited by Gerhard Kittel, translated by Geoffrey W. Bromiley, 3:933–54. Grand Rapids: Eerdmans, 1967.

Congregation for the Doctrine of the Faith. *Dominus Iesus*. The Holy See, Jun 16, 2000. https://www.vatican.va/roman_curia/congregations/cfaith/documents/rc_con_cfaith_doc_20000806_dominus-iesus_en.html.

Debrunner, Albert. "The Words λέγω, λόγος, ῥῆμα, λαλέω in the Greek World." In *Theological Dictionary of the New Testament*, edited by Gerhard Kittel, translated by Geoffrey W. Bromiley, 4:71–77. Grand Rapids: Eerdmans, 1967.

Derrida, Jacques. *Of Grammatology*. Translated by Gayatri Chakravorty Spivak. Baltimore: John Hopkins University Press, 1997.

Hegel, Georg. *Fenomenologia dello Spirito*. Milano: Bompiani Testi a Fronte, 2002.

———. *The Phenomenology of the Spirit*. Translated by A. V. Miller. New York: Oxford University Press, 1977.

Heidegger, Martin. *Being and Time*. Translated by John Macquarrie and Edward Robinson. Oxford: Blackwell, 2005.

———. *Ponderings II–VI: Black Notebooks 1931–1938*. Translated by Richard Rojcewicz. Bloomington: Indiana University Press, 2016.

Kasper, Walter. *The God of Jesus Christ*. New York: Crossroad, 1984.

———. *Jesus the Christ*. New York: Paulist, 1977.

Kisiel, Theodore. "The Drafts of 'Time and Being': Division III of Part One of *Being and Time* and Beyond." In *Division III of Heidegger's Being and Time: The Unanswered Question of Being*, edited by Lee Braver, 149–74. Boston: MIT Press, 2015.

Kittel, Gerhard. "Word and Speech in the New Testament." In *Theological Dictionary of the New Testament*, edited by Gerhard Kittel, translated by Geoffrey W. Bromiley, 4:100–143. Grand Rapids: Eerdmans, 1967.

Kleinknecht, Hermann. "The Logos in the Greek and Hellenistic World." In *Theological Dictionary of the New Testament*, edited by Gerhard Kittel, translated by Geoffrey W. Bromiley, 4:79–91. Grand Rapids: Eerdmans, 1967.

Michel, Otto. "μισέω." In *Theological Dictionary of the New Testament*, edited by Gerhard Kittel, translated by Geoffrey W. Bromiley, 4:683–94. Grand Rapids: Eerdmans, 1967.

Nestle, Eberhard, et al., eds. *Greek-English New Testament*. Stuttgart: Deutsche Bibelgesellschaft, 2012.

Nichols, Aidan. *Holy Order: Apostolic Priesthood from the New Testament to the Second Vatican Council*. Eugene, OR: Wipf & Stock, 2011.

Nietzsche, Friedrich. *Thus Spake Zarathustra*. Translated by Thomas Common. New York: Prometheus, 1993.

———. *The Will to Power*. Edited by Walter Kaufmann. New York: Vintage, 1968.

Painter, John. *1, 2, and 3 John*. Sacra Pagina. Edited by Daniel J. Harrington. Collegeville, MN: Liturgical, 2002.

Procksch, Otto. "The Word of God in the Old Testament." In *Theological Dictionary of the New Testament*, edited by Gerhard Kittel, translated by Geoffrey W. Bromiley, 4:91–100. Grand Rapids: Eerdmans, 1967.

Rahlfs, Alfred, and Robert Hanhart, eds. *Septuaginta*. Stuttgart: Deutsche Bibelgesellschaft, 2006.

Sartre, Jean-Paul. *Being and Nothingness*. Translated by Hazel Barnes. New York: Washington Square, 1972.

Sasse, Hermann. "κόσμος." In *Theological Dictionary of the New Testament*, edited by Gerhard Kittel, translated by Geoffrey W. Bromiley, 3:868–98. Grand Rapids: Eerdmans, 1967.

Stark, Thomas. "The Historicity of Truth: On the Premises and Foundations of Walter Kasper's Theology." In *The Faith Once for All Delivered: Doctrinal Authority in Catholic Theology*, edited by Kevin Flannery, 69–100. Steubenville, OH: Emmaus Academic, 2023.

Part I—*Munus Sanctificandi*

“Together with Dennis, Our Bishop”

The Bishop’s Name as a Sign of the Marks of the Church

—Ryan T. Ruiz

INTRODUCTION

THE FOUR IDENTIFYING MARKS of the church found in her Symbol of Faith—specifically the Niceno-Constantinopolitan Creed—unequivocally affirm the church’s status as “one, holy, catholic, and apostolic.” These marks, far from being self-appointed, are rooted in the very essence of the church by divine design. As the *Catechism of the Catholic Church* reminds us, “The Church does not possess them of herself; it is Christ who, through the Holy Spirit, makes his Church one, holy, catholic, and apostolic, and it is he who calls her to realize each of these qualities.”[1] It was this fact that led St. Augustine to declare that in the Catholic Church “there are many . . . things which most justly keep me in her bosom.” Expanding on this statement, the Doctor of Grace goes on to note exactly what those things are:

> The consent of peoples and nations keeps me in the Church; so does her authority, inaugurated by miracles, nourished by hope, enlarged by love, established by age. The succession of priests keeps me, beginning from the very seat of the Apostle Peter, to whom the Lord, after His resurrection, gave it in charge to feed His sheep, down to the present episcopate. And so, lastly, does the name itself of Catholic, which, not without reason, amid so many heresies, the Church has thus retained; so that, though all heretics wish to be called Catholics, yet when a stranger asks where the Catholic Church meets, no heretic will venture to

1. Catholic Church, *Catechism of the Catholic Church*, sec. 811.

> point to his own chapel or house. Such then in number and importance are the precious ties belonging to the Christian name which keep a believer in the Catholic Church.[2]

The purpose of this essay is to focus on a particular Christian's name, that of the bishop, and how this name serves to solidify the church's understanding of her identifying marks. Why is this important? A practical response is related to the nature of this present compendium: to honor a particular bishop who has faithfully served as "apostle" and "vicar of Christ" in the dioceses assigned to his pastoral care for upwards of twenty-three years.[3] However, a fuller response rests in the seemingly slow but steady erosion of two things in our contemporary context: identity and relationality.

Today the question of one's identity has come into heavy focus. With the push in many Western cultures to redefine certain constitutive realities of human society, a fluidity to one's sense of personal and corporate identity has become normative in the minds of many. As a bulwark against such constantly shifting realities is the name of a man who holds a particular office in a particular community that helps that particular community remember what it is in fact: a body of believers rooted in truth, united in love, and confident in mission.

Like identity, the question of relationality is equally important. The breakdown of the family in the West is not only a challenging pastoral issue but a societal one as well. Without knowing and appreciating to whom one belongs, one's ability to know oneself is compromised. In the ecclesial sphere, this is not just a matter of a flock not knowing and appreciating its bishop and its mission to build up the church in the local realm, but also of a bishop not knowing and appreciating his flock and his responsibility to them: "We are shepherds, and the shepherd listens and trembles not only at what is said to the shepherds but also at what is said to the sheep. . . . Because we are placed in charge, we are ranked among the shepherds, if we are good; but because we are Christians, we too are members of the flock with you."[4] What is more, the bishop, as the source of the local church's communion with the Roman Pontiff, provides an even higher level of relationality, helping to stave off St. Augustine's remark: "*Turpis est omnis pars universo suo non congruens*."[5] Thus, the articulation of the name of a man whose vocation

2. Augustine, *Contra epistolam Manichæi quam vacant*, 130.

3. Prior to being appointed archbishop of Cincinnati, Archbishop Schnurr served as bishop of Duluth (Minnesota) from 2001 to 2008.

4. Augustine, "Sermo 47," 423.

5. "For any part which is not consistent with its whole is unseemly." Augustine, *Confessions*, 65.

is to be spiritual father to a vast multitude is a corrective to a penchant for radical autonomy and individualism, connecting the individual members of the Mystical Body of Christ with the whole.

This essay will connect the liturgical and sacramental with the ecclesiological, seeking to deepen our appreciation of the role played by the bishop—or *antistite*, the word used in the Roman Canon to indicate the local pontiff as "high priest"—in establishing his local church as "one, holy, catholic, and apostolic." The first section of the essay will analyze the marks of the church individually, following insights given by Yves Congar,[6] and commented on by Aidan Nichols,[7] as well as those of Henri de Lubac[8] and Charles Journet,[9] explicating how these marks interact one with the other and contribute to the church's overall sense of mission and identity. The second section will reflect on the episcopal office and its relationship to the eucharistic sacrifice. Here insights from de Lubac and those who have analyzed his reflections, specifically Paul McPartlan,[10] will be employed. Points will also be taken from the liturgical record regarding the significance of the bishop's name being found in the eucharistic prayer, for which we will rely on the research of the learned Joseph Jungmann.[11] The conclusion of this essay will expound on the bishop's vocation and how, in his person and in his name, he symbolizes the characteristic marks of the church. This essay will limit its discussion of ecclesiological notions to how they pertain to the four marks, as well as limiting its review of the sacred liturgy to the placement of the bishop's name in the Eucharistic Prayer. Although the framework to engage this discussion is bound by a finite number of pages, our hope is to be both succinct and thorough in our analysis. While primary and secondary sources in their original languages will be used or cited when possible, authoritative English translations will be employed as needed.

APPROACHES TO THE MARKS

When we speak of the marks of the church, we speak of them in reference to the church as a whole, the Mystical Body of Christ. Here, it is important to keep in mind that the Mystical Body is a "*Corpus Christi mixtum*," a "mixed herd," a gathering of "wheat . . . with the straw, a field with tares growing

6. Congar, *L'Église*.
7. Nichols, *Figuring out the Church*.
8. De Lubac, *Splendor of the Church*. Also, de Lubac, *Catholicism*.
9. Journet, *Théologie de l'Église*; English translation: *Theology of the Church*.
10. McPartlan, *Eucharist Makes the Church*.
11. Jungmann, *Mass of the Roman Rite*.

in it . . . the ark which shelters clean and unclean animals," but still yet an "unspotted virgin, mother of saints, born on Calvary from the pierced side of Jesus."[12] These details are an aid to answer those who might go to great lengths to reveal the apparent imperfections in the church, something that would seemingly contradict her mark of holiness. Such critics might aim to point out something that the supreme shepherds of the church already readily admit: that the church in this temporal realm shows "the weakness of our human nature . . . that regrettable inclination to evil found in each individual, which its Divine Founder permits even at times in the most exalted members of His Mystical Body."[13] Pope Pius XII's prescient allusion to even "the most exalted members" of the church giving way to the "inclination to evil" would seem to be a particular offense against the church's constitutive holiness, as well as to her unity. The church, though, is not naïve. She recognizes that she lives in the City of Man and that she is engaged in a constant struggle against Satan: "Simon, Simon, behold Satan has demanded to sift all of you like wheat, but I have prayed that your own faith may not fail; and once you have turned back, you must strengthen your brothers" (Luke 22:31–32). The church is similarly aware, however, that the same society that "lives and painfully progresses in our poor world is the very same that will see God face to face."[14]

The Mystery of the Church: Eucharistic Presence and Hierarchic Order

In his work *Theology of the Church*, the Swiss theologian Charles Journet reflects on the diverse ages that either prefigured the church or served as the backdrop to the fulfillment of her divinely instituted mission.[15] In the "age of the Father," the grace of original innocence communicated directly by God to his creatures eventually gives way to another age in which "so glorious a Redeemer"—using the language of the *Exsultet*—was sent to rectify the *felix culpa*, thus inaugurating the "age of the Christ."[16] It was within this age of Christ that the Mystical Body of Christ, the church, was born. However, it is really in the succeeding age, the "age of the Spirit," where the church is

12. De Lubac, *Catholicism*, 69. For these reflections on the "*Corpus Christi mixtum*," de Lubac utilizes St. Hippolytus's *Elenchos*, bk. 9, ch. 12, as well as various writings from St. Augustine.

13. Pius XII, *Mystici Corporis Christi*, sec. 66.

14. De Lubac, *Catholicism*, 73.

15. Journet, *Théologie de l'Église*, 25–37.

16. Journet, *Théologie de l'Église*, 26–27.

most clearly operative. According to Cardinal Journet, the "age of the Spirit" is characterized by two essential elements related to Christ's Mystical Body: "The mystery of the eucharistic presence and the mystery of the institution of the hierarchy."[17] These two mysteries, instituted by Christ and infused by the Spirit, "leaves in our midst the mediation of the hierarchic powers and the sacramental rites," which prolongs Christ's "*sensible contact* with the whole world, and under the species of which he will send the fullness of grace and truth."[18]

When examining the mystery of hierarchic order, we find Journet identifying this reality as the proper cause of the church:

> The Father, Christ, the apostolic body composed of Peter and the apostles and empowered by the Holy Spirit (Acts 1:18), the people: such are the links in the chain revealed to us by the whole of the Gospels. . . . This extraordinary force, this spiritual power, which goes forth from God—having become, to a certain extent, visible through Jesus and continuing to be so through the apostolic body (whose members are constantly replaced as individuals, but which, nevertheless, subsists from one generation to the next as a unique living being), so that it can be called the virtue of apostolicity—is the proper cause of the Church, as fire is the proper cause of heat.[19]

The "mysterious" part to this equation is that "God could have acted alone" since he would have undoubtedly foreseen "well enough that, in having recourse to the ministry of men, he would all too often be badly served."[20]

17. Journet, *Théologie de l'Église*, 36: "Deux nouveaux mystères vont marquer l'avènement de l'âge de l'Esprit saint: le mystère de la présence eucharistique, et le mystère de l'institution de la hiérarchie." English translation: *Theology of the Church*, 24.

18. Journet, *Theology of the Church*, 25; *Théologie de l'Église*, 37: "Jésus va laisser au milieu de nous la médiation des pouvoirs hiérarchiques et des rites sacramentels qui prolongeront son *contact sensible* dans l'univers entier et sous les espèces desquels il enverra la plénitude de sa grâce et de sa vérité" (emphasis original).

19. Journet, *Theology of the Church*, 100; *Théologie de l'Église*, 120–21: "Le Père, le Christ, le corps apostolique composé de Pierre et des apôtres et revêtu de la force du Saint-Esprit (Act., 1, 8), le peuple: tels sont les anneaux d'une chaîne que tout l'Évangile dénonce. . . . Cette force extraordinaire, cette puissance spirituelle sortie de Dieu, devenue jusqu'à un certain point visible par Jésus et continuant de l'être par le corps apostolique (dont les membres sont constamment remplacés comme individus, mais qui néanmoins subsiste, comme un vivant unique, à travers les générations), en sorte qu'on peut l'appeler la vertu d'apostolicité, est la cause propre de l'Église, comme le feu est la cause propre de la chaleur."

20. Journet, *Theology of the Church*, 101; *Théologie de l'Église*, 121: "Voilà certes un grand mystère. Dieu pouvait agir tout seul. . . . Il prévoyait assez en recourant au ministère de l'homme, qu'il serait trop souvent mal servi."

The story of salvation history, thus, serves to remind us that God did *not* act alone, but invited imperfect actors to take part in the narrative, as coworkers in his vineyard.

In responding to this reality wherein Christ entrusted his message and mission to sinful men, Journet highlights two distinctive ways in which the Lord engaged his own ministry: occasionally at distance from those he was engaging, but more often by way of sensible contact. When reviewing the miracles recounted in the Gospels, one can note that our Lord occasionally performed these marvels without physical contact, and even often without close spatial proximity. One can recall the healing of the son of the royal official in John 4:46–54 and the curing of the centurion's servant in Matt 8:5–13 as two such examples.[21] However, it was more typical for Christ to engage his interlocutors and petitioners in a tangible way and with physical touch,[22] and it was through this preeminent means by which God communicated himself to man—via the tangible—that we find the true reason for the "mystery of the hierarchy." When Christ ascended to the Father,

> he willed that there would always be among us men endowed with divine powers, by which the action that he exercises from heaven could be sensibly transferred to us and continue to reach us in the manner that is most proper to our nature—by way of contact. These are the hierarchical powers: far from substituting for the action of Christ, they are subordinate to it in order to convey it, in a certain sense, across time and space.[23]

21. Journet, *Théologie de l'Église*, 123. Here Journet also notes the healing of the daughter of the Syrophoenician woman (Mark 7:24–30), and the curing of the ten lepers (Luke 17:11–19) as examples.

22. Journet, *Théologie de l'Église*, 123. Journet provides the following list of examples of Christ healing by way of "sensible contact": the touching of the leper (Mark 1:41); the commanding of the paralytic to rise and walk (Mark 2:11); the use of spittle to heal the sight of the man in Bethsaida (Mark 8:23–25); the touching of the eyes of the blind in Capernaum (Matt 9:29) and Jericho (Matt 20:34); the allowance of the woman with the hemorrhage to touch the hem of his garment (Luke 8:44); the touching of the stretcher carrying the dead man (Luke 7:14); taking the hand of Jairus's daughter (Luke 8:54); removing the stone from Lazarus's tomb (John 11:39); and the anointing of the blind man's eyes at Siloam with clay (John 9:6).

23. Journet, *Theology of the Church*, 105; *Théologie de l'Église*, 125: "Il a voulu qu'il y eût toujours, au milieu de nous, des hommes revêtus de pouvoirs divins, par lesquels l'action qu'il exerce du haut du ciel pourrait être conduite sensiblement jusqu'à nous et continuer de nous atteindre de la manière qui nous est le plus adaptée, par la voie d'un contact direct. Ce sont les pouvoirs hiérarchiques: loin de se substituer à l'action du Christ, ils se subordonnent à elle pour la véhiculer en quelque sorte à travers le temps et l'espace."

The role of the hierarchy as custodians of man's physical contact with God connects us with the other constitutive element of the Mystical Body of Christ, the Eucharist. When defining the church's "soul," the life force of her being, Journet points to the virtue of charity,[24] something that he notes is ultimately cultic since its efficacy is rooted in the sacrifice of Christ on the cross. Journet relates that "unlike the charity of the terrestrial paradise," Christian charity is "absolutely inseparable from Christian worship," since lacking it would be to lack the "reference to the redemptive act of Christ."[25] Journet makes the connection between the church, the virtue of charity, and the Eucharist all the more strong when he highlights the significance of the church, "formed around the Eucharist," as the "center of convergence of all the graces bestowed on the world," such that "if the Mystical Body were ever to disappear (which in reality is impossible), all graces would disappear at the same time."[26]

This present discussion serves as an entrée for how we can begin to reflect on the church—the Mystical Body of Christ, made sensible through the hierarchy and the Eucharist—as possessing the marks of unity, holiness, catholicity, and apostolicity. In one of his mystagogical homilies, St. Cyril of Jerusalem addresses neophytes in his church and reminds them of the Mystical Body to which they belong and, in so doing, advises them:

> If ever you are visiting in cities, do not ask simply where the Lord's house is (for the other sects of the profane also attempt to call their own dens houses of the Lord), nor merely where the church is, but where is the catholic church. For this is the peculiar name of this holy church, the mother of us all, which is the spouse of our Lord Jesus Christ, the only-begotten Son of God.[27]

24. Ultimately, though, there are two "souls," one that is uncreated—the Holy Spirit—and one that is rooted in the saving action of Christ—charity. See Journet, *Théologie de l'Église*, 193–94; *Theology of the Church*, 168–69.

25. Journet, *Theology of the Church*, 173; *Théologie de l'Église*, 198: "Une charité qui, à la différence par exemple de la charité du paradis terrestre, est, ici-bas, absolument inséparable du culte chrétien; supprimer le culte chrétien, supprimer la Messe ou les sacrements, ce serait, du même coup, supprimer la charité dans sa référence à l'acte rédempteur du Christ, ce serait supprimer la charité en tant que chrétienne."

26. Journet, *Theology of the Church*, 183; *Théologie de l'Église*, 209: "Dans l'économie chrétienne du salut, le Corps mystique, qui se forme autour de l'eucharistie, est lui-même le centre de convergence de toutes les grâces dispensées au monde, même des grâces sanctifiantes non sacramentelles, au point que, s'il venait par impossible à disparaître, toutes ces grâces disparaîtraient en même temps."

27. Cyril of Jerusalem, *Mystagogical Catechesis*, 18:26–27, quoted in di Berardino, *We Believe in One*, 69.

The direction St. Cyril offered these new Christians was essential: there is but one church of Christ, founded on the apostles, marked by holiness and destined for universal application. The way one can tell that he or she is in the right assembly is to be mindful of these marks.

Unity, Holiness, Catholicity, and Apostolicity

"The primordial feature of the Church of God" is the mark of unity—the church's "oneness."[28] The standard scriptural passage utilized to highlight this feature is Acts 2:42, which, when speaking of the church in the apostolic age, notes that the members of the church "devoted themselves to the teaching of the apostles and to the communal life, to the breaking of the bread and to the prayers." Commenting on Congar's treatment of this passage and how it relates to the unity of the church, Aidan Nichols highlights the three types of *vincula* (bonds) that connect the individual local churches, as well as individual members of those local churches, as one. The first is the *vinculum symbolicum*, or the bonding that is rooted in the common creed outlined in the Symbol of Faith. The second is the *vinculum liturgicum*, based on the "right worship" celebrated in the church throughout the world. The third is the *vinculum sociale* or the *vinculum hierarchicum*, that is, the ordering of the church under a common discipline and common pastors.[29] All three *vincula* are critical, but the fulcrum is found in the Eucharist, known firstly as the "Sacrament of Charity," but also associated with the Mystical Body as the "Sacrament of Unity."[30]

This sacrament, rooted in the *vinculum liturgicum*, in turn, helps to engage the church's second mark: holiness. The remarkable reality we encounter in the Eucharist is its being the supernatural food that transforms men into God: "With St. Augustine, they heard Christ say to them: 'I am your food, but instead of my being changed into you, it is you who shall be transformed into me.'"[31] It is this transformation by way of the eucharistic

28. Nichols, *Figuring out the Church*, 12.

29. Nichols, *Figuring out the Church*, 16–17. Cf. Congar, *L'Église*, 13–65, esp. 20.

30. See Congar, *L'Église*, 31. Here Cardinal Congar notes that "unanime, la Tradition affirme que l'Eucharistie est le sacrament de l'unité, que son effet spirituel est l'unité du Corps mystique." Further, in the footnote at the conclusion of this sentence, footnote 50, Congar cites a handful of other scholars, including Maurice de la Taille, A. M. Roguet, and Henri de Lubac, to reaffirm this point.

31. De Lubac, *Catholicism*, 99. In this section of his work, Cardinal de Lubac notes the gradual minimization that occurred from the medieval to the modern period wherein "the idea of the relationship between the physical body of Christ and his Mystical Body came to be forgotten."

sacrifice that particularly defines the church in her state of becoming the veritable "Bride of Christ," in place of her terrestrial status as the "Betrothed of Christ."[32] Following St. Thomas's insights, Cardinal Congar relates that the church's holiness is most clearly associated with her being the place where the worship God desires is rendered.[33]

Thus, one could say that the first two marks are somewhat ontologically determinate of the essence of the church: the church's unity and holiness identify what she is at the core of her being. If that is the case, the final two marks—the church's catholicity and apostolicity—could be the vehicles by which the essence of the church is most readily made known. We glean this insight from *Lumen Gentium*, which reminds us that "God . . . does not make men holy and save them merely as individuals, without bond or link between one another. Rather has it pleased Him to bring men together as one people, a people which acknowledges Him in truth and serves Him in holiness."[34] The church's oneness and holiness is revealed, then, by her "catholicity," where individuals from all walks of life are drawn together into union with Christ.

The church's catholicity is unique among the marks in that the actual word is not directly rooted in biblical language. We first encounter a direct correlation between the church and its "catholicity" in the *Epistulae* of St. Ignatius,[35] a series of documents that will also have great significance in our discussion on the episcopal office in the section that follows, and the *Martyrdom of St. Polycarp*.[36] Nichols highlights the scholarly debate about the

32. Nichols, *Figuring out the Church*, 53. On this page, Nichols comments on insights given by Louis Bouyer who highlights that the eschatological fulfillment of the church will only come to pass "in a future state . . . [at] the altar of the heavenly sanctuary." See Bouyer, *L'Église de Dieu*, 607.

33. Congar, *L'Église*, 127: "La première valeur que nous rencontrons dans l'affirmation de la sainteté de l'Église tient à ce qui fait, de cette Église, la chose *de Dieu*: élection, vocation, alliance, consécration, habitation; l'Église est le lieu où est rendu à Dieu le culte qu'il désire." Congar takes his insights from St. Thomas's *Expositio in Symbolum Apostolorum*, a. 9, where Aquinas gives four reasons for the holiness of the church: she is (1) consecrated by the blood of Christ, (2) anointed with the Holy Spirit, (3) the place where Divinity dwells, and (4) the place where Divinity is invoked.

34. Second Vatican Council, *Lumen Gentium*, sec. 9.

35. Ignatius of Antioch, "Letter to the Smyrnaeans," 248–61, esp. 254–55, sec. 8.2: "Wherever the bishop appears, there let the congregation be; just as wherever Jesus Christ is, there is the catholic church."

36. *Martyrdom of Polycarp*, 314–15, sec. 8.1; 324–25, sec. 16.2; 326–27, sec. 19.2. Other church fathers who contributed to the solidification of this mark in the church's understanding of herself include St. Irenaeus (*Adversus Haereses*, bk. 3, ch. 3, sec. 2), St. Clement of Alexandria (*Stromata*, bk. 7, ch. 17), and Tertullian (*De praescriptione haereticorum*, ch. 26, line 9; ch. 30, line 2; *Adversus Marcionem*, bk. 4, ch. 4). Cf. Congar,

nature of the *katholicos* and whether it is indicative of a qualitative aspect, that is, in the church's integrity as a corporate body, or a quantitative one, that is, in the church's engagement of her mission to spread the kingdom of God across the known world.[37] *Lumen Gentium*, for its part, provides a sense of both, seeing the church as the "visible sacrament of this saving unity" for all gathered together by God under Christ the Head, and that this "sacrament of unity" is "destined to extend to all regions of the earth" transcending "at once all times and all racial boundaries."[38] As St. Cyril of Jerusalem reminds us, "The Catholic Church is the distinctive name of this holy Church which is the mother of us all," as she "alone has a power without boundaries throughout the entire world."[39]

Of course, the means of demonstrating the church's unity and holiness—her catholicity—would be superfluous without her apostolicity. Cardinal Congar defines the church's apostolicity as "the property thanks to which the Church preserves across time the identity of her principles of unity as these were received from Christ in the persons of the apostles."[40] Nichols notes that while this mark certainly has a view to the past work of the Lord in founding the church on the apostles, it also has a future, eschatological outlook to "final salvation: the *ultimate* good God has in store for man."[41] "In this sense," Nichols further relates, "The purpose of apostolicity is to unite the Church's beginning to her last end. It is to assure the continuity of the saving revelation from the first, hidden, coming of Christ to his second and glorious coming."[42] St. Thomas speaks of the church's mark of "apostolicity" in terms of her *firmitas*, that is, "her permanence or solidity . . . teaching as she does the same doctrine as the apostles themselves."[43]

However, not only is this mark reflective of the church's continuity with apostolic doctrine—the deposit of faith—but also in the persons of

---

L'Église, 151.

37. Nichols, *Figuring out the Church*, 57.

38. Second Vatican Council, *Lumen Gentium*, sec. 9.

39. Cyril of Jerusalem, "Catechesis XVIII," 560.

40. Congar, *L'Église*, 181–82: "L'apostolicité est la propriété grâce à laquelle l'Église garde, à travers le temps, l'identité de ses principes d'unité tels qu'elle les a reçus du Christ en la personne des Apôtres." Translation from Nichols, *Figuring out the Church*, 74.

41. Nichols, *Figuring out the Church*, 74–75.

42. Nichols, *Figuring out the Church*, 75. Here Nichols credits his insights to the theological position of Orthodox bishop and theologian John Zizioulas in his essay entitled "Apostolic Continuity and Succession" found in Zizioulas's *Being as Communion*, 171–208.

43. Nichols, *Figuring out the Church*, 77, commenting on St. Thomas Aquinas's *In Symbolum apostolorum expositio*, a. 9.

the sacred ministers who, throughout history, have stood in place of the apostles in the local churches. Thus, the church's mark of apostolicity does not just preserve orthodox teaching, but also assures "true sacramental worship," thus securing "the entire confessional and liturgical structure of the Church as a whole."[44] Naturally, it is not merely a matter of the juridical appointment of one as a successor to the apostles that, by this fact alone, guarantees the purity of apostolic faith. Rather, it is the bishops joining together in a *collegium*, under the supreme governance of the successor of St. Peter, that establishes bonds of communion among the individual churches, with the two foci of this communion—the bishop on the local level and the pope on the universal level—as this reality's physical signs.

THE BISHOP: A SIGN OF THE MARKS

We can now begin to analyze how the church's "actual and visible reality" here on earth and her "invisible and final achievement" in heaven are brought together through these two *pontifici*, high priests and bridge builders of the *Domus Dei*.[45] The pontiff of the diocese—the bishop—is no mere chief executive officer or administrator of property and people, important as these functions may be; rather, he is, as noted in the section above, the source of ecclesial communion for the faithful living in his territory, connecting them to the universal church, both past and present. It is for this reason that bishops can be considered

> the more illustrious members of the Universal Church, for they are united by a very special bond to the divine Head of the whole Body and so are rightly called "principal parts of the members of the Lord"; moreover, as far as his own diocese is concerned, each one as a true Shepherd feeds the flock entrusted to him and rules it in the name of Christ.[46]

These men, though, are not independent contractors, but "subordinate to the lawful authority of the Roman Pontiff," while also "enjoying the ordinary power of jurisdiction which they receive directly from the same Supreme Pontiff" and "divinely appointed successors of the Apostles."[47]

This relationship between the successor of St. Peter and the successors of the apostles is most readily highlighted in the eucharistic prayer of the

44. Nichols, *Figuring out the Church*, 80.
45. De Lubac, *Catholicism*, 73.
46. Pius XII, *Mystici Corporis Christi*, sec. 42.
47. Pius XII, *Mystici Corporis Christi*, sec. 42.

Mass where the names of the two *pontifici* are articulated one after the other. As St. John Paul II taught, it would be "a great contradiction if the sacrament *par excellence* of the Church's unity [the Eucharist] were celebrated without true communion with the Bishop."[48] Similarly, since "'the Roman Pontiff, as the successor of Peter, is the perpetual and visible source and foundation of the unity of the Bishops and of the multitude of the faithful', communion with him is intrinsically required for the celebration of the Eucharistic Sacrifice."[49] Thus, in antiquity, and even to this day, the significance of hearing these two names mentioned in the great prayer of the Mass is the difference between communion or schism, orthodoxy or heresy. Much, then, can be found in these two proper names that the church includes whenever the eucharistic sacrifice is offered.

The Names of the Pope and Bishop in the Eucharistic Prayer

In both the Western and Eastern liturgical traditions, the naming of certain important personages in the eucharistic prayer had been a long-standing and significant custom. In the West, the acerbic St. Jerome, in a not-so-veiled critique of the common liturgical practice of his day, expressed concern regarding the public recitation of the names of living members of the church. St. Jerome's objection rested on the fact that those individuals often named in the liturgy had the means to contribute financially to the church's mission, thus creating the unfortunate scenario where the poor were shamed and the rich led into pride.[50] In the East, the practice to name certain deceased members of the church in the anaphora—not just the saints, but other important figures like past bishops—highlighted the significance of ecclesial communion as it endured into eternity. Sometimes, though, this created controversy, as when the name of St. John Chrysostom was at first *not* included, but then later included, in the anaphora of the Divine Liturgy in the fifth century.[51] Clearly, the "insertion or omission of a name," in the

48. John Paul II, *Ecclesia de Eucharistia*, sec. 39.

49. John Paul II, *Ecclesia de Eucharistia*, sec. 39.

50. Jerome, "Commentaria in Ezechielem," 175. Here St. Jerome comments on Ezek 18:5–9, where the prophet critiques those who act unjustly toward their neighbors. Jerome notes, "Publiceque [*sic*] diaconus in Ecclesiis recitet offerentium nomina: tantum offert illa, tantum ille pollicitus est, placentque sibi ad plausum populi, torquente eos conscientia. Damusque materiam miseris, ut gaudeant, ad ea quae tribuunt, et non lugeant ad ea quae rapuerint." Cf. Bishop, "Observations on the Liturgy of Narsai," 98.

51. In the somewhat volatile ecclesial and political landscape of the fourth and fifth centuries, the archbishop of Constantinople, Chrysostom, found himself falsely accused of both theological inaccuracies by the patriarch of Alexandria—Constantinople's

eucharistic prayer, could "cause a popular uproar . . . for the inclusion of a name in the diptychs indicated the attitude of the ecclesiastical community towards the person involved and its acknowledgement of his orthodoxy."[52]

Here, then, we find a kind of "theology of names" that came into focus early in the church's history. As Jungmann notes, the aforementioned diptychs were

> a sort of announcement book, which, because of their beautiful design, were presented as gifts by aristocratic peoples. In Church circles, they were used for a list of names, even if, as was often the case, they were of purely secular origin. The covers were often inlaid on the outside with plates of precious metal or ivory and adorned with sculptured ornaments.[53]

In the East, the use of the diptychs highlighted deceased members of the faithful, anywhere from the ranks of "patriarchs, prophets, apostles and martyrs," to the fathers of the first ecumenical councils, to prominent luminaries in the life of a local church.[54] Eventually, the inclusion of one's name on the diptychs became synonymous with canonization, and likewise, the removal of that name signified excommunication, hence the controversy with the initial lack of inclusion of St. John Chrysostom's name in the Eastern diptychs.[55] In the West, and specifically in the Roman Rite, the names of the living members of the church, in addition to the list of saints mentioned in the two commemorative sections of the Canon, were given prominence. Particularly the names of the pope and the local bishop were eventually highlighted, not so much in an ornate book, but in the action of the sacrifice of the Mass itself.

In the Roman Rite, the names of the reigning pope and bishop find themselves in the intercessory section of the eucharistic prayer. This section expresses "the fact that the Eucharist is celebrated in communion with the whole Church, of both heaven and of earth, and that the oblation is made for her and for all her members, living and dead."[56] In the First Eucharistic

ecclesiastical rival at the time—and political sabotage by the emperor's consort. Deposed of his see and dying in exile, John's name was not immediately inserted into the prayers for the dead of the Divine Liturgy, much to the uproar of his supporters. When his name was eventually added, there was then an outcry from an opposing camp, that is, those who questioned John's orthodoxy. See Bishop, "Observations on the Liturgy," 102–3.

52. Jungmann, *Mass of the Roman Rite*, 160.

53. Jungmann, *Mass of the Roman Rite*, 160.

54. Jungmann, *Mass of the Roman Rite*, 160.

55. Jungmann, *Mass of the Roman Rite*, 160.

56. Catholic Church, *General Instruction*, sec. 79c (hereafter *GIRM* and cited by

Prayer—the Roman Canon—the names of those "set in high places"[57] are noted almost immediately. After initiating the Canon with a blessing made over the offerings, the celebrant identifies those for whom the sacrifice is offered. In first place (*in primis*), the eucharistic sacrifice is offered for the entire church, which is then identified with the articulation of two of her four marks—"holy" and "catholic"—the second of which is further elucidated by the qualification that notes the church is spread throughout the known world (*toto orbe terrárum*).[58] In the other three principal eucharistic prayers, the intercessory section comes shortly after the "anamnesis" section, where the church recalls Christ's "blessed Passion, glorious Resurrection, and Ascension into heaven."[59] The conclusion of this anamnesis also includes a "communion epiclesis," where the church prays that all her members might benefit from the worthy reception of the sacrificial offerings.[60] The intercessions for the church as a whole, including her supreme pastor and local pastor by name, follow this communion epiclesis. We, thus, find a clear link between communion with the chief shepherds of the church—illustrating both the church's unity or "oneness" and her "apostolicity" through these present-day apostles who teach, sanctify, and govern the Mystical Body in the here and now—and communion with the Supreme Shepherd of the Sheep, the Lord himself.[61]

---

section number).

57. Aquinas, *Summa Theologiae*, III, q. 83, a. 4, resp. Here, St. Thomas is quoting from 1 Tim 2:2 where St. Paul directs prayers to be prayed for kings and all in authority, that they may lead quiet and peaceable lives.

58. Catholic Church, "Prex Eucharistica I," sec. 84: "In primis, quæ tibi offérimus pro Ecclésia tua sancta cathólica: quam pacificáre, custodíre, adunáre et régere dignéris toto orbe terrárum."

59. *GIRM*, 79e.

60. Jungmann, *Early Liturgy*, 218: "In each Mass, according to Christ's institution, there are two points where the divine omnipotence is conjoined to the action of the priest, thus causing a supernatural effect: the consecration and the communion. Hence it is very natural that in the priest's prayer some acknowledgment should be made of the fact that here God Himself has to act. And its natural form is a petition, a petition addressed to God, that He effect the consecration, that He sanctify our souls in communion. This petition we may call *epiclesis*, an invocation of God by which that effect is solicited. If the petition concerns the consecration we call it a consecration-*epiclesis*, if the communion, a communion-*epiclesis*."

61. Catholic Church, "Prex Eucharistica II, III, IV," secs. 105, 113, 122: **Prex Eucharistica II**—"Et súpplices deprecámur ut Córporis et Sánguinis Christi partícipes a Spíritu Sancto congregémur in unum. Recordáre, Dómine, Ecclésiæ tuæ toto orbe diffúsæ, ut eam in caritáte perfícias una cum Papa nostro N. et Epíscopo nostro N. et univérso clero" (cf. Catholic Church, *Roman Missal*: "Humbly we pray that, partaking of the Body and Blood of Christ, we may be gathered into one by the Holy Spirit. Remember, Lord, your Church, spread throughout the world and bring her to the

What the names of both the pope and bishop provide the church in this moment of the eucharistic sacrifice is a reaffirmation of all that makes the church *the* church. Cardinal de Lubac provides a rich synthesis of this when he references an important luminary of the liturgical movement's reflection on the matter: "To quote Fr. Louis Bouyer's blunt words (based on a formula of St. Ignatius of Antioch), 'an invisible Church is the same thing as no Church at all'; without the hierarchy, which is her point of crystallization, her organizer, and her guide, 'there can be no talk of the Church.'"[62] This reprises our earlier reflection of how the church's holiness and unity is framed by her catholicity and apostolicity. The notion of the *collegium episcoporum* reminds the individual bishop that he is not an autonomous overseer of a single church, but rather leads one that is grafted onto a much larger vine. St. Cyprian of Carthage related this well when he said of his fellow bishops:

> There are many bishops in the body; they are joined together by the cement of mutual concord and the bond of unity, so that if

fullness of charity, together with N. our Pope and N. our Bishop and all the clergy"). | **Prex Eucharistica III**—"Réspice, quǽsumus, in oblatiónem Ecclésiæ tuæ et, agnóscens Hóstiam, cuius voluísti immolatióne placári, concéde, ut qui Córpore et Sánguine Fílii tui refícimur, Spíritu eius Sancto repléti, unum corpus et unus spíritus inveniámur in Christo. . . . Hæc Hóstia nostræ reconciliatiónis profíciat, quǽsumus, Dómine, ad totíus mundi pacem atque salútem. Ecclésiam tuam, peregrinántem in terra, in fide et caritáte firmáre dignéris cum fámulo tuo Papa nostro N. et Epíscopo nostro N., cum episcopáli órdine et univérso clero et omni pópulo acquisitiónis tuæ" ("Look, we pray, upon the oblation of your Church and, recognizing the sacrificial Victim by whose death you willed to reconcile us to yourself, grant that we, who are nourished by the Body and Blood of your Son and filled with his Holy Spirit, may become one body, one spirit in Christ. . . . May this Sacrifice of our reconciliation, we pray, O Lord, advance the peace and salvation of all the world. Be pleased to confirm in faith and charity your pilgrim Church on earth, with your servant N. our Pope and N. our Bishop, the Order of Bishops, all the clergy, and the entire people you have gained for your own"). | **Prex Eucharistica IV**—"Réspice, Dómine, in Hóstiam, quam Ecclésiæ tuæ ipse parásti, et concéde benígnus ómnibus qui ex hoc uno pane participábunt et cálice, ut, in unum corpus a Sancto Spíritu congregáti in Christo hóstia viva perficiántur, ad laudem glóriæ tuæ. Nunc ergo, Dómine, ómnium recordáre, pro quibus tibi hanc oblatiónem offérimus: in primis fámuli tui, Papæ nostri N., Epíscopi nostri N. et Episcopórum órdinis univérsi, sed et totíus cleri, et offeréntium, et circumstántium, et cuncti pópuli tui, et ómnium, qui te quærunt corde sincéro" ("Look, O Lord, upon the Sacrifice which you yourself have provided for your Church, and grant in your loving kindness to all who partake of this one Bread and one Chalice that, gathered into one body by the Holy Spirit, they may truly become a living sacrifice in Christ to the praise of your glory. Therefore, Lord, remember now all for whom we offer this sacrifice: especially your servant N. our Pope, N. our Bishop, and the whole Order of Bishops, all the clergy, those who take part in this offering, those gathered here before you, your entire people, and all who seek you with a sincere heart").

62. De Lubac, *Splendor of the Church*, 88, quoting from Louis Bouyer in *Dieu Vivant*, 2:140.

> any one of our college attempts to frame a heresy, to wound and worry the flock of Christ, the others come to the rescue . . . for although we are many pastors, we feed the one flock, and we must gather together and care for all the sheep Christ won by his blood and passion.[63]

The fact that this very clear and obvious expression of communion is outlined in the church's great prayer is a key component to our understanding how the individual marks of the church coalesce in the eucharistic sacrifice.

"The Eucharist Makes the Church" and "the Church Makes the Eucharist"

In his reflection on the Mystical Body of Christ, Cardinal de Lubac observes, "The Church and the Eucharist make each other, every day, each by the other: the idea of the Church and the idea of the Eucharist must likewise be promoted and deepened each by the other."[64] Commenting on this, Paul McPartlan notes that "the *corpus mysticum*, which strictly is Christ's own glorified Body *in mysterio*, can by extension be the *ecclesial* Body of Christ, but only if this latter is being considered *precisely in her edification by the Eucharist*. Christ and the Spirit are at work in the Eucharist, forming the ecclesial Body, gathering the Church."[65]

However, if the Eucharist "makes the Church," the complementary principle to this reality is the fact that the church, in turn, "makes the Eucharist." It is for this reason that the priesthood was instituted.[66] Here we find a clear link to the church's mark of holiness. The universal call to holiness, highlighted in chapter 5 of *Lumen Gentium*,[67] ties the "one" to the "many," such that "the individuals who, each in his own state of life, tend

63. Cyprian of Carthage, *Epistula* 68, 3–4: "Copiosum corpus est sacerdotum concordiæ mutuæ glutino atque unitatis vinculo copulatum, ut si quis ex collegio nostro hæresim facere et gregem Christi lacerare et vastare temptaverit, subveniant ceteri qua pastores utiles et misericordes oves dominicas in gregem colligant. . . . Nam etsi pastores multi sumus, unum tamen gregem pascimus et oves universas quas Christus sanguine suo et passione quæsivit colligere et fovere debemus." Quoted in Botte, "Collegiate Character," 86–87.

64. De Lubac, *Corpus Mysticum*, 292–93, quoted in Paul McPartlan, *Eucharist Makes the Church*, 79.

65. McPartlan, *Eucharist Makes the Church*, 80 (emphasis original).

66. See de Lubac, *Splendor of the Church*, 133. Cf. McPartlan, *Eucharist Makes the Church*, 100.

67. See Second Vatican Council, *Lumen Gentium*, secs. 39–42.

to the perfection of love" help others "to grow in holiness."[68] Thus, in the Eucharist, the church highlights the varied occasions in which the faithful participate in their baptismal priesthood, offering sacrifice to God.[69] Nevertheless, de Lubac makes the necessary distinction between the baptismal priesthood and the ministerial priesthood: "the priesthood of the Christian people," although important, "is not concerned with the liturgical life of the Church, and it has no direct connection with the production of the Eucharist."[70] Rather,

> within the "holy nation," and for the purpose of making it holy, certain men are therefore "set aside" by a new consecration that is of a different order. They receive the imposition of hands, which has been handed down uninterruptedly from the first Apostles of our Lord, and hear in their turn the words that those Apostles heard: "Do this for a commemoration of me." It is the "hierarchic" Church that produces the Eucharist.[71]

The bishop as head of the local church, represents the holiness of his flock—both the baptismal priesthood of the faithful and the ministerial priesthood of the clergy—especially when they gather as one body. This is the insight of the *Ceremonial of Bishops* when it describes the bishop's "stational Mass." In this form of the liturgy, the "preeminent manifestation of the local Church is present when the bishop, as high priest of his flock, celebrates the eucharist and particularly when he celebrates in the cathedral, surrounded by his college of presbyters and by his ministers, and with the full, active participation of all God's holy people."[72] Here, the bishop serves as the focal point of the holy people gathered to worship God, and thus the bishop constitutes "the unity of his flock."[73] What's more, the bishop likewise represents the catholicity—as well as apostolicity—of the local church, since "each bishop is himself 'in peace and in communion' with all his brother bishops, who offer the same and unique sacrifice in other places

68. Second Vatican Council, *Lumen Gentium*, sec. 39.

69. For example, in *GIRM*, 54, we are told that the period of silence between the invitation to prayer ("let us pray") and the celebrant's chanting or reciting of the collect is designed to allow the faithful to place themselves in God's presence and to mentally gather their intentions to offer with those of the priest. Similarly, the Universal Prayer is envisioned almost entirely as a mechanism by which the faithful exercise "the office of their baptismal Priesthood" offering "prayers to God for the salvation of all" (*GIRM*, 69).

70. De Lubac, *Splendor of the Church*, 137.

71. De Lubac, *Splendor of the Church*, 137–38.

72. Catholic Church, *Ceremonial of Bishops*, 49, sec. 119.

73. De Lubac, *Splendor of the Church*, 149.

and make mention of him in their prayer as he makes mention of all of them in his."[74] Together, the local *antistite* and his brother bishops, members of the *collegium episcoporum*, form "one episcopate only and are all alike 'at peace and in communion' with the Bishop of Rome, who is Peter's successor and the visible bond of unity."[75]

CONCLUSION: THE IMPORTANCE OF A NAME

This essay has sought to reflect on how a particular aspect of the Mass, the eucharistic prayer, can deepen our understanding of the characteristic marks of the church as one, holy, catholic, and apostolic. The "oneness" and "apostolicity" of the church are rooted in the name of one man—the bishop—who, recognizing the mark of the church's "catholicity," joins himself to his brother bishops in communion with the supreme visible head of Christ's Mystical Body, the pope. Joined as one, and sharing in the "one Lord, one faith, one baptism" (Eph 4:5), the "holiness" of the church equally comes to the fore, bringing to fruition the great prayer of the great High Priest that we, his disciples, "may all be one" (John 17:21), and that we might be glorified and perfected (v. 22), and, thus, share in divine life (v. 24). The principal context in which we find exhibited the interplay between these four characteristic marks of the church is the Sacrament of Charity, the Eucharist. Whenever the name of the local successor of the apostles and the name of the universal successor of St. Peter are uttered, the former after the latter, we have a guarantee of standing in the midst of Christ's one, holy, catholic, and apostolic church.

As Cardinal Journet noted, the mystery of the church—composed as she is of these four essential marks—is ultimately rooted in the mystery of the Eucharist and the mystery of the hierarchic priesthood. It is within the divine drama of the eucharistic sacrifice that the whole Christ offers spiritual sacrifice to God. In doing so, the Mystical Body of Christ "really makes herself by the celebration of the mystery," where the "Church of this world is embodied in the Church of heaven, and the ministerial hierarchy, thus preparing that kingdom of priests which Christ wishes to make of us all to

74. De Lubac, *Splendor of the Church*, 149–50. Here, de Lubac is referencing the structure of the eucharistic prayer that, in addition to including the name of bishop and the pope, also prays in general for "all those who, holding to the truth, hand on the catholic and apostolic faith" (Catholic Church, "Eucharistic Prayer I," sec. 84).

75. De Lubac, *Splendor of the Church*, 150.

the glory of his Father, is, in the exercise of its most sacred function, thus entirely at the service of the hierarchy of sanctity."[76]

Any fear of exaggerating the significance of the name of a man—the bishop—spoken in a public ritual to signify the essence of a particular community can be calmed by the fact that the power of this man, whose presence is made known verbally even when physically absent from the ritual gathering, is restrained by Sacred Scripture and holy tradition, as well as by the *collegium* of which he is merely a part, and not the head. As Bernard Botte succinctly put it, "The mission which Christ gave to his apostles is to unite all men in a visible society having the same faith, the same hope, partaking in the same eucharist and living in the same charity. It is towards this unity that the efforts of the apostles and those who have continued their work have been directed. It is for this unity that the priesthood of today must strive."[77]

BIBLIOGRAPHY

Aquinas, Thomas. *Summa Theologiae*. Translated by the Fathers of the English Dominican Province. New York: Benzinger Brothers, 1947. https://aquinas101.thomisticinstitute.org/st-index.

Augustine. *Confessions*. In *Nicene and Post-Nicene Fathers of the Christian Church*, vol. 1, edited by Philip Schaff, translated by J. G. Pilkington. New York: Christian Literature, 1892.

———. *Contra epistolam Manichæi quam vacant fundamenti* [Against the epistle of Manichæus called fundamental]. In *Nicene and Post-Nicene Fathers of the Christian Church*, vol. 4, edited by Philip Schaff, translated by Richard Stothert and Albert H. Newman. Buffalo: Christian Literature, 1887.

———. "Sermo 47 (De ovibus)." In the *Liturgy of the Hours: Ordinary Time Weeks 1–17*, translated by the International Commission on English in the Liturgy, 3:422–24. Office of Readings, Monday, Thirteenth Week in Ordinary Time. New York: Catholic Book Publishing, 1975.

Bishop, Edmund. "Observations on the Liturgy of Narsai." In *The Liturgical Homilies of Narsai: Translated into English with an Introduction*, edited and translated by R. H. Connolly, 97–116. Cambridge: Cambridge University Press, 1909.

Botte, Bernard. "Collegiate Character of the Presbyterate and Episcopate." In *The Sacrament of Holy Orders: Some Papers and Discussions Concerning Holy Orders at a Session of the Centre de Pastorale Liturgique, 1955*, 79–97. Collegeville, MN: Liturgical, 1962.

Bouyer, Louis. *L'Église de Dieu, Corps du Christ et temple de l'Esprit*. Paris: Les Éditions du Cerf, 1970.

Catholic Church. *Catechism of the Catholic Church*. 2nd ed. Vatican City: Libreria Editrice Vaticana, 2000.

76. De Lubac, *Splendor of the Church*, 153–54.

77. Botte, "Collegiate Character," 97.

———. *Ceremonial of Bishops*. Collegeville, MN: Liturgical, 1989.

———. *General Instruction of the Roman Missal*. Washington, DC: United States Conference of Catholic Bishops, 2011.

———. "Ordo Missae: Prex Eucharistica I seu Canon Romanus." In *Missale Romanum*, editio typica tertia, 495–504. Vatican City: Typis Vaticanis, 2002.

———. "Order of Mass: Eucharistic Prayer I." In *The Roman Missal*, 3rd typical ed., translated by the International Commission on English in the Liturgy, 487–95. Totowa, NJ: Catholic Book Publishing, 2011.

———. "Order of Mass: Eucharistic Prayers II, III, IV." In *The Roman Missal*, 3rd typical ed., translated by the International Commission on English in the Liturgy, 497–514. Totowa, NJ: Catholic Book Publishing, 2011.

Congar, Yves. *L'Église: Une, sainte, catholique, et apostolique*. Paris: Les Éditions du Cerf, 1970.

Cyril of Jerusalem. "Catechesis XVIII." In *Liturgy of the Hours: Ordinary Time Weeks 1–17*, translated by the International Commission on English in the Liturgy, 3:560–61. Office of Readings, Thursday, Seventeenth Week in Ordinary Time. New York: Catholic Book Publishing, 1975.

De Lubac, Henri. *Catholicism: Christ and the Common Destiny of Man*. Translated by Lancelot C. Sheppard and Elizabeth Englund. San Francisco: Ignatius, 1988.

———. *Corpus Mysticum*. Paris: Aubier, 1949.

———. *The Splendor of the Church*. Translated by Michael Mason. San Francisco: Ignatius, 1999.

Di Berardino, Angelo, ed. *We Believe in One Holy Catholic and Apostolic Church*. Ancient Christian Doctrine 5. Downers Grove, IL: InterVarsity, 2010.

Ignatius of Antioch. "Letter to the Smyrnaeans." In *The Apostolic Fathers: Greek Texts and English Translations*, 3rd ed., edited and translated by Michael W. Holmes. Grand Rapids: Baker Academic, 2007.

Jerome. "Commentaria in Ezechielem." In *Patrologia Latina*, edited by J. P. Migne, 25:15-490. Paris: J. P. Migne, 1845.

John Paul II. *Ecclesia de Eucharistia*. The Holy See, Apr 17, 2003. https://www.vatican.va/content/john-paul-ii/en/encyclicals/documents/hf_jp-ii_enc_20030417_eccl-de-euch.html.

Journet, Charles. *The Theology of the Church*. Translated by Victor Szczurek and Michael J. Miller. San Francisco: Ignatius, 2004.

———. *Théologie de l'Église*. 18th ed. Paris: Desclée/Mame, 1987.

Jungmann, Joseph. *The Early Liturgy: To the Time of Gregory the Great*. Translated by Francis Brunner. Notre Dame, IN: University of Notre Dame Press, 1959.

———. *The Mass of the Roman Rite: Its Origins and Development (Missarum Sollemnia)*. Vols. 1–2. Translated by Francis A. Brunner. Notre Dame, IN: Christian Classics, 1950.

Martyrdom of Polycarp. In *The Apostolic Fathers: Greek Texts and English Translations*, 3rd ed., edited and translated by Michael W. Holmes, 298–333. Grand Rapids: Baker Academic, 2007.

McPartlan, Paul. *The Eucharist Makes the Church: Henri de Lubac and John Zizioulas in Dialogue*. Edinburgh: T&T Clark, 1993.

Nichols, Aidan. *Figuring out the Church: Her Marks, and Her Masters*. San Francisco: Ignatius, 2013.

Pius XII. *Mystici Corporis Christi*. The Holy See, Jun 29, 1943. https://www.vatican.va/content/pius-xii/en/encyclicals/documents/hf_p-xii_enc_29061943_mystici-corporis-christi.html.

Second Vatican Council. *Lumen Gentium*. The Holy See, Nov 21, 1964. https://www.vatican.va/archive/hist_councils/ii_vatican_council/documents/vat-ii_const_19641121_lumen-gentium_en.html.

Zizioulas, John. *Being as Communion: Studies in Personhood and the Church*. New York: St. Vladimir's Seminary Press, 1985.

The Bishop as the Regulator of Concelebration in His Diocese

—Andrew J. Moss

INTRODUCTION

WITH THE DECREE *ECCLESIÆ Semper*,[1] the Congregation of Rites in 1965 promulgated the first fruits of the liturgical reform initiated by the Second Vatican Council: the rite of eucharistic concelebration called for by the *Constitution on the Sacred Liturgy*.[2] In recent years, the practice of eucharistic concelebration has been no stranger to controversy, with reappraisals of concelebration emerging from all shades of theological opinion.[3] The diocesan bishop plays a unique role within the liturgical life of the diocese. He is the *summus sacerdos* of his flock, the "principal dispenser of the mysteries of God."[4] As such, his role is not to intervene in scholarly disputes, but rather to oversee the liturgical life of his diocese. As the overseer of his flock, the law is indispensable. The bishop does not impose his own will in an arbitrary fashion, but oversees his diocese in accordance with the law of the church.[5]

The *General Instruction of the Roman Missal* singles out four areas that are especially entrusted to the regulation of the diocesan bishop. These areas are concelebration, altar servers, communion under both kinds, and

1. Sacred Congregation of Rites (Consilium), "Ecclesiæ Semper."
2. Second Vatican Council, "Sacrosanctum Concilium."
3. For a critique of the praxis of concelebration from a "traditional" perspective, see Kwasniewski, *Resurgent in the Midst of Crisis*, 139–47. For a critique of the praxis of concelebration from a "progressive" perspective, see Huels, *Disputed Questions*, 39–45.
4. Catholic Church, *Code of Canon Law*, c. 387 (hereafter *CIC/1983*).
5. John Paul II, *Sacrae Disciplinae Leges.*

the construction and ordering of churches.[6] This essay examines the first of these—the discipline of concelebration. The *General Instruction of the Roman Missal* states, "It is for the Bishop, *in accordance with the norm of law*, to regulate the discipline for concelebration in all churches and oratories of his diocese."[7] The bishop's duty is not confined to the cathedral and parish churches; it is to all churches and oratories, including those used by institutes of consecrated life and other communities. To fulfill this duty, the bishop therefore requires a comprehensive knowledge of the liturgical law on concelebration. But what is the law? This essay seeks to provide an answer to this question.

In order to assess the current law in the context of the canonical tradition, this essay will first examine the law on celebration that was operative in the 1917 code and the pre-conciliar liturgical books and examine developments in this area up to and including the *Constitution on the Sacred Liturgy* at the council. Second, the essay will examine developments in the regulation of concelebration that occurred in the years immediately following the council. Third, the essay will seek to delineate the current law on concelebration through an examination of the 1983 *Code of Canon Law*, the *General Instruction of the Roman Missal*, the liturgical books themselves, and documents of the Holy See. In the fourth part, the essay will examine more closely the tasks of the bishop as regulator of the discipline of concelebration in his diocese.

THE PRE-CONCILIAR LAW ON CONCELEBRATION AND THE CONCILIAR DEBATE

The Pio-Benedictine Code of 1917 contains one canon which regulates concelebration and that forbids its use except for presbyteral and episcopal ordinations. Canon 803 states, "It is not licit that several priests concelebrate, beyond the Mass of ordination of priests and in the Mass of consecration of Bishops according to the Roman Pontifical."[8] While the practice was restricted, it is also pertinent to note that the one occasion when the rite was permitted was not merely a peripheral rite, but that of the solemn ordination of the church's priests. Thus, although restricted, the rite of concelebration nevertheless had a prominent place in the church's liturgy; every newly ordained began his priestly life by concelebrating Mass with the bishop.

6. Catholic Church, *General Instruction*, sec. 387 (hereafter *GIRM* and cited by section number).

7. *GIRM*, 202 (emphasis added).

8. Peters, *Pio-Benedictine Code*, 292, c. 803.

In Cardinal Pietro Gasparri's footnotes for the code of 1917, he offers only two sources for the canon.[9] First, the 1755 encyclical *On the Observance of Oriental Rites* by Pope Benedict XIV states the following:

> The rite of concelebration is now out of fashion in the western church, except at priestly ordinations performed by the bishop and at episcopal consecrations where two bishops assist the consecrating bishop. But this rite continues to thrive in the Oriental Church, and priests often concelebrate with the bishop or with the priest as chief celebrant. . . . And wherever this custom is practiced among Greeks and Orientals, it is approved and to be preserved.[10]

Scholars associated with the liturgical movement posed the question as to whether concelebration might once more be fashionable in the Western church.

The second source is an extract from a decretal of Pope Gregory IX from the collection compiled in 1230. In this decretal, the pope repudiates the practice of a newly consecrated bishop immediately administering the minor orders in the same ceremony. Having established that only the pope has this prerogative, he states:

> Other bishops, however, who are consecrated between the epistle and the gospel, ought not to celebrate ordinations at that time, because those consecrated concelebrate directly with the celebrant, so that the mystery of unity is not divided.[11]

The pope's words reveal the *raison d'être* for the praxis of concelebration: to manifest the *mysterium unitatis* of the church. Scholars noted that neither of the sources for canon 803 in the 1917 code contain a rationale as to why concelebration had to be restricted to the rite of ordination of priests and bishops. Scholars also noted that St. Thomas Aquinas offers a theological basis for several priests to consecrate one species: "Since a priest does not consecrate except in the *persona* of Christ, and the many are one in Christ, therefore it does not matter whether this Sacrament is consecrated through one or through many."[12]

9. Gasparri, *Codex Iuris Canonici*, 269, c. 803.

10. Benedict XIV, *Allatae Sunt*, sec. 38.

11. "Ceteri vero, qui inter epistolam et evangelium consecrantur, quia consecrati concelebrant principaliter celebranti, ne dividatur mysterium unitatis, non debent tunc ordines celebrare" (author's translation). Gregory IX, "Decretal," 71.

12. Aquinas, *Summa Theologiae*, III, q. 82, a. 2.

Thus the liturgical movement of the early twentieth century saw a lively debate on the issue of concelebration, with scholars arguing for the renewal of the practice.[13] By the 1920s, the terms "ceremonial concelebration" and "sacramental concelebration" had acquired a technical meaning: the former indicated a form of concelebration where the concelebrants did not simultaneously pronounce the words of consecration with the main celebrant; the latter described the form of concelebration where they did. Some scholars considered that the more ancient form—ceremonial—was the more authentic form.[14] Pope Pius XII intervened to indicate the direction which the Latin Rite was to take. In 1944 the pope revised the rite of the ordination of bishops, adjusting the rite to establish that the assisting bishops were true co-consecrators—they were to participate in the laying on of hands over the candidate, recite the prayer of consecration with the principal celebrant, and were to have the requisite intention.[15]

The pope intervened again in 1956 when, in an address to participants of the International Congress on Pastoral Liturgy, Pius XII described "true concelebration" as when the assembled priests recite the words of consecration: "The concelebrants must themselves say over the bread and the wine, 'This is my Body,' 'This is my Blood.' Otherwise, their concelebration is purely ceremonial."[16] Moving the Latin Rite in the direction of sacramental concelebration rather than a ceremonial one was consistent with the practice of the Latin Church. From the eighth to the twelfth century, the custom at Rome had been for the concelebrants to recite together the words of consecration, a custom which continued in the Mass at which the newly ordained concelebrated.[17] These interventions of Pius XII thus set the stage for a renewal of the praxis of sacramental concelebration at the Second Vatican Council.

The *Constitution on the Sacred Liturgy* devotes two paragraphs—fifty-seven and fifty-eight—to the issue of concelebration. In examining the

13. In 1946 Dom Lambert Beauduin, one of the fathers of the liturgical movement, stated, "One has the right to hope with filial confidence and respectful submission for a return to the ancient practice." Beauduin, "La Concelebration," quoted in Jounel, *Rite of Concelebration*, 25.

14. For a discussion of the origin of the terms "sacramental" and "ceremonial," see Manders, "Concelebration," 138–40.

15. Pius XII, *Episcopalis Consecrationis*.

16. Pius XII, "Address to the International Congress," 273. This was to be confirmed in a "Decree of the Holy Office of March 8, 1957": Denzinger, *Compendium of Creeds*, 818.

17. For an account of the development of sacramental concelebration in Rome, see Lang, "Sacramental Concelebration," 59–62.

versions prior to the final text,[18] two motivations are given for expanding the occasions when concelebration might be used. The first motivation was to provide the church with a liturgical manifestation of the church's unity, but the second was as a solution to the practical difficulty of providing for individual Masses at a gathering of priests. The liturgical movement had emphasized the importance of the priest offering the eucharistic sacrifice each day, and increasingly priests were not content to merely assist *in choro* at the bishop's Mass at a diocesan gathering. Moreover, the liturgical movement also emphasized that the reception of Communion at Mass constitutes a more perfect mode of participation, something the priest was unable to do when assisting *in choro* at the bishop's Mass when he had previously celebrated an individual Mass. Thus, eucharistic concelebration was seen as a solution to these difficulties.

The final text of *Sacrosanctum Concilium* emphasizes first that concelebration is not an innovation in the life of the church: "Concelebration . . . has remained in use to this day in the Church in the East and in the West."[19] In the final text, only one motivation is given for the expansion of concelebration, and that is priestly unity: "Concelebration, by which the unity of the priesthood is appropriately manifested."[20] The additional motivation of convenience, which had appeared in the previous versions of the text, was discarded. In the mind of the council fathers, therefore, the value of concelebration is not in any sense a practical solution, but rather its value is that it makes manifest a particular aspect of the church—its hierarchical unity.

Concerning when concelebration may be used, the council gives only four situations when it is to be permitted by the law itself: the Chrism Mass on Holy Thursday, the Mass of the Lord's Supper on Holy Thursday, at councils and synods, and at the Mass for the Blessing of an Abbot. The inclusion of the Mass of the Lord's Supper on Holy Thursday, not in the initial text, was the occasion of lively debate at the council.[21] The custom in the Latin Church had been that on Holy Thursday, if not presiding at Mass themselves, priests would assist *in choro* at another Mass and receive Holy Communion from the hands of the presiding priest, as symbolic of the action at the Last Supper.[22]

18. For an account of the evolution of the text that was to become sections 57–58 of *Sacrosanctum Concilium*, see de Sainte-Marie, *Holy Eucharist*, 212–54.

19. Second Vatican Council, "Sacrosanctum Concilium," sec. 57.

20. Second Vatican Council, "Sacrosanctum Concilium," sec. 57.

21. Jungmann, "Commentary on the Constitution," 44.

22. McGowan, *Concelebration: Sign of Unity*, 58.

The mind of the council is revealed in these four situations when the law itself gives permission for concelebration. Each of these are significant and solemn occasions, and each of these manifest in a particular way the hierarchical unity of the church since the presbyters are gathered around their bishop or abbot while exercising their sacerdotal power. The inclusion of the Mass of the Lord's Supper on Holy Thursday appears to be an exception, but one justified by the custom of priests coming together on such a solemn occasion.

Having established a small number of situations when permission was given by the law itself, the council then adds two further situations where permission can be granted by the ordinary. These are the daily Mass for priests living in community—the conventual Mass or principal cathedral Mass—and the Mass at a gathering of priests. Although there is potentially no hierarchical superior as the main celebrant, these Masses can only take place with the permission of the superior, and so the link with the hierarchic aspect of the church is maintained.

The penultimate version of the text of these paragraphs of *Sacrosanctum Concilium* afforded this faculty of granting permission to the "ordinary," who would decide on the opportuneness of concelebration and the number of concelebrants.[23] Since the word "ordinary" could indicate both the diocesan bishop and the major superior of a clerical religious community, this would mean that the bishop would effectively lose his authority concerning concelebration in the communities of religious in his diocese. Following further debate, the final text maintained the prerogative of the religious ordinary but added that "rules concerning concelebration within a diocese are under the control of the bishop."[24]

From examining these occasions when concelebration is either permitted by the law itself or by the hierarchical superior, we can discern two aspects of the mind of the council with regard to concelebration: first, there is to be a moderate expansion of the use of concelebration; second, the intrinsic link between concelebration and the hierarchic aspect of the church is to be preserved.

Two further norms in the text of *Sacrosanctum Concilium* underline the moderateness of the conciliar approach: the ordinary is only to grant permission for priests in community to concelebrate if the needs of the laity have been provided for, and the ordinary is to recognize that the priest always retains his "right to celebrate individually."[25] These caveats serve to

23. Text reproduced in de Sainte-Marie, *Holy Eucharist*, 228.

24. *Sacrosanctum Concilium*, sec. 57.

25. *Sacrosanctum Concilium*, sec. 57. Two exceptions are made to this right; the

protect both the right of the laity to the sacraments and the right of the priest to choose to celebrate individually. At the same time, these caveats also serve to protect the integrity of the rite itself. In the following section, the essay will examine how the conciliar reform on concelebration was modified in subsequent documents.

POST CONCILIAR DEVELOPMENTS IN THE REGULATION OF CONCELEBRATION

Nine months following the promulgation of the *Constitution on the Sacred Liturgy*, the Consilium and the Sacred Congregation of Rites jointly promulgated, in September 1964, the first instruction on the proper implementation of *Sacrosanctum Concilium*. Regarding concelebration, the document includes a norm which considerably alters the directives of the *Constitution on the Sacred Liturgy*: "Once the new rite has been published, concelebration is permitted for priests, especially on more solemn feasts, if pastoral needs do not require individual celebration."[26] This norm abrogates a significant element of *Sacrosanctum Concilium*, that of the need for the permission of the hierarchic superior. While ordinarily an instruction that contradicts a constitution would have no force (c. 34 sec. 2), *Inter Œcumenici* was confirmed *in forma specifica*[27] by Pope Paul VI, giving it the force of law and abrogating the norm of *Sacrosanctum Concilium*. The directive of *Sacrosanctum Concilium* that the bishop regulate concelebration in his diocese, however, is left intact.

This change found in *Inter Œcumenici* is a significant change since it weakens the link of concelebration to the hierarchic aspect of the church, which the rite is intended to make manifest. Moreover, the removal of the need for the permission of the hierarchical superior ought not to be interpreted to mean the priest should concelebrate at every opportunity since *Sacrosanctum Concilium* had only signalled a moderate expansion of the practice. Rather, following *Inter Œcumenici*, it is now for the priest himself to decide whether concelebration is opportune.

Sacrosanctum Concilium 58 directed that a new rite of concelebration was to be devised. Following a period of experimental use of the rite both

---

priest may not celebrate an individual Mass on Holy Thursday—due to the long established custom of priests attending Mass *in choro* at this Mass—and the priest may not celebrate his individual Mass while a concelebrated Mass is taking place in the same church. The current law adds the Easter Vigil to these exceptions. See *GIRM*, 199d.

26. Sacred Congregation of Rites (Consilium), *Inter Œcumenici*, sec. 15.

27. Sacred Congregation of Rites (Consilium), *Inter Œcumenici*, sec. 99.

during the council and elsewhere,[28] the new rite of concelebration—the first of the postconciliar rites—was promulgated in March 1965. The members of the consilium did not use the preconciliar rite as a model. In the rite used at priestly ordinations, the newly ordained presbyter remained kneeling throughout the Mass of the Faithful, recited with the bishop-celebrant each and every prayer from the offertory onwards to the Last Gospel, did not receive the Precious Blood from the chalice, and concelebrated with his chasuble pinned up at the back until he had received the "commission to absolve" at the end of the Mass. By contrast, the new rite of concelebration emphasizes that the assembled priests are truly co-consecrators. Accordingly, the concelebrants sit and stand with the main celebrant, gather around the altar at the eucharistic prayer, extend their hands at the epiclesis over the elements, recite together with the main celebrant the "core" of the Roman Canon (the *Hanc igitur* to the *Supplices te rogamus*), recite other parts of the Canon as directed, receive the Body and Blood in the same manner as the main celebrant, and wear the chasuble and stole as is usual for Mass.[29] That the priest is a co-consecrator is underlined by the provision that the priest concelebrant can accept a stipend.[30]

The 1965 decree promulgating the new rite of concelebration, *Ecclesiae Semper*, also strengthened the doctrinal rationale for its use. Whereas *Sacrosanctum Concilium* referred only to the unity of the priesthood, *Ecclesiae Semper* refers to a three-fold unity—that of the cross, the priesthood, and the church.[31] At the same time, any sense of concelebration being a practical solution is minimized:

> The rite of concelebration thus strikingly presents and deeply inculcates truths of utmost importance regarding the spiritual life and the pastoral formation of priests and faithful. These are the reasons, much more than any at a practical level, that concelebration of the eucharistic mystery has been accepted in the Church.[32]

Thus, again, a certain development of *Sacrosanctum Concilium* is in evidence. Whereas the *Constitution* justified concelebration on the basis of its preexistence in the church, in *Ecclesiae Semper* it is justified by reason of

28. For an account of the various experiments that preceded the promulgation of the new rite of concelebration, see Chiron, *Annibale Bugnini*, 110–13.

29. For a commentary on the 1965 *Rite of Concelebration*, see Jounel, *Rite of Concelebration*, 71–165.

30. Jounel, *Rite of Concelebration*, 93.

31. Sacred Congregation of Rites (Consilium), "Ecclesiæ Semper," sec. 1791.

32. Sacred Congregation of Rites (Consilium), "Ecclesiæ Semper," sec. 1792.

its ability to present and inculcate truths of the spiritual life in a superior manner.

This direction of travel is further developed in the instruction *Eucharisticum Mysterium* promulgated by the Sacred Congregation of Rites in 1967. While replicating the two caveats of *Sacrosanctum Concilium*, that of the needs of the faithful having being met and the right of the priest to celebrate alone, the instruction states that it is "desirable that priests should celebrate the Eucharist in this eminent manner."[33] Moreover, the document also states that "competent superiors should, therefore, facilitate and indeed positively encourage concelebration, whenever pastoral needs or other reasonable motives do not prevent it."[34] Thus, this instruction seems to recommend concelebration anytime two or more priests gather together. Whereas the role of the competent superior was merely to permit concelebration in *Sacrosanctum Concilium*, in *Eucharisticum Mysterium* his role is to positively encourage concelebration. To be recalled here, however, is that this document is an instruction that was confirmed *in forma communi*,[35] not *in forma specifica*, and therefore, that which is not in conformity with the *Constitution on the Sacred Liturgy* cannot be considered as binding.

The perspective of *Eucharisticum Mysterium* was counterbalanced in a 1972 *Declaration on Concelebration* issued by the Sacred Congregation for Divine Worship. The declaration includes a strikingly positive assessment of the individual Mass:

> Although concelebration is to be regarded as the most excellent form of eucharistic celebration in communities, private celebration without a congregation also "remains as the center of the entire life of the Church and at the heart of the priest's existence."[36]

The *Declaration* serves to remind us that the council did not seek to devalue or render illegitimate the individual Mass, since this had traditionally been understood "at the heart of the priest's existence," but rather sought to open up new possibilities for the manifestation of the church's unity in a renewed rite of eucharistic concelebration.

The church's eucharistic theology, therefore, recognizes both the excellence of concelebration and the perennial value of the individual Mass. These two aspects are not to be placed in opposition to each other, but

33. Sacred Congregation of Rites, *Eucharisticum Mysterium*, sec. 47.
34. Sacred Congregation of Rites, *Eucharisticum Mysterium*, sec. 47.
35. Sacred Congregation of Rites, *Eucharisticum Mysterium*, sec. 67.
36. Sacred Congregation for Divine Worship, "In Celebratione Missæ," sec. 1816.

rather are to be seen as complementary. Moreover, the council's words on concelebration in *Sacrosanctum Concilium* retain their value: there was to be a moderate expansion of concelebration while preserving the link with the hierarchical aspect of the church. It is the task of the law to express these aspects in juridical terms, which will be examined in the following section.

THE CURRENT LAW ON CONCELEBRATION

In continuity with *Sacrosanctum Concilium*, the *General Instruction of the Roman Missal* designates the diocesan bishop as the one who is to regulate concelebration in all the churches and oratories in the diocese, including those of institutes of consecrated life and other communities.[37] The *GIRM* specifies, however, that the bishop is to do this "in accordance with the norm of law." The task of the bishop is not to impose his own opinions or preferences concerning concelebration, but rather to implement the law of the church.

There are four sources of norms for the church's law on concelebration. These consist of the *Code of Canon Law* of 1983, the third typical edition of the *General Instruction of the Roman Missal* of 2002, the rubrics of the ritual books themselves, and additional documents promulgated by the Holy See.

Paragraph 310 of the *General Instruction of the Roman Missal* contains the following norm: "Seats should be arranged in the sanctuary for concelebrating Priests as well as for Priests who are present at the celebration in choir dress but without concelebrating."[38] This norm is especially informative. It tells us that there are two possibilities for the priest who assists at Mass: either he concelebrates or he assists *in choro*. Although this latter way of participating at Mass has become rare, it is by no means excluded by the law. Indeed, this paragraph of the *GIRM* informs us that for a priest to assist at Mass *in choro* is a usual and legitimate option.

At the same time, the *GIRM* also states that when the bishop presides it is "most fitting" that the other priests in attendance concelebrate the Mass, not for the sake of adding solemnity, but to "signify more vividly the mystery of the Church, the sacrament of unity."[39] Thus, when the bishop presides, the law anticipates that the other priests will participate as concelebrants.

37. *GIRM*, 202.

38. *GIRM*, 310.

39. *GIRM*, 92. The doctrine that the church is the sacrament of unity is the rationale for the prohibition of concelebration not only with ministers of ecclesial communities but also with ministers of churches with valid holy orders. See John Paul II, *Ecclesia de Eucharistia*, sec. 44.

Nevertheless, the law also foresees certain situations when the priest does not concelebrate—even when the presider is the bishop—and attends the Mass in choir dress.

A first situation is when the priest himself chooses not to concelebrate. Canon 902, repeating the clause of *Sacrosanctum Concilium*, is careful to enshrine the priest's right to always choose this option:

> Unless the welfare of the Christian faithful requires or suggests otherwise, priests can concelebrate the Eucharist. They are completely free to celebrate the Eucharist individually, however, but not while a concelebration is taking place in the same church or oratory.

The previous schema of 1982 had the following:

> Unless the welfare of the Christian faithful requires or suggests otherwise, it is *recommended* that priests concelebrate the Eucharist. Intact, however, is [the fact] that priests might celebrate the Eucharist singularly, but not while a concelebration is taking place in the same church or oratory.[40]

In the final revision of the code by Pope John Paul II, two significant changes were made:[41] the *recommendation* of concelebration in a general sense is removed and, instead, priests are afforded the general *possibility* of concelebration. In this the pope adjusts the canon to reflect more closely the intentions of *Sacrosanctum Concilium* rather than the subsequent perspective of the 1967 instruction *Eucharisticum Mysterium*. Also, the priest's freedom to celebrate individually is heightened in the final draft of canon 902: he is said to be "completely free." The law does not inquire into the reason for the priest's choice, but simply underlines the right of the priest to make this choice, a right which the bishop is obliged by the law to uphold.[42]

Nevertheless, as noted above, it is important to understand that this norm is not only for the good of the individual priest, but it is also for the integrity of the rite of concelebration. The 1972 *Declaration on Concelebration* states, "To increase the spiritual benefits for those who take part, the

40. "§1. Nisi utilitas christifidelium aluid requirat aut suadeat, commendatur ut sacerdotes Eucharistiam concelebrant. §2. Integrum tamen est sacerdotibus, ut singuli Eucharistiam celebrant, quo in eadem ecclesia aut oratorio concelebratione habetur" (author's translation, emphasis added). Text reproduced in Peters, *Incrementa in Progressu*, 827.

41. For an account of the process of compiling the 1983 *Code of Canon Law*, see Peters, *Incrementa in Progressu*, xi–xix.

42. See *CIC/1983*, c. 384.

freedom of the concelebrants must always be respected."[43] In the same vein, a priest cannot accept an offering for a concelebrated Mass which is his second Mass of the day,[44] for the same reason that his motivation for participating at that Mass must be simply that of desiring to concelebrate rather than to obtain an offering.

A second situation when a priest should not concelebrate is when he does not have the faculty to do so. The *Code of Canon Law* foresees that the priest will celebrate one Mass each day: "A priest is not permitted to celebrate the Eucharist more than once a day except in cases where the law permits him to celebrate or concelebrate more than once on the same day."[45] At paragraph 204, the *GIRM* lists liturgical days when the law itself gives the faculty to celebrate or concelebrate three Masses (Christmas Day, All Souls) or two Masses (Holy Thursday, Easter Vigil). On these days, it would also be licit for the priest to concelebrate twice or, when permitted, three times in one day. The last norm in the paragraph states, "A Priest who concelebrates with the Bishop or his delegate at a Synod or pastoral visitation, or concelebrates on the occasion of a gathering of Priests, may celebrate Mass again for the benefit of the faithful."[46] Thus a priest who celebrates Mass for the faithful in his parish, and then later attends a gathering of priests, would have the faculty to concelebrate on that occasion. However, a priest who celebrates Mass for the faithful in his parish, and then later attends a nuptial Mass, would not have the faculty to concelebrate. In this situation the priest should attend *in choro*.

Many priests in the United States will enjoy in their list of faculties the permission of the bishop to celebrate twice on the same weekday, permission which will have been given because of a shortage of priests.[47] In promulgating this norm, the legislator was not concerned to boost opportunities for concelebration, but rather to provide for the needs of the faithful. Since the norm of paragraph 2 of canon 905 provides an exception to the norm of paragraph 1, it should be read strictly, according to the norm of canon 18.[48] Since the canon explicitly refers to "celebration" rather than "concelebration," the canon is not to be interpreted as granting a greater

43. Sacred Congregation for Divine Worship, "In Celebratione Missae," sec. 1816.

44. *CIC/1983*, c. 951, sec. 2.

45. *CIC/1983*, c. 905, sec. 1.

46. *GIRM*, 204.

47. *CIC/1983*, c. 905, sec. 2.

48. *CIC/1983*, c. 18 states that "laws which . . . contain an exception from the law are subject to strict interpretation."

freedom to concelebrate than that given in the universal law contained in the *GIRM*, 204.

A third situation when the priest should not concelebrate is when the priest is not familiar with the language in which the Mass is celebrated. The 2004 instruction *Redemptionis Sacramentum* states:

> Where it happens that some of the Priests who are present do not know the language of the celebration and therefore are not capable of pronouncing the parts of the Eucharistic Prayer proper to them, they should not concelebrate, but instead should attend the celebration in choral dress in accordance with the norms.[49]

This norm underlines that concelebration is not merely ceremonial, but truly sacramental since the concelebrant is a co-consecrator. The *GIRM* reiterates that the concelebrants are obliged to say the words of consecration,[50] and therefore, those priests who cannot pronounce these words are unable to concelebrate validly and so should attend *in choro*.

A fourth situation in which a priest may not be able to concelebrate is when there is a large number of priests in attendance at the Mass. Two paragraphs in the *GIRM* allude to the possible necessity of limiting the number of concelebrants. Paragraph 294 describes the norms for the placement of seats for the concelebrants, which should be in the sanctuary. The paragraph also states, "If their number is great, seats should be arranged in another part of the church, though near the altar."[51] The concern that the concelebrants be near the altar stems from the nature of the rite itself—the concelebrants are true co-consecrators. Also, paragraph 215 directs that the concelebrants should not prevent the faithful from having a clear view of the sacred action. This norm underlines that the laity are truly participants at the Mass and not merely "silent spectators."[52]

This concern that the rite of concelebration should not be overwhelmed by the number of concelebrants was present from the inception of the rite. Writing in 1963, the liturgical scholar and pioneer A. G. Martimort stated,

> We cannot imagine the indefinite multiplication of the number of concelebrants, with the danger of rendering celebration impossible; the theologian will worry about the recitation in

49. Congregation for Divine Worship and the Discipline of the Sacrament, *Redemptionis Sacramentum*, 113.

50. *GIRM*, 218.

51. *GIRM*, 294.

52. Second Vatican Council, "Sacrosanctum Concilium," sec. 48.

> common, the master of ceremonies will be concerned with the minimum required for dignity.[53]

That the concelebrants might not consist of all of the priests in attendance is also acknowledged in the rubrics of the *Ordo Missae* for the Chrism Mass: "To signify the unity of the presbyterate of the diocese the Priests who concelebrate with the Bishop should be from different regions of the diocese."[54] Even though concelebration forms an integral part of the Chrism Mass, as it does in the Rite of Ordination of a Bishop and of Presbyters, and at the Rite of the Blessing of an Abbot, this does not mean that all priests in attendance are obliged to concelebrate.

These various norms in the church's law serve as a reminder that concelebration is not part of the liturgical life of the church for the sake of priest's liturgical preference, nor for the sake of convenience, but rather is to make manifest the hierarchical ordering of the church which is the sacrament of unity.[55] Accordingly, if that unity is in danger of being obscured due to an excessive number of concelebrants, the number of concelebrants should be limited and the rest of the priests should attend *in choro*.[56]

One paragraph of the *GIRM* deserves special commentary. Paragraph 114 concerns the daily Mass in communities of priests; for this paragraph the following words were added:

> For it is preferable that Priests who are present at a celebration of the Eucharist, unless excused for a just reason, should usually exercise the function proper to their Order and hence take part as concelebrants, wearing sacred vestments. Otherwise, they wear their proper choir dress or a surplice over a cassock.[57]

Taken out of context, this paragraph could be read as a quasi-obligation for all priests to concelebrate the Eucharist whenever they are not the main celebrant. It is important, however, to remember the context: the paragraph deals with the daily community Mass in a community of priests and seeks to address a specific problem—that of priests choosing not to concelebrate in the sacred vestments, nor to attend *in choro*, but rather to sit in the congregation in the manner of a layman. In such communities, an alternate

53. Martimort, "Le rituel de la concélébration," quoted in Jounel, *Rite of Concelebration*, 86.

54. Catholic Church, "Chrism Mass," 147, sec. 4.

55. Second Vatican Council, *Sacrosanctum Concilium*, sec. 26.

56. For a discussion of the difficulties with large-scale concelebrations, see Benedict XVI, *Sacramentum Caritatis*, sec. 61.

57. Compare with sec. 76 of the fourth edition of the *General Instruction of the Roman Missal* published in Catholic Church, *Sacramentary*, 31.

concept of concelebration has emerged, one which prefers to speak of the "concelebration" of the entire assembly rather than only the priests, and therefore considers that priestly concelebration serves to distract from this broader concept of "concelebration."[58]

This understanding of concelebration is difficult to reconcile with the council's understanding of concelebration, since in the latter, the hierarchical aspect is intrinsic to the rite, as the rite is meant to make manifest the hierarchical unity of the church. When the hierarchical aspect is obscured—as occurs when priests attend in the manner of the lay faithful—so the unity of the church is obscured. The instruction *Redemptionis Sacramentum* therefore expressly repudiates this practice: "It is not fitting, except in rare and exceptional cases and with reasonable cause, for [priests] to participate at Mass, as regards to externals, in the manner of the lay faithful."[59] Moreover, the words added to paragraph 114 of the *GIRM* cannot be read in isolation from the rest of the law. The added words do not impinge on the priest's right to choose to celebrate individually, nor do they render licit the examples of illicit concelebration given above.

In summary, the law of the church upholds the integrity of the rite of concelebration and the right of the priest to celebrate individually; concelebration is commended in certain instances, but is never imposed; and the law grants the faculty to concelebrate on some occasions, but not on others. Moreover, the church's law finds an important place for the custom of the priest attending Mass *in choro*, wherein he remains part of the liturgical assembly even when prevented from concelebrating.

The law, therefore, faithfully expresses in juridical terms the mind of the council with regard to concelebration—a call for a moderate expansion of concelebration while preserving the link with the hierarchical aspect of the church. It is the bishop to whom is entrusted the delicate task of regulating the discipline on concelebration.

THE BISHOP AS THE REGULATOR OF CONCELEBRATION IN HIS DIOCESE

Before discussing the bishop as the regulator of concelebration in his diocese, it is pertinent to call to mind certain difficulties in the current praxis in the Latin Church.

58. For an explanation of this alternative praxis, see Baldovin, "Jesuits, the Ministerial Priesthood," 17–35.

59. Congregation for Divine Worship and the Discipline of the Sacraments, *Redemptionis Sacramentum*, sec. 128.

The first difficulty rests in the fact that large-scale concelebrations are now a common feature of the contemporary church, with papal liturgies often featuring hundreds of concelebrants.[60] Many of these priests will be at a considerable distance from the altar, and thus, the concelebrant's role as a co-consecrator will be obscured. Moreover, the coordination of the words of consecration and essential gestures is rendered difficult, if not impossible, calling into question the integrity of the rite.[61]

The second difficulty, as noted above, is that there is the phenomenon of groups of priests, especially in religious communities, abandoning both concelebration and assisting *in choro*, choosing instead to sit in the nave and participate in the Mass in the manner of the laity. Indeed, in some communities of consecrated life, priests are not permitted to concelebrate since it is perceived as manifesting a clericalist attitude.

Third, there is the problem of habitual concelebration among diocesan clergy, even when the law does not grant the faculty to concelebrate. It has become normative for a priest simply to always concelebrate at a Mass at which he is not the main celebrant, without any reference to liturgical norms, to the point where assisting *in choro* is perceived as displaying a traditionalist mindset.[62]

Such practices are difficult to reconcile with liturgical law, but more fundamentally, are difficult to reconcile with an authentic spirit of the Second Vatican Council. The vision of concelebration given in *Sacrosanctum Concilium* is not merely a starting point from which the church has moved on, but rather the words of the *Constitution* retain their value as a point of reference for the praxis of today.

The bishop is the *summus sacerdos* of his diocese and therefore the regulator of the praxis of concelebration. Moreover, his regulation is seen to be a means of renewal. There are two actions the bishop can take to promote the renewal of concelebration. The first is to issue his own particular law for his diocese. This would assist the priests of the diocese by collating together the various sources for norms on concelebration and would also serve to underline both the integrity of the rite and the freedom of the priest to celebrate individually. The norms would serve to remind priests that the most effective way to encourage the active participation of the faithful is that of

60. For example, hundreds of concelebrants were present at Benedict XVI's funeral on January 5, 2023.

61. For further discussion of these issues, see Derville, *Eucharistic Concelebration*, 91–93.

62. For a discussion of this mindset, see Kocik, "Preaching through the Choir," 204–11.

fidelity to the rite itself,[63] most especially in concelebrations with potentially a large number of concelebrants. Where appropriate, the bishop could use his norms to give guidelines on the maximum number of concelebrants for a concelebration in a parish church. Such norms would also assist communities of consecrated life to rediscover the riches of the council's vision of concelebration through fidelity to the liturgical law as well as their own duty of obedience to the local ordinary as the Vicar of Christ.[64]

The second action the bishop can take is to use the annual Chrism Mass as an exemplar for the rite of concelebration since he is to be the "celebrant par excellence in his diocese."[65] Where the number of priests is large, the bishop could limit the number of concelebrants to a representative portion of the priests, as foreseen in the rite, with the remainder assisting *in choro*. This would manifest the unity of the presbyterate while respecting the integrity of the rite and so assist the active participation of the faithful. The bishop's own example of submission to the universal law will assist his priests in their obedience to his particular law.

CONCLUDING REMARKS

This essay has sought to examine the role of the bishop as the regulator of concelebration in his diocese. As the *GIRM* states, he is to do this "in accordance with the norm of law."[66] Having surveyed the law on concelebration from its various sources—the *Code of Canon Law*, the *GIRM*, the *Ordo Missae*, and documents of the Holy See—the law can be seen to faithfully translate into juridical terms the conciliar vision for eucharistic concelebration that is presented in *Sacrosanctum Concilium*, that is to say, a moderate expansion of the use of the rite of concelebration while preserving the rite's intrinsic link to the hierarchic aspect of the church. A more faithful application of the law is therefore the best way to implement the authentic spirit of the council and the surest path to renewal of the church's liturgy.

BIBLIOGRAPHY

Aquinas, Thomas. *Summa Theologiae*. Latin/English ed. Edited by J. Mortensen and Enrique Alarcón. Translated by Laurence Shapcote. The Works of St. Thomas Aquinas 14. Lander, WY: Aquinas Institute for the Study of Sacred Doctrine, 2012.

63. Benedict XVI, *Sacramentum Caritatis*, sec. 38.
64. *CIC/1983*, c. 678, sec. 1.
65. Benedict XVI, *Sacramentum Caritatis*, sec. 39.
66. *GIRM*, 202.

Baldovin, John F. "Jesuits, the Ministerial Priesthood and Eucharistic Concelebration." *Studies in the Spirituality of Jesuits* 51.1 (2019) 17–35.

Benedict XIV. *Allatae Sunt*. Jul 26, 1755. Papal Encyclicals Online. https://www.papalencyclicals.net/ben14/b14allat.html.

Benedict XVI. *Sacramentum Caritatis*. The Holy See, Feb 22, 2007. https://www.vatican.va/content/benedict-xvi/en/apost_exhortations/documents/hf_ben-xvi_exh_20070222_sacramentum-caritatis.html.

Catholic Church."The Chrism Mass." In *The Roman Missal*, 3rd typical ed., translated by the International Commission on English in the Liturgy. Totowa, NJ: Catholic Book Publishing, 2011.

———. *Code of Canon Law, Latin-English Edition: New English Translation Fourth Printing*. Washington, DC: Canon Law Society of America, 2023.

———. *General Instruction of the Roman Missal*. Washington, DC: United States Conference of Catholic Bishops, 2011.

———. *The Sacramentary: The Roman Missal*. 2nd typical ed. Translated by the International Commission on English in the Liturgy. Washington, DC: United States Conference of Catholic Bishops, 1985.

Chiron, Yves. *Annibale Bugnini: Reformer of the Liturgy*. Brooklyn: Angelico, 2018.

Congregation for Divine Worship and the Discipline of the Sacraments. *Redemptionis Sacramentum*. The Holy See, Mar 25, 2004. https://www.vatican.va/roman_curia/congregations/ccdds/documents/rc_con_ccdds_doc_20040423_redemptionis-sacramentum_en.html.

Denzinger, Heinrich. *Compendium of Creeds, Definitions, and Declarations on Matters of Faith and Morals*. 43rd ed. Edited by Peter Hünermann. San Francisco: Ignatius, 2012.

Derville, Guillaume. *Eucharistic Concelebration: From Symbol to Reality*. Montreal: Wilson and Lafleur, 2011.

De Sainte-Marie, Joseph. *The Holy Eucharist: The World's Salvation*. Leominster, England: Gracewing, 2015.

Gasparri, Pietro, ed. *Codex Iuris Canonici Pii X Pontificis Maximi Iussu Digestus, Benedicti Papae XV Auctoritate Promulgatus*. Westminster, MD: Newman, 1957.

Gregory IX. "Decretal." In *Corpus Iuris Canonici: Edition lipsiensis secunda post Aemilii Ludovici Richteri curas ad librorum manu scriptorium et editionis romanae fidem recognovit et adnotatione critica*, 71. 1879. Reprint, Graz, Austria: Akademische Druck-U. Verlagsanstalt, 1995.

Huels, John M. *Disputed Questions in the Liturgy Today*. Chicago: Archdiocese of Chicago, 1988.

John Paul II. *Ecclesia de Eucharistia*. The Holy See, Apr 17, 2003. https://www.vatican.va/content/john-paul-ii/en/encyclicals/documents/hf_jp-ii_enc_20030417_eccl-de-euch.html.

———. *Sacrae Disciplinae Leges*. The Holy See, Jan, 25, 1983. https://www.vatican.va/content/john-paul-ii/en/apost_constitutions/documents/hf_jp-ii_apc_25011983_sacrae-disciplinae-leges.html.

Jounel, Pierre. *The Rite of Concelebration of Mass and of Communion under Both Species*. New York: Desclee, 1967.

Jungmann, Joseph A. "Commentary on the Constitution on the Sacred Liturgy." In *Commentary on Documents of Vatican II*, edited by Herbert Vorgrimler, 1:44. New York: Crossroad, 1989.

Kocik, Thomas M. "Preaching through the Choir: The Merits of Assisting at Mass *in Choro*." *Antiphon* 10.2 (2006) 204–11.

Kwasniewski, Peter. *Resurgent in the Midst of Crisis*. Kettering, OH: Angelico, 2014.

Lang, Uwe M. "Sacramental Concelebration: Historical and Theological Perspectives on Contemporary Practice." *Antiphon* 27.1 (2023) 59–62.

Manders, Hendrik. "Concelebration." In *Concilium*, 2:138–40. Glen Rock, NJ: Paulist, 1965.

McGowan, Jean C. *Concelebration: Sign of Unity in the Church*. New York: Herder and Herder, 1964.

Peters, Edward N., ed. *The 1917 or Pio-Benedictine Code of Canon Law in English Translation*. San Francisco: Ignatius, 2001.

———, ed. *Incrementa in Progressu 1983 Codicis Iuris Canonici*. Montreal: Wilson and Lafleur, 2005.

Pius XII. "Address to the International Congress on Pastoral Liturgy." *The Pope Speaks* 3.3 (Winter 1956–1957) 273.

———. *Episcopalis Consecrationis*. The Holy See, Nov, 30, 1945. https://www.vatican.va/content/pius-xii/la/apost_constitutions/documents/hf_p-xii_apc_19441130_episcopali-consecrationis.html.

Sacred Congregation for Divine Worship. "In Celebratione Missæ." In *Documents on the Liturgy 1963–1979 Conciliar, Papal, and Curial Texts*, 561–64. Collegeville, MN: Liturgical, 1982.

Sacred Congregation of Rites (Consilium). "Ecclesiæ Semper." In *Documents on the Liturgy 1963–1979 Conciliar, Papal, and Curial Texts*, 553–64. Collegeville, MN: Liturgical, 1982.

———. *Inter Œcumenici*. Adoremus, Sep 26, 1964. https://adoremus.org/1964/09/inter-oecumenici.

Sacred Congregation of Rites. *Eucharisticum Mysterium*. Adoremus, May, 25, 1967. https://adoremus.org/1967/05/eucharisticum-mysterium/.

Second Vatican Council. "Sacrosanctum Concilium." In *The Documents of Vatican II*, edited by Walter M. Abbot, 137–78. New York: Herder and Herder, 1966.

Part II—*Munus Docendi*

The *Munus Docendi* in Biblical, Patristic, and Conciliar Perspectives

—Alan D. Mostrom

WITHIN THE CONTEXT OF a post-Christian and biblically illiterate society, a renewed commitment to the church's teaching office is needed. Renewal of the teaching office is aided by understanding the biblical basis of the clergy's teaching office. This office, prefigured in the Levitical ministry, is a divinely ordained instrument of the divine *munera* of teacher, priest, and king. Jesus Christ's priesthood and teaching office are correctly viewed as the source of the ecclesial sanctifying and teaching *munera*, but this essay argues that the teaching office and its purpose are also prefigured in the Old Testament, and specifically in the Levitical priesthood.[1]

The theological premise of this essay, broadly speaking, is that the divine economy from its beginning is equally intellectual as it is affective, and that the saving truths of the deposit of faith are principally communicated through the teaching office. Biblical revelation provides a theological basis of the teaching office—typological in the Old Testament, fulfilled in the New Testament—as a source of ecclesial edification and renewal that is

1. Jean-Pierre Torrell's study *A Priestly People: Baptismal Priesthood and Priestly Ministry* argues that Jesus Christ's priesthood has no natural nor Old Testament predecessor, but is *sui generis*. In a certain sense this is true, but part of the purpose of looking for typologies is to show progressive nature of revelation, even when there are discontinuities. When studying the mode of divine revelation in salvation history, it is arguable that the divine will privileges the use of instruments/mediators to communicate divine word and presence. Priesthood as an official means for the communication of divine revelation and presence makes it a unique instrument among instruments and a worthwhile course of study to trace the continuities and discontinuities between Old Testament and New Testament priesthoods.

often untouched in the tradition and the modern magisterium but should and can be developed today, in a time when renewal is desperately needed.

The essay is composed of three parts: the first part will survey the Levitical priest-Catholic priest typology in the tradition up to Vatican II; the second will survey Old Testament texts on the teaching office of the Levitical priesthood; and finally, a conclusion will offer a proposal for how to develop the Levitical priest-Catholic priest typology to incorporate the aspect of the teaching office.

CLARIFICATION OF TERMS AND THEIR SIGNIFICANCE FOR TYPOLOGY

Historical-critical scholarship on the Levites and the priesthood is vast and convoluted.[2] Scholars are divided as to the origins of the Levites, how they were divided in terms of their function in Israelite society and cult in different eras in history. Since the nature of this study is theological and dogmatic, this essay does not address such issues. The perspective taken here is that the high priesthood, priests, and their attendants were all male members of the tribe of Levi. Thus, the "high priest" and his "priests" were also Levites in the sense that they were members of the tribe of Levi, though they were distinctive by their ordination to offer sacrifice in the inner parts of the sanctuary, which were considered holier than the outer parts.[3]

2. For an overview of the scholarship on the Levites, see D. A. Garrett's entry "Levi, Levites" in *Dictionary of the Old Testament*, 519–22. Garrett describes the state of scholarship as "reflecting on the diversity of viewpoints in the Bible, many scholars follow J. Wellhausen's lead and assert that although the Old Testament presents a confused and unreliable account of the background of the Levites, the biblical texts are nevertheless not without value in reconstructing Israel's religious history. In particular, most scholars see in the Bible the redacted fragments of texts that were used by rival claimants to Israel's priesthood to bolster their cases. The story of Israel's priesthood is thus a dialectical historical process in which rival groups . . . contended for the right to officiate at Israel's altars," 520. For another perspective on the scholarship, see Merlin Rehm's entry "Levites and Priests" in *The Anchor Bible Dictionary*, 297–310. See also Anthony Giambrone's recently published work *The Bible and the Priesthood: Priestly Participation in the One Sacrifice for Sins*, 76–80.

3. D. A. Garrett contrasts the scholarly position that all Levites were priests with what he calls the "traditional view" of the Levite/priest distinction: "The Levites served as special assistants who cared for the sacred articles of the tent of meeting whereas the Aaronites actually functioned as priests. Thus the Levites had sanctuary duties but were not actually priests (they are sometimes described as a *clerus minor*, or 'lower clergy'). This interpretation is derived primarily from texts in Exodus, Leviticus and Numbers. For example, the priestly consecration of Aaron and his sons in Leviticus 8 starkly contrasts with the commands regarding the Levites in Numbers 3–4. The former sets the Aaronites apart for officiating in sacrifice and worship, whereas the latter prescribes

When referring to the other cultic personnel, the non-priestly attendants in the tabernacle or temple are designated as "Levites," though it is also a term for tribal members in general. The "Levite" non-priestly cultic personnel were males of a certain age, and they were ordained to serve liturgical functions distinct from the priests and the high priest in the outer parts of the sanctuary. Thus, there are three distinct orders of service in the sanctuary that are descended from the same tribe. They are both a unified group in terms of tribal origin and ministry, but they are divided by the type of work they perform in the sanctuary and the parts of the sanctuary to which they are permitted access.

As will be shown below, the divine command for Levites to teach is not delineated according to this threefold division. The command to teach seems to belong to every Levite male who serves in the sanctuary, regardless of his ordained tasks. Thus, Levite attendants, priests, and high priests are all enjoined to teach the law.[4] The texts studied below and the subsequent history of Judaism may raise the question whether the ordained clergy alone were teachers. This is certainly not the case. The Old Testament attests to parents (Deut 6:7), judges (Deut 16:18–19; 17:9–12), kings,[5] and prophets as teachers of the law, regardless of tribal origin. The Second Temple period saw the development of new socioreligious groups of teachers, including the scribal class and the Pharisees, who eventually evolved into the rabbis (again, regardless of tribe).

Christian typology does not necessitate strict continuity in the comparisons being made across testaments; there are often discontinuities between type and antitype.[6] For example, the Gospel of Matthew has an extensive Moses-Christ typology, even though Jesus Christ was not a

---

for the other clans of Levi (the Gershonites, the Kohathites and the Merarites) specific duties in caring for and transporting the tent, the altar and the other sacred vessels" (Garrett, "Levi, Levites," 519–20). Cf. Giambrone, *Bible and the Priesthood*, 77.

4. For an alternate view, see Rehm's dictionary entry which argues, "This writer believes that Wright is correct in his belief that 'Levitical priests' and 'Levites' are not synonymous terms in Deuteronomy. However, he does not think that the distinction that Wright assumes, namely, that one group was altar clergy and the other teaching clergy is valid. Emerton is no doubt correct in his view that all Levites were in principle altar priests and that they could also serve as teachers. If there is nevertheless a distinction between 'Levitical priests' and 'Levites,' what is it? We propose the theory that the two names do not represent two different groups living and working at the same time, but that they represent (essentially) the same group working at two different times" (Rehm, "Levites and Priests," 297–310).

5. Ecclesiastes, traditionally attributed to Solomon, opens, "The words of David's son, Qoheleth, king in Jerusalem."

6. For an overview of typology per se and specific examples of patristic typology, see Daniélou, *From Shadows to Reality*. Also see O'Keefe and Reno, *Sanctified Vision*.

Levite like Moses.[7] In terms of the typology between the teaching office of "Levite, priest, high priest" and that of "deacon, presbyter, bishop," there are continuities and differences. As an example of divergence, the teaching authority of the Old Testament does not delineate any distinction of degree between the non-priestly Levites, the priests, and the high priest. In Catholic theology, however, teaching authority is possessed by the bishop in full and in the priest and deacon by participation, and, therefore, by degree. Nevertheless, both the Old Testament ordained clergy and the New Testament ordained clergy were authorized to teach.

LEVITICAL PRIESTHOOD AND CATHOLIC PRIESTHOOD: A CATHOLIC TRADITION OF TYPOLOGY

Patristic Sources

The basis of a Levitical priesthood-Christian priesthood typology was established in the early ecclesial tradition but has not developed subsequently. Clement of Rome is arguably the first Christian thinker to employ a typology between the two forms of priesthoods, though it appears only once in his writings.[8] Other early typological usages appear in the *Apostolic Tradition*, Tertullian of Carthage, Cyprian of Carthage, and the *Didascalia Apostolorum*.[9]

Clement of Rome is possibly the first Christian writer to use this form of typology in chapter 40:3–5 of his First Letter to the Corinthians:

> In his [the Master's] superior plan he set forth both where and through whom he wished them to be performed, so that everything done in a holy way and according to his good pleasure might be acceptable to his will. Thus, those who make their sacrificial offerings at the arranged times are acceptable and blessed. And since they follow the ordinances of the Master, they commit no sin. For special liturgical rites have been assigned to the high priest, and a special place has been designated for the regular priests, and special ministries are established for the Levites. The lay person is assigned to matters enjoined on the laity.[10]

7. See Allison, *New Moses*.

8. Clement of Rome, "First Letter of Clement," 107.

9. The patristic usage of the Levitical priesthood-Christology typology is covered in depth in Bryan Stewart's *Priests of My People*, which is my guide through the patristics.

10. Clement of Rome, "First Letter of Clement," 107.

Clement is concerned with the proper ministrations allotted to the high priest, the priests, the Levites, and the layman. The reference to threefold temple ministry in the temple liturgy in Judaism is not to be taken literally, however, but as an analogy or typology being drawn between Christian ministers and their Jewish prefigurations.

Clement follows this comparison by drawing out another comparison, or typology, between the organization of the apostolic church as built on the preaching of apostles, their successors—the bishops—and deacons, and Moses giving structure to the Israelites as unified tribes centered around liturgical worship in the tabernacle. Clement does not explicitly explain how teaching or preaching under the old law is fulfilled in the new covenant, but it implicitly suggests such a typology.

In the Ethiopic version of the *Apostolic Tradition*[11]—which purports to record apostolic authoritative statements about Christian morality, liturgical norms, and ecclesiastical organization and discipline—the section dealing with the ordination of bishops contains no references to the Old Testament, but in the section concerning the ordination of presbyters, the text compares the Holy Spirit's outpouring in a priestly ordination to Moses's appointment of seventy elders. It is in the text on the ordination of deacons that the deacon is compared to the Levites who assist the high priest in his sanctuary in the temple. The emphasis is on the deacon as one who serves alongside the higher order of clergy, specifically the bishop, though perhaps Christ's high priesthood is in view as well:

> Over the deacon then, let the bishop say thus: "O God, you who created all things, and who adorned [them] by the Word . . . Father of our Lord Jesus Christ, whom you sent to minister to your will, that all the human race might be saved, and you made known to us and revealed your Thought, your Wisdom . . . give the spirit of grace and earnestness to this your servant . . . *Enlighten, Lord, the one you have loved and chosen to minister to your church, offering in holiness to your sanctuary those things offered to you from the inheritance of your high priesthood, so that ministering without blame and purely and in a holy fashion and with a pure conscience, he may be counted worthy of this high and exalted office*, by your good will, praising you continually through your only begotten Son Jesus Christ our Lord, by whom

11. Bradshaw et al., *Apostolic Tradition*. It was originally written as a Greek work, which is no longer extant. The translation cited is a reconstruction of a variety of translations, from Latin, Sahidic, Arabic, Ethiopic, and Bohairic. The Ethiopic version is a critical edition based on eight manuscripts, and the text cited below is unique to the Ethiopic version.

> [be] praise and might to you forever and ever." The people: "Amen."[12]

Thus, the priestly typology in the *Apostolic Tradition* is located in the texts about the ordination of presbyters and deacons, though in the ordination prayer over the deacon, the bishop is the antitype to the Levitical high priest. In neither of these ordination prayers, however, is the Levitical teaching office referenced.

Tertullian of Carthage holds a complicated place among the church fathers considering his criticism of the episcopal office after he joined the schismatic Montanists. However, it has been demonstrated that Tertullian viewed the episcopacy as a priesthood[13] and deployed typological reasoning to demonstrate it.[14] Most of Tertullian's references to the typology are tacit and complex, which Bryan Stewart's work demonstrates in detail. He demonstrates through a variety of texts that Tertullian linked the Christian bishop to the Levitical priesthood.[15]

In Tertullian's work *An Exhortation to Chastity*, for instance, he compares the "priestly order" of Christian priesthood to the Levitical priests in order to deny Christians' justification for remarriage. Stewart argues that Tertullian's reference to a priestly order is restricted to Christian bishops who are described in the Pastoral Epistles as men with only one wife: "For behold in the old law I observe the license of repeated marriage being restricted. A caution is given in Leviticus: 'My priests shall not marry several

12. Bradshaw et al., *Apostolic Tradition*, 63–65; ellipses in original.

13. Many of the third-century fathers of the church identified the episcopal office with a teaching function (Irenaeus of Lyons is one example; cf. *Against Heresies*, IV, 26:2), but the work of "teaching," especially catechesis, was also taken up by non-clerical teachers like Pantaenus, Clement, and Origen of Alexandria, all who taught in Alexandria's catechetical school. For a brief overview of the scholarship on the Alexandrian catechetical school, see Osborn, *Clement of Alexandria*, 19–24.

14. This summary is found in Stewart, *Priests of My People*, 28n2: "It is important to note that Tertullian's Montanist conception of the bishop as a priest does not differ from his pre-Montanist days. As David Rankin has demonstrated, Tertullian freely designates the Christian bishop a priest in texts written from both time periods. Therefore, for my purposes, a careful distinction between pre- and post-Montanist works is unnecessary." See Rankin, "Tertullian's Consistency of Thought on Ministry," 271–76. See also Rankin, *Tertullian and the Church*. Rankin does note that Tertullian does not explicitly associate the episcopal office with a teaching function: "Irenaeus had associated the office of bishop (and that of the presbyterate) with the role of teacher. Tertullian does not explicitly do so. His association of the succession of the episcopal office with the authentic handing down of unadulterated apostolic doctrine does not require the conclusion of a specific teaching role either for the bishop or for either of the other major clerical offices" (Rankin, *Tertullian and the Church*, 174).

15. Stewart, *Priests of My People*, 27–43.

times.' . . . Therefore, the apostle more fully and more closely orders that the one who is chosen into the priestly order (*ordinem sacerdotalem*) must be a man of one marriage."[16]

Cyprian of Carthage, a mid-third-century bishop, is known for his thematization of Christian priesthood along Old Testament Levitical lines. In letter 8, Cyprian compares episcopal ministry to that of their "predecessors," who might include Levitical priests since he is directly quoting Ezekiel's famous diatribe against the shepherds of Judah:

> And since it is incumbent upon us who seem to be in charge and in the place of shepherds to guard the flock, if we should be found negligent, there will be said to us what was said to our predecessors who were such negligent leaders that "we did not seek the lost and we did not bring back the strayed and we did not bind up the injured and we have fed off their milk and worn their wool."[17]

Even if he is not clearly comparing bishops to Levitical priests, Cyprian elsewhere explicitly compares Christian priests to Levites who

> first held the form of this ordination and religion in the law so that, when the eleven tribes divided the land and distributed the possessions, the tribe of Levi, which had time for the temple and the altar and the divine ministries, received nothing from that apportionment of the division but, while others cultivated the land, that tribe honored God only and received from the eleven tribes for its food and nourishment tithes of the crops which were growing. This whole matter was carried out by divine authority and arrangement so that those who devoted themselves to divine services should, in no way, be distracted nor be forced to consider or to transact secular business.[18]

In letter 72, Cyprian compares the holiness of the priest's service to that of Levite priests in Lev 21:21 and Exod 19:22 and 28:43.[19] In an example

16. Stewart, *Priests of My People*, 31. See Tertullian, *De Exhortatione Castitatis*, 2:1024.

17. Cyprian, *Letters (1–81)*, 21. The biblical quotation is from Ezek 34:3–4. Anthony Giambrone describes the leaders in Ezek 34 as not only royal leaders but priests as well: "The plural 'shepherds' might target several or all of Israel's kings considered together (cf. Jer. 23:1); or, more likely, it might embrace a wider circle of ruling officials—thus indicting the priestly establishment as well, priests belonging integrally to the whole state apparatus, of course" (Giambrone, *Bible and the Priesthood*, 182).

18. Giambrone, *Bible and the Priesthood*, 3–4.

19. Giambrone, *Bible and the Priesthood*, 267.

brought out by Stewart, Cyprian encourages a fellow bishop, Rogatian, to address a rebellious deacon by drawing on the logic of Deut 17:12. Cyprian seeks to galvanize Rogatian to use his episcopal authority to punish the wayward deacon in the way a Levite priest was to correct a wayward Israelite seeking to avoid his legal prescriptions in Deut 17:12, a text that does refer to Levite civil authority, but an authority rooted in their authority to teach Torah, a point Cyprian does not address:

> And you, indeed, have acted honorably and in accordance with your usual humility toward us in that you preferred to complain to us concerning him although you had power, by virtue of the strength of the episcopate and the authority of the see, by which you could immediately punish . . . insolent deacon, having in mind the divine precepts concerning men of this type, since the Lord God says in Deuteronomy: "And any man who has the insolence to refuse to listen to the priest or judge, whoever he may be in those days, that man shall die."[20]

Cyprian's ecclesiology is based, at least partially, on an Israel-church typology, and his theology of holy orders is based on a typology of Levite priesthood-Christian bishop and priest. It does not seem Cyprian addresses a typology that directly includes the diaconal role, but perhaps that is more tacit. He is direct in offering these typologies and unequivocally applies them to the bishop's sacerdotal and royal functions, though he does not seem to apply it to the teaching function explicitly. Nevertheless, Cyprian understands the episcopal office to have a teaching function, even if he does not thematize it on typological grounds.[21]

The *Didascalia Apostolorum*, from the third century, has about a dozen references to Levite and high priesthood typology, though indistinctive from Clement and the *Apostolic Tradition*. The first set of references compares the bishop to the Levites who labored and served in the tabernacle, with the tabernacle serving as a type of the church. The comparison aids an argument that the bishop should be supported by the church's proceeds. The logic of episcopacy being supported by church funds is based on a

20. Giambrone, *Bible and the Priesthood*, 6–7. See Stewart, *Priests of My People*, 162–63.

21. That the bishops were not only kings and priests but also teachers (prophets) is not particularly controversial, especially for a prominent bishop like Cyprian, who led a see that was a regional court of appeal, even to the bishop of Rome. Cyprian held three synods in Carthage to deal with disciplinary (governance) and doctrinal (teaching) matters. See Novatian of Rome's appeal to Cyprian for episcopal advice concerning reconciliation with the lapsed. For example, letters 44 and 45 in the collection of his letters in Cyprian, *Letters (1–81)*. Also see Papandrea, *Novatian*, 141–66.

comparison to "priests and Levites and deacons," which may be an equation of non-priestly Levites to deacons or a mixture of old law ministerial offices with ecclesial ministerial office:

> You bishops may be supported from the revenues of the church but you are not to devour them, for it is written: "You shall not muzzle a threshing ox." Thus, just as the ox which labours without a muzzle on the threshing floor eats, but does not consume it all, so you likewise, labouring on the threshing floor which is the church of God, may be supported by the church, in the same manner as the Levites who served in the tent of witness, which was entirely a type of the church.[22]
>
> For if you are serving in the office of the episcopate you should be supported from that very office of the episcopate as are the priests and Levites and deacons who minister before God, just as it is written in the book of Numbers.[23]

This text compares bishops to priests and Levites serving in the tabernacle as well as a variety of mediatorial figures—prophets, leaders, nobles, and kings—who go between God and his people, particularly in their ministry of preaching God's word and demonstrating knowledge of Scripture. The text does not directly connect preaching to the priestly Levitical office but to the roles of prophets, leaders, nobles, and kings:

> In this way you bishops are [*sic*] today are priests to your people, and Levites who serve the tent of God, the holy catholic church, who stand continually before the Lord God. So you are now priests and prophets and leaders and nobles and kings to your people, mediating between God and his faithful ones, receiving his word and proclaiming and declaring it, knowledgeable of the Scriptures and the sayings of God, bearing witness to his will, bearing the sins of all as you are to give answer on behalf of all.[24]

The next text is the most elaborate reference to the typology and is the most difficult to square with previous references. It also includes the first typological reference to the bishop as high priest, who is a teacher of divine truths. The bishop is typed as a chief, king, and even godlike. Yet, for our purposes, it is his comparison to the Levitical high priest who "ministers the word to you and is your mediator, your teacher" that is most striking. The priests, deacons, widows, and orphans are typed as Levites, but the deacon

22. Stewart-Sykes, *Didascalia Apostolorum*, 146.
23. Stewart-Sykes, *Didascalia Apostolorum*, 147.
24. Stewart-Sykes, *Didascalia Apostolorum*, 147.

is later typed as Christ too. This text, as far as I know, is the only time in the tradition that a sacramental minister—i.e., the bishop—is compared to a Levitical priest, in this case the high priest, and a Levite attendant, which is, then, connected to their authority to teach:

> Listen then, sacred and catholic church. . . . There are prayers and petitions and thanksgivings where there were sacrifices, and now are there offerings which are offered through the bishops to the Lord God where there were firstfruits and tithes and portions and gifts. For they are your high priests, and there are deacons and presbyters and widows and orphans where there were Levites, but the bishop is high-priest and Levite. He it is who ministers the word to you and is your mediator, your teacher, and, after God, is your father who has regenerated you through the water. He is your chief, he is your master, he your powerful king. He is to be honoured by you in the place of God, since the bishop sits among you as a type of God. The deacon, however, is present as a type of Christ, and is therefore to be loved by you. . . . Therefore just as it was not allowed to a stranger, that is to anyone who was not a Levite, to go up to the altar, or to make any offering without the high priest, so you likewise should do nothing without the bishop.[25]

The *Didascalia Apostolorum* offers a straightforward typology of priests and deacons as Levites. Subdeacons are compared to "those who carried the vessels of the court of the Lord's sanctuary," and the bishop called a "watchman" is compared to the high priest:

> Again the apostles decreed: There shall be presbyters, and deacons like the Levites, and subdeacons like those who carried the vessels of the court of the Lord's sanctuary, and a watchman, the guide of all the people, like Aaron, the head and the chief of all the priests and Levites in the whole camp.[26]

The *Didascalia Apostolorum* has the most extensive usage of the Levitical priesthood typology, though it is also the most idiosyncratic in terms of consistently assigning the antitype, that is, the fulfillment of the Old Testament ministerial offices in the church's ranks of sacred ministers.

25. Stewart-Sykes, *Didascalia Apostolorum*, 151.

26. Stewart-Sykes, *Didascalia Apostolorum*, 271.

The Second Vatican Council

Having presented the Levitical priesthood-Christian priesthood typology as an established feature of patristic theology of holy orders, this essay will consider the Second Vatican Council's *Lumen Gentium* and *Presbyterorum Ordinis*, the most recent magisterial text to invoke the typology for our understanding of holy orders.

Presbyterorum Ordinis, the *Decree on the Ministry and Life of Priests*, opens by defining the presbyterate as a particular sharing in Christ's *munera* of teacher, priest, and king. Priests are described as sharing, through the outpouring of the Spirit received in ordination,[27] in the office and authority of the episcopal order, though to a lesser degree, and are, thus, cooperators with the episcopal ministry and mission. Like bishops, priests share in the tasks of governing, sanctifying, and teaching. Their teaching office and power, which is their "primary duty,"[28] is like the bishop's, but to a lesser degree, and is derived from Christ's original authority and power as teacher. The faithful, in turn, can "rightfully . . . expect this [the Word of God] from their priests."[29] *Presbyterorum Ordinis*'s specification of a "right" to the word footnotes three biblical citations: Mal 2:7; 1 Tim 4:11–13; and 1 Tim 1:9. The Malachi reference is to Levitical priests who bear the responsibility to teach Israel: "For a priest's lips preserve knowledge, and instruction is to be sought from his mouth, because he is the messenger of the Lord of hosts."[30]

The decree directly uses the Levitical priest-Christian priest typology in paragraph 17, where a comparison is made between the Catholic priest's usage of ecclesiastical goods to the Levitical priesthood, who have the

27. See *Presbyterorum Ordinis*, which draws from the *Apostolic Tradition* text cited earlier: "Therefore, by reason of the gift of the Holy Spirit which is given to priests in Holy Orders, bishops regard them as necessary helpers and counselors in the ministry and in their role of teaching, sanctifying and nourishing the People of God. Already in the ancient ages of the Church we find liturgical texts proclaiming this with insistence, as when they solemnly call upon God to pour out upon the candidate for priestly ordination 'the spirit of grace and counsel, so that with a pure heart he may help and govern the People of God,' just as in the desert the spirit of Moses was spread abroad in the minds of the seventy prudent men, 'and using them as helpers among the people, he easily governed countless multitudes'" (Second Vatican Council, *Presbyterorum Ordinis*, sec. 7).

28. See Second Vatican Council, *Presbyterorum Ordinis*, sec. 6.

29. Second Vatican Council, *Presbyterorum Ordinis*, sec. 4.

30. It should be noted, however, that this passage from Mal 2:7 is presenting the ideal Levite/priest, whereas the actual Levite/priest during the writing of Malachi is specified in negative terms in 2:8: "But you have turned aside from the way, and have caused many to stumble by your instruction; You have corrupted the covenant of Levi, says the Lord of hosts." See Giambrone, *Bible and the Priesthood*, 132–33.

Lord as their portion: "For priests who have the Lord as their 'portion and heritage,' (Num 18:20) temporal goods should be used only toward ends which are licit according to the doctrine of Christ and the direction of the Church."[31]

Lumen Gentium, the *Dogmatic Constitution on the Church*, deploys typology in paragraphs 21–22 where episcopal consecration is described as conferring the fullness of power of orders and is referenced as the antitype of the Aaronic high priesthood: "The fullness of the sacrament of Orders is conferred, that fullness of power, namely, which both in the Church's liturgical practice and in the language of the Fathers of the Church is called *the high priesthood*, the supreme power of the sacred ministry."[32]

The contemporary magisterium and the ancient tradition of the church fathers, together, teach a typology that compares the threefold priesthood of the old law—high priest, priest, and Levites—to the sacramental priesthood of the new law—bishops, priests, and deacons. This typology is generally used to signify the unity-in-difference between the orders, with an added emphasis on analogous offices to govern and sanctify God's people. With the exception of a single reference in the *Didascalia Apostolorum* to a Levite priest-Christian priest teaching office, the typology generally does not include reference to the teaching office.

THE TEACHING OFFICE OF LEVITES

The methodical approach of this section examines the relevant texts according to their final canonical form. This approach will not address the historical development of the Levites as a group (especially the distinction between Levites and Levitical priests), the historical and lexical difficulties found in texts about Levites (especially as they relate to their liturgical role within the kingdoms of Israel and Judah), nor the redactional process and provenance of the texts considered. However, it will address the Levitical ministry within the matrix of the beliefs of Judaism and Christianity and will consider a variety of biblical references to a Levitical teaching office, which are found in the Torah, the Historical Books, and the Prophets.

31. Second Vatican Council, *Presbyterorum Ordinis*, sec. 17.

32. Second Vatican Council, *Lumen Gentium*, sec. 21 (emphasis added).

Torah References to Levitical Teachers

While the composition of the Torah is generally argued to have occurred in the exilic period, there is no argument as to the centrality of the Torah for Jewish belief vis-à-vis the maintenance of the covenant, liturgical ritual, and the kind of holiness needed to bring an end to the "exile," even exile on their own land. So, even if the Torah was composed into its final form in the exilic period and represents an ideal form of Israelite history and practice, the legislation on the Levitical priesthood, including teaching responsibilities, still represents what Judaism views to be the ideal for priestly ministry with or without a temple.

The first text to consider is Lev 10:8–11: "The Lord said to Aaron. . . . You must be able to distinguish between what is sacred and what is profane, and between what is clean and what is unclean; and you must be able *to teach* the Israelites *all the statutes* that the Lord has given them through Moses." Leviticus 10 narrates several laws in the tragic aftermath of Nadab and Abihu's "unholy" sacrifice, which led to their destruction by the divine presence. Moses, in response, has their bodies removed and instructs Aaron and his remaining sons to avoid the same fate by maintaining the necessary distinctions between holy and non-holy things. Aaron, in turn, is warned directly by the Lord[33] to altogether avoid intoxication in the tabernacle, arguably another example of how Levite priests might fail to distinguish holy things (tabernacle service) from common behavior (strong drink). This commandment is followed by the Lord, for the first time, instructing Aaron (and his sons) to teach his law to all of Israel. The term for teaching, *ūləhōwrōṯ*, is a term that is indicative of special authority by which the Lord commands the Levitical priesthood to take on this role or office.

Jacob Milgrom argues that the legislation following the tragic incident, verses 10–11, has in view the priesthood's essence.[34] Even though priests were not otherwise the direct recipients of divine law—i.e., their teaching role does not suggest new legislation—they were tasked with communicating the entirety of the Torah to the people. Leviticus 10:8–11 thus affirms that the ministry of Levitical priests is both liturgical and pedagogical; that

33. This is, perhaps, the only time someone other than Moses receives divine law. Jay Sklar summarizes this passage in the following way: "At this point, for the only time in Leviticus, *the Lord* speaks directly to *Aaron* alone, perhaps to emphasize that the priests in particular must pay attention to the following commands: to avoid intoxication, to distinguish ritual categories, and teach the Israelites divine law" (Sklar, *Leviticus*, 159).

34. Milgrom claims the "making of distinctions is the essence of the priestly function" and that the imperative to teach all the law to Israel also entails "one of the main functions of the priesthood (Deut 24:8)." See Milgrom, *Leviticus*, 96. Cf. Giambrone, *Bible and the Priesthood*.

is, they were ordained to offer true sacrifice and to instruct Israel in divine things. Priesthood is holy but not exclusively cultic; it is ordered to God in the form of sacrifice and as a mediation of divine law.[35]

The most extensive texts establishing the Levitical priesthood as teachers of Israel are found in Deut 17:8–13; 24:8; 33:8–10. Modern biblical scholars emphasize Deut 17's mitigated view of kingship as evidence of a post-exilic provenance, but verses 8–13 are not concerned with royal authority as it is of priestly and judicial authority to adjudicate between disputants in a legal and social case, which likely would require *interpretation* of Torah legislation. The priests and judges indicated in this text are clearly not the original Levite priests alone, but subsequent generations who carry forward the authority of the original generation of priests.

Deuteronomy 17 depicts the disputants being commanded to bring their case, at the Lord's choosing, to the Levitical priest or the juridical officeholder who will then decide the case. The thrust of the text focuses on the care to which the disputants are to give the decisions of the priests or judges. The disputants, with no distinction between acquitted or condemned, are required to follow the entirety of the judge's or priest's decision. No modifications of the verdict are permitted lest the innovator suffer death.[36]

The word "instruct," וּלְהוֹרֹת (*ulehorot*), is the same term found in Lev 10:11 and clearly has the sense of the priest and/or judge possessing officially and divinely sanctioned authority. Deuteronomy 16–17 describes appointed judges and officers engaging in righteous judgment, showing impartiality and fairness as a way to restore peace and justice.[37] Thus, it would not be surprising for a postexilic Jewish community to view the goal of these leaders' adjudicating cases between Israelites as an ideal of established righteousness and holiness, and not necessarily a system of human governance. It is noteworthy that the priests' teaching role in Deut 17 is more specific than that found in Lev 10, particularly in that priests serving as judges are not instructing the faithful in divine law but offering judgments on practical matters in light of divine law. The Levitical priest's cultic mediation is therefore complemented by his authority to interpret God's word for his people.

35. Milgrom offers an insightful summary of the rationale for this legislation that Levitical priests are to teach: "There can be no esoteric doctrine hidden away in the priestly archives: 'The Torah commanded us by Moses is the heritage of the congregation of Jacob (Deut 33:4)'" (Milgrom, *Leviticus*, 96).

36. Stephen Cook provides a fine summary of the details of this process. See Cook, *Reading Deuteronomy*, 138–39.

37. For an excellent study of the *rîb*, or contention, as a way to reestablish justice in Israel, see Bovati, *Re-Establishing Justice*.

In Deut 24:8, building on the legislation in Lev 13–14 and using the same term as Lev 10:11 and Deut 17:8, the Levitical priests are depicted as instructing[38] sufferers of skin disease how to be restored to ritual purity: "In an attack of scaly infection you shall be careful to observe exactly and to carry out all the *instructions* the Levitical priests give you, as I have commanded them: observe them carefully. Remember what the Lord, your God, did to Miriam on the journey after you left Egypt." The commandment to carefully follow the priest's instruction requires the sufferer to know the detailed legislation in Lev 13–14 as well as the Exodus narrative that includes the story of Miriam contracting leprosy. The requirement is especially applicable to the priest who must know how to apply the legislation before instructing the sufferer.

The final reference to a Levitical teaching office in Deut and the Torah as a whole is found in Moses's farewell address in chapter 33 where he blesses each tribe before dying. In his blessing over the tribe of Levi, Moses first references the Thummim and Urim—i.e., "a device for obtaining God's decision on important questions"[39]—and the original generation's ordination in their fight against the golden-calf worshipers. Next, Moses blesses Levi by saying, "They teach your ordinances to Jacob, your law to Israel" (Deut 33:10). Jeffrey Tigay's comment on this line is illuminating:

> This refers to the full range of priestly instruction in ritual, judicial, and civil matters, such as worship, distinction between sacred and profane, clean and unclean, judicial decisions, and division of territory. . . . Priests gave some of their instructions as ad hoc rulings, sometimes probably obtained from the Urim and Thummim, in response to specific inquiries. We do not know what further institutional form their instruction took, such as teaching in schools or at festivals or other gatherings.[40]

The Torah texts on the Levitical teaching office exhibit the Levite priests teaching in several contexts: through interpreting and applying legislation in difficult circumstances; through maintaining cultic boundaries in ritual contexts; and in seeking to understand and communicate the divine plan to the people.

38. Jeffrey Tigay comments that *torah* in Hebrew means "instruction" and conveys a wide range of meanings, including "rules of civil and ritual procedure, prophetic teaching and reproof, moral exhortation, and didactic narrative." See Tigay, *JPS Torah Commentary*, 323.

39. Tigay, *JPS Torah Commentary*, 324.

40. Tigay, *JPS Torah Commentary*, 325.

Levitical Teachers in the Historical Books

The Historical Books narrate the history of Israel from the conquest of Canaan to the beginning of the postexilic period. Judges 17–18 is a marginal example of the Levitical teaching office in that it is not a straightforward narration of priestly teaching but rather a negative portrayal of Levitical priesthood both in terms of cult and teaching.

The narrative depicts a Judahite noble sojourning in Ephraim, who is also a Levitical priest consecrated[41] by a thief, the Ephraimite Micah. Eventually, the priest is hired to serve in a counterfeit shrine in the territory of the relocated tribe of Dan. He is described as providing the Danites with theological justification for relocating their tribe, and he leads them in their worship of an idol of the Lord that they stole from Micah. The episode has an ominous tone as the Levite, Micah, the Danites, and the people at large are all described as doing "what was right in their own eyes" (Judg 17:6).

In Judg 18:3–6, the Danite spies ask the unnamed[42] Levite priest to "*consult* God, that we may *know* whether the journey we are making will lead to success" (v. 5). The Levite priest answers in the affirmative and blesses them in the name of the Lord. Some commentators understand the Levite's blessing not to have been a result of him seeking counsel from God but rather of him telling the Danites what they wanted to hear.

The entire episode is perplexing and difficult for several reasons. First, the Levite priest may not have been a Levite, but rather a Judahite, which would have disqualified him from ordination. Second, it is obvious that his ordination at the hands of Micah, a non-Levite who is nowhere near the tabernacle, is invalid. Third, the Levite priest's ministry to an idol is a blatant transgression of Torah legislation. Finally, the Levite priest's counsel to the inquiry of the Danites about whether to take the land for themselves is, on the one hand, a tacit acknowledgement of Levitical priests as teachers and guides in legal and civic matters, but on the other hand, his response falls short of the integrity required of Levitical priests. This narrative functions as part of an exilic-era Judean polemic against the Israelite cult and

41. Barry Webb summarizes this event as: "The expression 'to fill the hand' is idiomatic for 'consecrate' (see, e.g., Exod. 28:41; 29:9, 29, 33, 35; Lev. 8:33), and probably refers to the ceremonial filling of the appointee's hand with some token of his office. But the use of the term *hired* (kr) here in 18:4 suggests that it is filling of the hand in quite another sense that occupies the Levite's mind!" (Webb, *Book of Judges*, 433).

42. At the end of Judg 18, the Levite is finally named as Jonathan, the descendant of Moses's son Gershom, though some texts say Manasseh. Commentators are divided on both the purpose for leaving the priest unnamed until the end of the narrative and the significance of him being a descendant of Moses.

priesthood, which is depicted as illegitimate in its consecration and unjust in its teaching office.[43]

First and Second Samuel include several sustained references to Levitical priests, particularly as agents involved in the drama between Saul and David, as well as idiosyncratic references to figures that are difficult to categorize, such as the role of Samuel, who serves in the tabernacle but does not seem to be a Levite,[44] and David's sons, who are described as priests even though their father was a Judahite.[45] The most idiosyncratic reference is 2 Sam 22–23, where David asks a priest to consult the Lord through an ephod after which the Lord instructs David directly apart from the priest. With the exception of the divine communication through the ephod, 1 and 2 Samuel have no instances of Levitical priests engaging in the teaching of law.

First Kings 1–8 follows in line with 1 and 2 Samuel and depicts the Levitical priesthood as essentially subordinate to the royal authority of David and Solomon, taking direction in the coronation of Solomon in a role that was complementary to Nathan, the court prophet. Solomon even threatens to kill the high priest, Abiathar, but spares him for his service to King David. Yet he still replaces him with Zadok, suggesting that Solomon takes precedence over the high priesthood's line of succession. The remainder of 1 Kgs 1–8 depicts the high priest, priests, and Levite engaging exclusively in cultic roles, specifically during the dedication of Solomon's temple. After the dedication of the temple, Levitical priests are no longer mentioned during the reign of Solomon. It is only after the division of the kingdom that the Levites and priests return in 1 Kings and 2 Kings, though in a largely negative light with the exception of the story of Jehoiada, which is more extensively covered in 2 Chr 22–23.

Second Chronicles depicts the southern kingdom of Judah undergoing five periods of renewal and one case of Levitical priests withstanding idolatry in alignment with their sacerdotal and teaching office. For the sake of conciseness, this section will only treat the final period related to the reigns of Hezekiah and Josiah.[46] During this fifth period of renewal, King Hezekiah institutes a project to restore the temple after the reigns of the idolatrous kings Jotham and Ahaz. He is described as addressing the Levites to return

43. Webb, *Book of Judges*, 449–50; Butler, *Judges*, 397–99. See also Cody, *History of Old Testament Priesthood*, 52–54.

44. See Bar, "Was Samuel a Priest?," 16–21.

45. Torah legislation defines Levite descent according to one's father and mother being part of the tribe of Levi.

46. The other four periods treat the reigns of Kings Asa (2 Chr 15), Jehoshaphat (2 Chr 17–20), Joash (2 Chr 24; cf. 2 Kgs 12), and Uzziah (2 Chr 26).

to the temple, to sanctify themselves and purge the sanctuary of the myriad of impurities and evil previously performed inside: "They abandoned him, turned away their faces from the Lord's dwelling, and turned their backs on him" (2 Chr 29:6).

Hezekiah desires to make a covenant with God to turn away his wrath. The Chronicler describes the Levites as fulfilling the king's request in sixteen days, which is followed by Hezekiah reinstituting temple sacrifice, particularly burnt and sin offerings, so that the sins of Judah could be atoned. The scene then shifts to Hezekiah inviting the "assembly" of people to bring their various sacrificial offerings to the priests in the temple (2 Chr 29:20–24). The influx of sacrifices reveals an unforeseen problem: there were too few priests in a state of ritual purity to slaughter the animals. This required the "more conscientious" Levite attendants (non-priests) to assist in the slaughtering.[47] Hezekiah's zeal for worship inspired him to call for a "great Passover" (2 Chr 30) at the temple. The themes of ad hoc liturgical, festal, and national renewal are intertwined throughout this part of the narrative of 2 Chronicles.[48]

The narrative then highlights that Hezekiah, the Levite priests and their Levite attendants, and the people as a whole, though quite zealous, had misunderstood the Torah legislation. For instance, when the priests are sacrificing the Passover lambs during the great Passover, they are portrayed as "ashamed." It seems likely the priests became conscious during the performance of the ritual slaughter that they were ritually unclean.[49]

The assembly also realizes that they, too, are ritually unclean and, therefore, in need of the Levites to intervene. Hezekiah, who realizes that his and the assembly's zeal overreached their observance, pleads with God to forgive their error and accept their offering. The Lord shows mercy to the assembly and "heals" them.[50] Gratitude for the outpouring of divine mercy led the assembly, Levites, and priests to continue to celebrate the festival for one more week. The great Passover is followed by an extensive destruction of idolatrous shrines, a nationwide revival of sacrificial offerings, and national commitment to financially support the priests and Levites so they could study divine law:

47. Dillard, *2 Chronicles*, 237.

48. Japhet, *I and II Chronicles*, 931.

49. Dillard, *2 Chronicles*, 245.

50. Japhet, *I and II Chronicles*, 953. Japhet notes that the "healing" involved here was a preventative healing that kept the people from eating the ritual meal in a state of uncleanness.

> And the priest Azariah, head of the house of Zadok, answered him [Hezekiah], "Since they began to bring the offerings to the house of the Lord, we have eaten, been satisfied, and had much left over, for the Lord has blessed his people. This great supply is what was left over." (2 Chr 31:10)

The Hezekiah narrative ends on a positive note, unlike the kings who governed in the other periods of renewal, and notes that in his death his legacy was honored.

The reforms of Josiah are the culmination of the renewal events in 2 Chronicles. Josiah's reforms parallel those of the figures previously discussed in this section, especially Hezekiah. Josiah, noted for his piety, attacks idolatry, inaugurates temple repairs, and restores the Levites to their temple service, which leads to the famous rediscovery of the book of the law. In response to the rediscovery of the law, Josiah convokes an assembly of all of Judah and Levi and leads the people in a renewal of the covenant. The final part of Josiah's renewal program is a great Passover. In comparison to Hezekiah's great Passover, Josiah is liturgically and legally sound. In his preparations, Josiah appoints Levites and priests to serve in the temple, who are described as those who instruct "all Israel." The Levites and priests are not described as engaging in the work of teaching, only that they fulfilled that role. The Chronicler, then, compares the great Passover to all the Passovers offered since Samuel the prophet and notes that it surpassed all others.

The notion that Josiah's Passover was the greatest to have ever happened since Samuel carries major significance for the importance of the Levitical teaching office. The fact that the Levites and priests taught the people in preparation for the great feast day, and that this Passover was the greatest liturgical event of its kind, likely means that the Passover is causally connected to the quality of the priests and Levites' teaching leading up to the feast. If we consider that the Chronicler is also likely comparing this liturgically sound Passover to Hezekiah's zealous but flawed great Passover, this point is even clearer.

Josiah's work to reform and renew Judah legally and liturgically coincided with the last restoration of the Levitical teaching office in Judah's history. In the Second Temple period, the scribes, the Pharisees, and the rabbis take over the role of Torah instruction.

The Levite Teaching Office in the Prophets

References to the Levitical teaching office can be found in the Major Prophets: Isaiah, Jeremiah, and Ezekiel.[51] Some scholars have suggested the prophets had antinomy for the priesthood, even arguing that the prophets in general envisioned an eclipsing of the cultic priesthood. This section argues, however, that prophetic critique of the priesthood and Levitical teaching office was motivated to renew the priesthood—both in terms of cult and instruction.[52]

Isaiah 28–33 was likely composed in or near the reigns of Josiah and Jehoiakim (640–605 BC), with chapter 28 covering the Lord's "woe" by reminding them of the northern kingdom's (i.e., Ephraim) destruction a century prior. Isaiah describes the northern kingdom as a whole as being once a "crown," and then becoming a "drooping flower" and a "drunkard," which is a "figure of Israel's stumbling, bumbling life during the last decades of its existence."[53] Verses 7–8 specify groups within Ephraim that are also "drunkards," including priests and prophets.

Leviticus 10 addresses the specific problem of priestly drunkenness, which excluded priests from serving in the tabernacle. This law is followed by the command for Levites to teach. Isaiah 28:9, describing both drunken priest and prophet, says, "To whom would he impart knowledge? To whom would he convey the message?" The answer to both questions is that neither could have instructed a nursing child (Isa 28:9). The condemnation of drunken priests and prophets suggests that Israel's leaders, who were to provide them with knowledge of God's word, have neglected their duties to the detriment of all.[54]

The second prophet to examine is Jeremiah. Jeremiah 2 is a *rîb*, a contention or court case, where the Lord accuses Judah of crimes against the covenant—described as a marriage covenant—in front of witnesses that will end with a condemnation and punishment. In the initial part of the contention, verses 2–7, the Lord remembers the Exodus event under the imagery of a marriage and a field, and his fondness for his bride and field, even protecting her against her enemies. He then recounts their ancestors' unfaithfulness in the desert, and even in the land of Israel. The legal and moral rationale of appealing to the ideal past gone wrong is to suggest that

51. For purposes of space, I have excluded relevant references in Hos 4:4–9, Mic 3:11–12, and Hag 3:10–14.

52. See Tiemeyer, *Priestly Rites and Prophetic Rage*, for a full-scale critique of the notion that the prophets disparaged the priesthood per se and envisioned its replacement.

53. Watts, *Isaiah 1–33*, 362.

54. Brueggemann, *Isaiah 1–39*, 222; Wildberger, *Isaiah 28–39*, 22.

the present can proceed either toward destruction or renewal. The Lord next addresses the failures of the leaders, starting with the priests who he describes as "the priests—they have not said, 'Where is Yahweh?' the people controlling instruction—they have not acknowledged me."[55]

Jeremiah's reference to priests controlling or wielding instruction (*tôrâ*) in the context of the Exodus generations may indicate Lev 10:11 is in view. The verse depicts their failure in two ways. The first way is the priests' failing to ask "Where is Yahweh?" which is precisely what they are supposed to do, i.e., to inquire of the Lord's presence and word.[56] The failure to acknowledge God is, secondly, a deeper critique in that it suggests the priests failed to recognize the Lord as their master, which negatively impacts their "instruction."[57] Hence, Jeremiah, a singular Levite priest and prophet, reveals that, once again, the failure of the priesthood to properly instruct God's people leads to the opposite of renewal: exile.

A third point of reflection comes from Ezek 22, which is an elaborate indictment against Jerusalem, its people, and land. The first sixteen verses contain an entire court case: arraignment, summons, announcement of charges, presentation of evidence, and announcement of the sentence.[58] Verses 17–22 expand on the sentence by comparing Jerusalem under divine judgment to smelter that burns and melts metals. The result of divine judgment is knowledge of God whom the people of Jerusalem seem to have forgotten. Ezekiel 22:23–31 serves as the rationale for the judgment of Jerusalem, which is the location of the relevant verses. The purpose of permitting the Babylonians to siege and destroy Jerusalem is due to the fact that the land is unclean,[59] the rule of evil princes (a reference to Judean nobles and royal family), and that

55. Translation taken from Goldingay, *Book of Jeremiah*, 102.

56. Goldingay's comments are instructive: "Their particular responsibility was to ask *Where is Yahweh?* on [the] people's behalf. But they are not doing so. The people *controlling*, holding, or wielding (*tāpaś*) *the instruction* (the *tôrâ*) might be the theologians or scribes, the experts who possess Yahweh's instruction, in 8:8–9. They appear with priest and prophet in 18:18. But there, *instruction* is the business of priests, and here, the parallelism would work well if *the people controlling the instruction* is another way of describing the priests. They hold onto the *tôrâ*" (Goldingay, *Book of Jeremiah*, 110–11).

57. See Thompson, *Book of Jeremiah*, 168.

58. Block, *Book of Ezekiel*, 701.

59. "Uncleanness" generally refers to ritual impurity which means the ritually impure cannot enter the temple spaces—if they do enter those spaces, they pollute the temple's part and whole, and commit sin—but it also refers to moral impurity. Jerusalem under siege is in need of cleansing for these reasons to an extreme measure.

> her priests have done violence to my Torah. They have desecrated what is sacred to me, failed to distinguish between the holy and the profane, and to teach the difference between the clean and the unclean, and have closed their eyes to my Sabbaths. As a result, I am profaned in their midst. (Ezek 22:26)[60]

The "violence" of the Jerusalem priests—the only time Ezekiel directly condemns priests in the entire book—is explained by Ezekiel: these corrupt priests teach the Jerusalemites to treat God like a common thing and they have also ignored the sanctity of the Sabbath. In other words, they have failed to keep their original charter in Lev 10:10–11, which is to teach the Israelites to distinguish holy and non-holy things for the sake of civic harmony and cultic holiness and purity. Thus, the destruction of Jerusalem and the eventual exile of her inhabitants is tied to moral and intellectual corruption. One of Ezekiel's major tropes is that the Judeans are marked by ignorance of God, his will, and his law. Here in 22:26, corrupt priests' failure to teach correctly causes the people of Jerusalem to neglect God.

In turn, Ezekiel envisions the renewal of things in the eschatological age in chapters 40–48. In chapter 44:21–24, he depicts a renewal of Lev 10:10–11 and Deut 17:8–13:

> No priest shall drink wine before he enters the inner court. They shall not take as wives either widows or divorced women, but only unmarried women from the line of Israel; however, they may take as wives widows who are widows of priests. They shall *teach* my people to distinguish between sacred and profane and make known to them the difference between clean and unclean. *In legal cases they shall stand as judges, judging according to my ordinances.* They shall observe all my laws and statutes regarding all my appointed feasts, and they shall keep my sabbaths holy.

CONCLUSION

This study proposes the Levite priesthood-Christian priesthood typology found in the tradition from the early church fathers to the present can be developed to include the Levitical priesthood's teaching office as a type, or analogy, for the differing degrees of teaching authority found in episcopal, presbyteral, and diaconal orders. In fact, there is at least one instance in the tradition where it is used along the lines proposed.

The second part of the essay surveyed the Old Testament, from Leviticus to the latter prophets, for a theology of Levitical priesthood that defines

60. Translation taken from Block, *Book of Ezekiel*, 721.

the office of the priesthood as sacerdotal and instructional, and as an instrument for liturgical and legal/moral renewal. The Torah establishes the Levitical teaching office as an essential aspect of civic, social, and religious life. In the Historical Books from Judges to 2 Chronicles, the Levites and priesthood decline and rise alongside the kingdom as a whole (north and south). Yet, the Historical Books also depict specific periods of renewal—cultic and legal/moral—that coincide and are even caused by the Levitical priesthood teaching the people the word of God and leading them into cultic purity and liturgical renewal.

The conclusion of this study, then, is two distinct but related questions: (1) If there is a Levitical priesthood-Christian priesthood typology, but the usage of the typology does not reference the church's teaching office, and the biblical data on the Levitical priesthood strongly shows they possessed a teaching office, then why not add this to the typology?[61] (2) If we live in a time of religious decline that includes growing biblical illiteracy, is it incumbent on the church's teaching office to give greater attention to the tasks of ecclesial teaching, which should always be complementary to the sanctifying office? This study would strongly support this strengthening of the teaching office, and, in fact, recommend that the history of renewal in the Old Testament is (almost) always connected to a combined revitalization of the teaching office and cultus.

BIBLIOGRAPHY

Allison, Dale C. *The New Moses: A Matthean Typology*. Minneapolis: Fortress, 1993.
Bar, Shaul. "Was Samuel a Priest?" *Jewish Biblical Quarterly* 51.1 (2023) 16–21.

61. Anthony Giambrone's recent work on the biblical theology of the Catholic priesthood (*The Bible and the Priesthood*, 200) raises an issue that might indirectly challenge this essay's proposal. Giambrone refers to Christ's trial and condemnation at the hands of Levitical priests, including the high priest, as the fulfillment of Malachi's prophecy about the possible nullification of the Levite covenant if the Levites fail to listen to God and glorify his name. While Giambrone does not directly address the validity of a typology between Levites as teachers of the divine law and the church's hierarchical ministers as teachers, his interpretation of these events and texts might seem to suggest that Levites' rejection of Christ nullifies their typological value. However, the Levite priesthood is already (negatively) typologized in the letter to the Hebrews and, as noted, in the tradition at large. Further, while the Levitical priests were wrong in their assessment of Christ, their error seems to be more a manner of governance than instruction. I will add that Christ himself severely polemicizes and typologizes the temple in the Gospels (see Gray, *Temple*), and yet the apostle Paul and the letter to the Hebrews deploy a temple-church typology. In sum, negative aspects in typology are typical and do not necessarily nullify the positive comparisons.

Block, Daniel I. *The Book of Ezekiel, Chapters 1–24*. The New International Commentary on the Old Testament. Grand Rapids: Eerdmans, 1997.

Bovati, Pietro. *Re-Establishing Justice: Legal Terms, Concepts and Procedures in the Hebrew Bible*. Translated by Michael J. Smith. Journal for the Study of the Old Testament Supplement Series 105. Sheffield, UK: JSOT, 1994.

Bradshaw, Paul F., et al., eds. *The Apostolic Tradition: A Commentary*. Minneapolis: Fortress, 2002.

Brueggemann, Walter. *Isaiah 1–39*. Louisville: Westminster/John Knox, 1998.

Butler, Trent C. *Judges*. Word Biblical Commentary 8. Nashville: Thomas Nelson, 2009.

Clement of Rome. "First Letter of Clement." In *The Apostolic Fathers*, vol. 1, *I Clement, II Clement, Ignatius, Polycarp, Didache*, edited and translated by Bart D. Ehrman, 18–153. Loeb Classical Library 24. Cambridge, MA: Harvard University Press, 2003.

Cody, Aelred. *A History of Old Testament Priesthood*. Rome: Pontifical Biblical Institute, 1968.

Cook, Stephen. *Reading Deuteronomy: A Literary and Theological Commentary*. Macon, GA: Smyth & Helwys, 2014.

Cyprian. *Letters (1–81)*. Translated by Rose Bernard Donna. Fathers of the Church: A New Translation 51. Washington, DC: Catholic University of America Press, 1964.

Daniélou, Jean. *From Shadows to Reality: Studies in the Biblical Typology of the Fathers*. London: Burns & Oates, 1960.

Dillard, Raymond B. *2 Chronicles*. Word Biblical Commentary 15. Grand Rapids: Zondervan, 1986.

Garrett, D. A. "Levi, Levites." In *Dictionary of the Old Testament: Pentateuch*, edited by T. Desmond Alexander and David W. Baker, 519–22. Downers Grove, IL: Intervarsity, 2003.

Giambrone, Anthony. *The Bible and the Priesthood: Priestly Participation in the One Sacrifice for Sins*. Edited by Timothy C. Gray and John Sehorn. A Catholic Biblical Theology of the Sacraments. Grand Rapids: Baker Academic, 2022.

Goldingay, John. *The Book of Jeremiah*. The New International Commentary on the Old Testament. Grand Rapids: Eerdmans, 2021.

Gray, Timothy C. *The Temple in the Gospel of Mark*. Grand Rapids: Baker, 2010.

Japhet, Sara. *I and II Chronicles: A Commentary*. Louisville: Westminster/John Knox, 1993.

Milgrom, Jacob. *Leviticus: A Book of Ritual and Ethics; A Continental Commentary*. Minneapolis: Fortress, 2004.

O'Keefe, John J., and R. R. Reno. *Sanctified Vision: An Introduction to Early Christian Interpretation of the Bible*. Baltimore: Johns Hopkins University Press, 2005.

Osborn, Eric. *Clement of Alexandria*. New York: Cambridge University Press, 2006.

Papandrea, James, trans. *Novatian: On the Trinity, Letters to Cyprian of Carthage, Ethical Treatises*. Turnhout, Belgium: Brepols, 2015.

Rankin, David. *Tertullian and the Church*. New York: Cambridge University Press, 1995.

———. "Tertullian's Consistency of Thought on Ministry." In *Studia Patristica* 21:271–76. Leuven: Peeters, 1989.

Rehm, Merlin. "Levites and Priests." In *The Anchor Bible Dictionary*, edited by David Freedman, 4:297–310. New York: Doubleday, 1992.

Second Vatican Council. *Lumen Gentium*. The Holy See, Nov 21, 1964. https://www.vatican.va/archive/hist_councils/ii_vatican_council/documents/vat-ii_const_19641121_lumen-gentium_en.html.

———. *Presbyterorum Ordinis*. The Holy See, Dec 7, 1965. https://www.vatican.va/archive/hist_councils/ii_vatican_council/documents/vat-ii_decree_19651207_presbyterorum-ordinis_en.html.

Sklar, Jay. *Leviticus: An Introduction and Commentary*. Tyndale Old Testament Commentaries 3. Downers Grove, IL: IVP Academic, 2014.

Stewart, Bryan. *Priests of My People: Levitical Paradigms for Early Christian Ministers*. New York: Peter Lang, 2015.

Stewart-Sykes, Alistair, ed. *The Didascalia Apostolorum: An English Version*. Turnhout, Belgium: Brepols, 2009.

Tertullian. *De Exhortatione Castitatis 7.1*. Edited by A. Kroymann. Corpus Christianorum, Series Latina 2. Turnhout, Belgium: Brepols, 2010.

Thompson, J. A. *The Book of Jeremiah*. The New International Commentary on the Old Testament. Grand Rapids: Eerdmans, 1980.

Tiemeyer, Lena-Sofia. *Priestly Rites and Prophetic Rage*. Tübingen: Mohr Siebeck, 2006.

Tigay, Jeffrey H. *The JPS Torah Commentary: Deuteronomy*. Philadelphia: Jewish Publication Society, 1996.

Torrell, Jean-Pierre. *A Priestly People: Baptismal Priesthood and Priestly Ministry*. New York: Paulist, 2013.

Watts, John D. W. *Isaiah 1–33*. Word Biblical Commentary 24. Nashville: Thomas Nelson, 1985.

Webb, Barry. *The Book of Judges*. Grand Rapids: Eerdmans, 2012.

Wildberger, Hans. *Isaiah 28–39: A Continental Commentary*. Translated by Thomas Trapp. Minneapolis: Fortress, 2002.

The Teaching Ministry of the Diocesan Bishop as a Dialectical Recollection of Divine Revelation

—Tracy W. Jamison

THIS ESSAY EXAMINES THE sacred ministry of the Catholic episcopate in interpreting and teaching the supernatural deposit of faith and compares it to the philosophical ministry of the Aristotelian practice of dialectic in interpreting and teaching the natural deposit of reason. My hope is that the essay will contribute to a better understanding of the teaching functions of both the Catholic bishop and the Aristotelian dialectician by placing their proper activities side by side and attempting to link them together in a hierarchical configuration analogically and thus to provide some practical guidance to those who are called to engage in them.

Between the teaching function of the Catholic bishop and the teaching function of the Aristotelian dialectician, there are some important operational similarities which—upon being recognized—are very effective toward eliminating many of the puzzles that we regularly encounter in the interpretation of these two forms of active recollection. Dialectic is an intellectual process of remembrance and reconciliation which is effectively able to take us from an initially implicit and unclear knowledge of the fundamental content of faith and reason to an explicit and well-defined knowledge of it. This claim presupposes that there is a real analogical commonality between natural human knowledge and divinely revealed knowledge, but it does not entail that the content of divine revelation is reducible to or derivable from the content of human reason. The analogies become apparent only in the light of faith, which transcends the light of reason and reveals dissimilarities as well as similarities.[1]

I will begin by describing the teaching function of the Catholic bishop and proceed in the second half of the essay to describe the teaching function of the Aristotelian dialectician. The epistemological and theological assumptions which are guiding this endeavor are largely but not exclusively Thomistic. The conclusions of the analysis are grounded in analogical resemblances but are intended to hold true for the majority of ancient, medieval, modern, and contemporary philosophical realisms currently employed in Catholic theology.

The sacrament of holy orders has three degrees of participation in the ministry of Christ. Between the episcopate, the presbyterate, and the diaconate, the commonalities of the acts of teaching, sanctifying, and governing are analogical, not univocal. The same is true of the commonalities of the divine acts which are exercised analogically by the Persons of the Holy Trinity. The same eternal act of existing, for example, is exercised essentially by all three Divine Persons, but they each exercise that act in a personally distinct manner in accord with their three distinct relations.[2] The Divine Persons are really distinct from each other, but they are also the very same pure act, exercised in three different ways according to the three different subsistent relations that they are. Aristotelians understand by reason that the divine is essentially pure act, but by faith in Christ we know that the divine is also essentially a Trinity of Father, Son, and Holy Spirit, to which the trinity of the episcopate, the presbyterate, and the diaconate is analogous in exercising the common acts of governing, sanctifying, and teaching. But whereas the Divine Persons are coequal in all their acts, the episcopate, the presbyterate, and the diaconate are hierarchically related in their respective ways of exercising their common activities, and they constitute three different ways of participating in the governing, sanctifying, and teaching activity of Christ. This seems fitting, for Christ's human acts are always theandric and trinitarian.[3]

PARTICIPATING IN CHRIST'S MISSION VIA SACRAMENTAL CHARACTER

The ontological foundation of participating in the activity of Christ in general is sacramental character, which is given in the sacraments of baptism

1. White, *Principles of Catholic Theology*, 85.
2. Aquinas, *Quaestiones Disputatae de Potentia*, q. 3, a. 15, ad. 17.
3. Legge, *Trinitarian Christology*, 106–22.

and confirmation, as well as ordination. By baptism and confirmation, the lay faithful likewise participate in the mission of the church to govern, sanctify, and teach as living instruments of Christ's saving work on earth.[4] The question about the causal nature of sacramental character is answered by St. Thomas Aquinas and Bl. John Duns Scotus on the basis of Aristotle's philosophy of nature. Their slightly different answers are good examples of how theology is guided by philosophical theory.

In his *Summa Theologiae*, Aquinas says that sacramental characters are instrumental powers (*potestates*) received in the human soul's cognitive power, which is really distinct from the human will.[5] Scotus says that these powers are judicial and received in the human will, which he conceives as only formally distinct from the human intellect.[6] In either case, such infused accidents perfect our souls and incorporate us into Christ. As infused accidents, the powers ontologically change us and thus enable us to participate in Christ's activity as his human instruments and personal representatives, but they do not substantially change us as human persons. To receive an infused power in a rational faculty is to undergo an ontological change and to be indelibly "marked." The baptized, the confirmed, and the ordained are all thus indelibly marked by Christ, but in different ways, and for different purposes.

In Catholic doctrine, the infusion of grace is a real ontological change, but it is the infusion of an accident, not a change in substance. As a supernatural or judicial power, sacramental character is an infused accident and is thus a real ontological change by inherence, but it is additionally an indelible inherence, one that cannot ever be lost. Grace is either a permanent (habitual) or temporary (actual) inherence, but it is not indelible since it can be lost. Some Catholic theologians do not describe the infusion of grace into the soul as a fully ontological change, but certainly both of these accidental changes are ontological, though only the character is indelible.

Aquinas also says that sacramental characters are analogous to the instrumental powers of the sacraments themselves to convey grace, insofar as they are not properly in a genus.[7] In order to be properly in a genus, a power or an act must instantiate an essence completely. The causal power of a principal agent exists in its nature completely and perfectly, but the causal power of an instrument is actualized by another agent and does not exist in the nature of the instrument completely and perfectly. Aquinas explains that

4. Second Vatican Council, *Lumen Gentium*, sec. 31.
5. Aquinas, *Summa Theologiae*, III, q. 63. a. 4.
6. Duns Scotus, *Ordinatio*, 4.1.3–6; 4.2.1.
7. Aquinas, *Summa Theologiae*, III, q. 62, a. 4; q. 63, a. 2.

both sacramental character and the power to impart grace are analogous to motion, which is also not properly in a genus, since it is the act of a thing in motion coming from a mover.[8]

The analogy to motion seems good and useful, but how exactly are we to understand motion? According to Aquinas, the reason why motion is not properly in a genus is that it is neither completely a potentiality nor an actuality. This understanding of motion is formulated in the definition offered by Aristotle in the *Physics*: "Motion is the actualizing of what exists in potency insofar as it is in potency."[9] Aristotle believes that motion as such is an incomplete act and therefore is an accidental being that passes from agent to patient. Likewise, sacramental character can be understood as a being that passes from Christ as the principal agent acting through the person possessing the character for the supernatural purpose of building the kingdom of God on earth. In terms of Aristotle's *Categories*, it is an accident, specifically a kind of quality (an infused spiritual and municipal power), but it does not completely instantiate an accidental essence, so it is not properly in a genus. The natural powers of the human intellect which are non-instrumental, by contrast, do belong properly in a genus (e.g., the powers of abstraction, judgment, and inference), and such natural powers are exercised essentially, not merely by an instrumental participation.

The human nature (body and soul) of Christ is an instrument of his Divine Person and participates as such in his divine power. Likewise, the sacraments participate in his divine power, and the presence of sacramental character in our intellects or in our wills makes us living instruments of the Person of Christ, to some degree. We become members of Christ by baptism and are thus ontologically changed, but the change is accidental, not substantial or hypostatic. We remain what we are by nature but acquire an instrumental participation in the activity and power of Christ by virtue of the hypostatic union of his human nature with his divine nature. This participation is strengthened and increased by confirmation and ordination.

Aquinas maintains that even an accidental form such as a quality or power is wholly present in each part of its subject of inherence by the totality of its essence.[10] This is a positive aspect of his metaphysical commitment to the doctrine of holenmerism, which is implicit in the real essentialism of Plato and Aristotle and is often invoked to explain how a soul is wholly present in every part of the body that it animates, and how God is wholly present at every place in creation. Sacramental character truly inheres in

8. Aquinas, *Quaestiones Disputatae de Veritate*, q. 27, a. 4.

9. Aristotle, *Physics*, 201a10–11, 27–29; 201b4–5.

10. Aquinas, *Summa Theologiae*, I, q. 8, a. 2, ad 3.

the intellect or in the will, just as motion truly inheres in the moving object. The fact that motion is an incomplete act does not mean that it is not a true act. The same goes for the exercise of instrumental powers, and every sacramental character is an instrumental power that is possessed in full or in part and perfects the natural powers of the human soul.

As instrumental powers, whenever sacramental characters are exercised, they are also actualized by Christ as the principal agent. The baptized, the confirmed, and the ordained truly possess these powers in one degree or another and actively participate in the threefold office of Christ by freely exercising them. According to Aquinas, it follows that the divine power of Christ is truly present in our actions whenever we are exercising a sacramental character. Such actions are thereby supernatural, able to bring about what is metaphysically possible in the order of grace but physically impossible in the order of nature.

Whenever we exercise sacramental character, Christ acts through us, and we are his instruments. Qualifying conditions, however, always accompany the exercise of sacramental character. Most of the human acts of the baptized, the confirmed, and the ordained are not exercises of sacramental character, and some are even contrary to the will of Christ. We are not acting in the Person of Christ when we are acting in a merely human manner or committing sin. The agency of the church is divine, but its members on earth are still sinful. Whenever a member of the Mystical Body of Christ sins, it does not involve the direct will or agency of Christ. That said, the exercise of a sacramental character always involves the direct will and agency of Christ in accord with the specific office that he has sacramentally bestowed on that member through his church.

In the church there is a *common* priesthood of the baptized, along with a *ministerial* priesthood of those who are ordained to absolve sin and to make Christ substantially present in the sacrifice of the Mass. There is also a *common* charism of prophecy for the confirmed, along with a *ministerial* charism of prophecy for those who are ordained to proclaim the word of God liturgically and to transmit and interpret the deposit of faith and morals propositionally. We can also speak of a *common* charism of authority for the baptized and confirmed, along with a *ministerial* charism of authority for the ordained.

Every Christian is given a true indelible potency to participate partially in the threefold office of Christ as priest, prophet, and king through the sacramental character of baptism, but only bishops participate fully in that threefold office. The queenship of the Blessed Virgin Mary is similarly a full participation in the kingship of Christ, and whenever she commands, "Do whatever he tells you," as at the wedding feast in Cana (John 2:5), she is the exemplar of how the church exercises the divine authority of Christ in order to practice love of neighbor.[11] Baptized parents exercise this authority over their children in the family, which is the domestic church, but all the baptized possess the divine authority to command others to believe and observe all that Christ has commanded in the deposit of faith and morals, as he called the church to do in his Great Commission (Matt 28:19–20).

Obedience to the church, like obedience to the Blessed Virgin Mary, is obedience to Christ, and in the church there is a chain of divine authority that flows from Christ through apostolic succession. All the baptized are priests by participating in divine liturgy and the sacrifice of praise; they are all prophets by proclaiming the word of God and bearing witness to truth about Jesus Christ; and they are all royal subjects by imitating the Blessed Virgin Mary and commanding others to obey all that Christ tells us to do through his church, Sacred Scripture, and sacred tradition. Whoever listens to the baptized and the confirmed in faith and freely obeys the word of God is brought to Christ through the sacraments and ministers of the church. This is the activity of evangelization, which Christ wills to exercise through his church in every age and in every culture, and all the members of the church are called to participate lovingly and self-sacrificially in the divine mission of Christ in the world, without proselytizing or coercing.

THE PRIMACY OF THE BISHOP

Acting in the Person of Christ is therefore analogically common between the baptized, the confirmed, and the three degrees of ordination, but Christ directly wills to act through the faithful as living instruments of his divine power only in organic relation to his bishops. Christ prays, preaches, teaches, sanctifies, commands, and governs through all the faithful, but always relative to the proper exercise of the specific sacramental characters that they have received. The episcopate is the primary analogate of participating contingently in the threefold office which Christ alone possesses and exercises essentially. The secondary exercise of the threefold office of Christ by the presbyterate, the diaconate, the confirmed, and the baptized is thus subject to and conditioned by the primary exercise of that office by the episcopate, but this hierarchy is an instance of intrinsic analogical attribution. The various members of the presbyterate, the diaconate, and the lay faithful participate in the threefold office of Christ in ways that are more limited than the episcopal participation in it, but each degree of participation is an analogical perfection having real and proper causal power.

11. Francis, "Angelus," para. 3.

This analogical analysis of sacramental character is the doctrinal understanding of the primacy of the episcopate that is implicit in the seven letters of St. Ignatius of Antioch, with regard to which St. John Henry Newman affirmed even before he entered into full communion with the Roman Catholic Church: "It is hardly too much to say that almost the whole system of Catholic doctrine may be discovered, at least in outline, not to say in parts filled up, in the course of them."[12] The conviction of St. Ignatius that the unity of the church depends on respect for those ordained in apostolic succession is the reason why he begs the faithful in each city to heed their bishop. He explicitly claims that it was the Holy Spirit who proclaimed the words which he had spoken prophetically in the presence of the Christians in Philadelphia: "Apart from the bishop do nothing."[13] The principle that is present in this doctrine implies the equally divine command, "Apart from the pope do nothing." The more that Newman studied the various doctrinal affirmations of the Apostolic Fathers, the closer he came to accepting the full teaching of the Roman Catholic Church.

The municipal service that the church on earth possesses for the salvation of souls is the proper exercise of the threefold office of Christ as priest, prophet, and king. The public ministries, or *munera*, provided by the members of the church in various degrees are sanctifying (*munus sanctificandi*), teaching (*munus docendi*), and governing (*munus regendi*) for the natural and supernatural common good of all people, and they include public works of mercy and charity. The church exists as an organized and intentional community of divine liturgy and worship, divine preaching and teaching, and divine mercy and charity, under the local guidance and direction of its bishops, priests, and deacons. The bishop is the primary human agent whose objective and official public participation in the ministerial activity of Christ makes a local diocese one, holy, catholic, and apostolic. His exercise of the sacramental character of episcopal ordination is what conditions and regulates all the exercises of sacramental character within his jurisdiction. God illuminates, inspires, guides, and assists people through the local diocesan community: *fundamentally* through its bishop and *supplementally* through its other preachers, teachers, and catechists.

In order to obtain salvation and an abiding union with God in this life by theological faith, everyone in every age is bound to believe the word of God at least *implicitly*, but not everyone is bound to know, consider, and believe the *full* content of divine revelation, and not everyone is bound to

12. Newman, "Theology of St. Ignatius," 255.

13. Ignatius of Antioch, "Letter to the Philadelphians" sec. 7, quoted by Newman, "Theology of St. Ignatius," 255.

believe the word of God *explicitly* in the form of propositions. In *De Veritate*, Aquinas quotes the inspired author of Hebrews (11:6) and asserts that two basic dogmas must be believed *explicitly* by everyone in every age: "God exists, and God rewards those who love him."[14] These two truths can be known by reason, but they are generally known by faith, and thus they are potentially salvific. Theological faith, of course, requires grace. God offers the gift of theological faith to everyone for their happiness, and everyone at some point either explicitly or implicitly encounters the two basic revealed truths which are necessary for salvation. God always works to illuminate and inspire people to recognize and believe the truths which he has revealed to them. God wants everyone to be happy, and the ultimate happiness in this life is friendship and communion with God through the grace of faith. Believing and trusting God is also the path to everlasting happiness in the next life.

As Aquinas explains in *De Veritate*, the specific moral obligation which a minister of the church has regarding explicit assent to the full content of the deposit of faith and morals is rather challenging and certainly requires the grace of God. In the present age of grace, anyone who is appointed a teacher or leader in the church has a duty to believe and profess all matters of faith explicitly, to know all matters of faith explicitly in order to be able to recall and teach them to the faithful, and to study all matters of faith thoroughly in order to be able to guide the faithful in avoiding common errors in faith. The duty of members of the Catholic Church who are not appointed as teachers or leaders is far less rigorous, requiring explicit assent not to all matters of faith but only to the general articles of the Creed. Of course, an *implicit* assent to all matters of faith is always required of all the faithful, but a person who is appointed a teacher or a leader has a responsibility to have a faith that is completely *explicit*, knowing and believing all the divinely revealed truths defined as such and proposed as the first principles of the Catholic faith.[15]

The principles which Aquinas has in mind are all the infallibly taught truths of the deposit of faith and those which necessarily follow from the deposit of faith, which all the faithful are obligated to believe at least *implicitly*, and which teachers and leaders are obligated to believe *explicitly*. Among these irreformable principles, the dogmas of the Catholic Church are above all the first principles of the Catholic faith. The deposit of faith that is known by the church, however, does not consist merely of propositionally defined truths; more fundamentally, it consists of all the already defined and still

14. Aquinas, *Quaestiones Disputatae de Veritate*, q. 14, a. 11.

15. Aquinas, *Quaestiones Disputatae de Veritate*, q. 14, a. 11.

undefined aspects of the whole salvific reality that God revealed and gave to the church through Christ.

THE *MUNUS DOCENDI* OF THE DIOCESAN BISHOP

In light of these general requirements, let us now consider the *munus docendi* of the diocesan bishop, who is the primary educator of all the teachers of the faith who serve in his diocese. We have only one Teacher essentially (viz., Christ), but the bishop is the primary participant in the teaching ministry of Christ in a diocesan community. What is the specific ministry of the diocesan bishop in the exercise of preaching and teaching the apostolic deposit of faith and morals? It is to provide prescriptive norms of content and practice for homiletics and catechesis in his diocese, to provide suitable training in the arts of homiletics and catechesis for potential practitioners, to facilitate moral and spiritual growth and maturity in the members of his diocesan community, and to maintain full communion with the pope, the bishop of Rome.[16] He should also maintain "a cordial collaboration and a fruitful dialogue *in mutual respect and charity*"[17] with theologians, but he need not engage personally in the scientific work of theology. His specific teaching role as a bishop is necessarily that of an uncompromising prophet, high priest, and benevolent governor, but not necessarily that of a theologian.[18] By episcopal ordination, he is called not to theologize but to evangelize and catechize; nevertheless, he must collaborate with theologians and be able to discern whether works of theology are compatible with the deposit of faith and morals.

The fathers of the Second Vatican Council assert that "the common priesthood of the faithful and the ministerial or hierarchical priesthood" are essentially different but "interrelated": "They differ from one another in essence and not only in degree," and "each of them in its own special way is a participation in the one priesthood of Christ."[19] Similar principles would also seem to hold for the prophetic and kingly offices of Christ: the manner in which the lay faithful participate in these offices is essentially different from the manner in which the ordained ministers of the church participate in them. If this essential difference is ontologically based in their essentially different sacramental characters, then it also follows that among the lay faithful themselves the manner in which those both baptized and

16. Congregation for Bishops, *Apostolorum Successores*, secs. 118–41.

17. Congregation for Bishops, *Apostolorum Successores*, sec. 126.

18. Congregation for Bishops, *Apostolorum Successores*, secs. 123–26.

19. Second Vatican Council, *Lumen Gentium*, sec. 10.

confirmed participate in the priestly, prophetic, and kingly offices of Christ is essentially different from those who are only baptized.

There are, then, three essentially different kinds of participation in the priestly, prophetic, and kingly offices of Christ, which we can specify as the baptismal form, the confirmational form, and the ordinational form. The latter has three degrees which are identified as the episcopal, the presbyteral, and the diaconal. Thus, in the church there are five distinct levels of instrumental participation in the theandric activity of Christ, which can be graphically represented as a set of concentric circles centered around Christ, hierarchically radiating his salvific activity out into the world through sacramental character in the following interrelated order: bishops, priests, deacons, the confirmed, and the baptized. All divine authority exercised by priests, deacons, the confirmed, and the baptized in their proper activities comes from Christ through the bishops who are ordained in apostolic succession and in fraternal communion with the pope, the successor of St. Peter the Apostle.

Regarding the ordained form of participation in the threefold office of Christ, Catholic theologians often debate whether priority should be given to the priestly ministry of the sacraments, or to the prophetic ministry of the word, or to the kingly ministry of government.[20] This debate typically terminates in an impasse. One way around this would be to relativize the functional priority of ordination analogically to each of its three degrees, recognizing the priority of one of the *munera* in each case without excluding the other two. As three degrees of ordination, the episcopal, the presbyteral, and the diaconal species should be understood analogically, not univocally.[21] If this analogical analysis is valid, then the most logical division would recognize that in the episcopal degree of ordination the priority lies with the *munus regendi*; in the presbyteral degree the priority lies with the *munus sanctificandi*; and in the diaconal degree the priority lies with the *munus docendi*. The most basic and universal level of hierarchical ministry in the church is the ministry of the word. The deacon, the priest, and the bishop all share in the hierarchical ministry of Christ specifically because Christ has commissioned them to preach and teach his word to the faithful (Col 1:25). But they do not share equally in this mission.

The highest level of hierarchical ministry in the church is the ministry of governing and shepherding, which is the bishop's primary task. The bishop governs the teaching of his priests, deacons, and lay catechists. The intermediate level of hierarchical ministry in the church is the cultic

20. Dulles, *Priestly Office*, 4–5.

21. Cf. Aquinas, *Quaestiones Disputatae de Veritate*, q. 12, a. 12.

administration of the sacraments, which is the primary task of the priest. The episcopal degree of ordination is primarily for the sake of acting in the Person of Christ the King (as *basileus*, shepherd, pastor, governor, ordainer, overseer, authorizer, confirmer, and mystagogue) in order to cultivate hearts for growth in love. The presbyteral degree of ordination is primarily for the sake of acting in the Person of Christ the Priest (as *hiereus*, sanctifier, sacerdos, mediator, presider, consecrator, absolver, reconciler, and anagogue) in order to cultivate hearts for growth in hope. The diaconal degree of ordination is primarily for the sake of acting in the Person of Christ the Prophet (as *euaggelistes*, preacher, teacher, accompanier, servant, catechist, herald, proclaimer, and pedagogue) in order to cultivate hearts for growth in faith. These three priorities are apparent in Sacred Scripture and sacred tradition, and they are present in sacred liturgy.[22] The bishop is the ordinary minister of ordination and confirmation, who leads the faithful to maturity through the gift of the Holy Spirit. The priest is the ordinary minister of baptism, reconciliation, anointing of the sick, and the Eucharist, who leads the faithful in worship through the sacrifice of Christ. The deacon is the ordinary minister of evangelization and catechesis, who leads the faithful in proclaiming the kingdom of God and bearing witness to the Gospel of Christ.

In what follows, my goal will be to facilitate a better understanding specifically of the diocesan bishop's proper exercise of the *munus docendi*, and my contribution will consist of a comparison and contrast with the traditional purpose of Aristotelian dialectic in philosophical education. St. Vincent of Lérins formulates and incorporates Aristotelian principles and the dialectical method into his first canon:

> In the Catholic Church herself we must be careful to hold to what has been believed everywhere, always and by all (*quod ubique, quod semper, quod ab omnibus creditum est*); for that alone is truly and properly Catholic, as the word itself indicates, which embraces the universality of things. This will be brought about if we follow universality, antiquity, general consent. We shall follow universality if we confess as the sole truth the faith confessed by the whole Church throughout the world; antiquity, if we depart in nothing from the views of our holy predecessors and of our fathers; and lastly general consent, if, within this antiquity itself, we adopt the definitions and doctrines of all, or at least the greater part, of the bishops and doctors.[23]

22. Cf. International Theological Commission, *From the Diakonia of Christ*.

23. Vincent of Lérins, *Commonitorium*, ch. 2, para. 5–6, quoted in Journet, *Church of the Word Incarnate*, 554.

Discovering the ancient Athanasian and Roman Catholic interpretation of this canon was one of the preambles that freed John Henry Newman from modern misunderstandings and facilitated his entrance into the full communion of the Roman Catholic Church.

THE ARISTOTELIAN ART OF DIALECTIC

Let us now briefly consider the method of dialectic employed by Aristotle in his philosophical treatises in general and take a specific example from his treatises on ethics.[24] The sort of dialectical investigation that Aristotle conducts in philosophy is one that reasons from generally accepted opinions and arrives at clearly formulated definitions and principles. Each concept or principle is represented by means of a proposition specifying either the essence of a thing or some necessary property of it as a thing of its kind. These propositions are laid down as the first principles of knowledge, and accordingly, they are not directly supported or defended with any positive reasons why they are true, but they are indirectly confirmed and defended by reductions to the absurd. The discussions and arguments which lead up to these definitions and principles are therefore purely dialectical and do not attempt to demonstrate them from any prior causes.

As first principles of the sciences, the primary definitions and principles that are derived by means of dialectical reasoning must command belief of themselves and thus be self-evident in themselves. Dialectic proceeds toward each self-evident proposition through a reflective criticism of the generally accepted opinions relevant to it that organizes these opinions and establishes coherence among them by eliminating the assorted difficulties, ambiguities, and contradictions which appear in them. The self-evidence of the first principles in themselves does not, however, entail that these principles are actually evident to us, and this is the distinction that Aristotle employs specifically to describe the significance of his dialectical methodology for the clarification of concepts and truths in general.

Dialectic is understood as a movement of reason that advances from what is known to us toward what is known in itself but less clearly to us. In accord with this distinction, Aristotle is attempting in his study of the fundamental concepts and axioms of ordinary human reasoning to make clearly known to us by means of dialectically established definitions and propositions what we already spontaneously know by abstractive induction

24. The following interpretation of Aristotle's dialectical method was successfully defended in my dissertation "Wittgenstein and the Dialectical Representation of Concepts," 207–14.

and habituation prior to rational argument. From the very starting point of the dialectical investigation, it is assumed that the basic concepts and truths, which through a process of reasoning are being recovered and clarified, are already known in themselves and are implicit in the generally accepted opinions and things commonly said in ordinary reasoning, even though the opinions and things said are sometimes apparently contradictory or contrary. There is no doubt in Aristotle's mind that there is a conceptual content that is spontaneously given to human reason by nature, and that human knowledge has a firm foundation in real essences.

Aristotle adopts as a first principle the proposition that in each of the sciences certain principles are known immediately without rational inferences and cannot be justified by any form of demonstration. The goal of his various philosophical treatises is to formulate these principles dialectically and explicitly. He consistently maintains that while dialectical arguments are necessary in each branch of study to sort through and to clarify the things that we know and to recognize which of these things are fundamental to the science, it remains impossible for a process of reasoning to do anything more for these fundamental principles once they are adequately defined than to make apparent what the various refusals to accept them as known in themselves specifically entail. Such indirect evidence is not intended to guarantee the truth of the definitions.

Accordingly, the method of dialectical examination presupposes an immediate knowledge of the principles it formulates and therefore does not attempt to justify them, for what is known immediately in itself by abstractive induction is incapable of being justified from any other propositions. Aristotle frequently constructs dialectical arguments that explain the reasons why to some of us, or even to most of us, a particular definition or basic principle appears false. However, arguments of this sort are carried out under the assumption that the definition or principle is true, and they do not place it on any kind of rational foundation apart from the specific essence or necessary property that it represents. If Aristotle were to offer a justification for the definition or principle, he would thereby reject its status as primary and would at the same time award this status to some alternative principle.

Hence, for Aristotle a dialectical investigation into a specific subject-genus involves not a justification of our basic inductive knowledge of that subject-genus, but an organization of it, and this is done primarily by means of establishing its elementary definitions and principles. Any properly dialectical approach clarifies for us our fundamental alternatives with regard to defining the first principles of an order of knowledge and explores the logical consequences of defining them in one way rather than another, along with the possibilities for resolving apparent puzzles and problems through the definitions and further clarifications and distinctions. The dialectical choices to be made are so basic that it is impossible to evaluate them from any supposedly neutral perspective, for there are no standards external to a first principle by which to judge the truth of its definition or formulation. Dialectic simply makes apparent to us a significant portion of what is necessarily involved in a particular fundamental decision about defining a first principle and then calls forth a commitment from us based upon what we already know by the highest forms of abstractive induction such as *nous* or *synderesis*, especially in regard to the most fundamental judgments that we spontaneously make about being qua being.

In the philosophical science of ethics, for example, one of the most fundamental alternatives we regularly encounter is whether to identify the highest human good with pleasure or to define it instead as some form of activity that seems specific to human beings. Accordingly, Aristotle begins his dialectical investigation into the first principles of ethics by immediately raising the question as to whether some good that we pursue in our actions is wanted for itself alone. We all spontaneously think that there must be a good like this, for we agree that it is called "happiness," but even though we have a name for it, we disagree about what it is. Aristotle therefore describes in more detail what sort of good the highest human good must be: if there is some highest good, then it must be something that we pursue always and only for its own sake and never also for the sake of anything else, since nothing else can make it more desirable than it already is in itself.[25]

After having clarified the good that we should seek, Aristotle then recommends that we simply proceed by dialectical recollection and ask ourselves whether we know of anything pursued in this absolutely unconditional manner. In the *Eudemian Ethics* as well as the *Nicomachean Ethics*, Aristotle suggests that upon rational reflection it soon becomes apparent that only two serious possibilities exist: either happiness is found in some kind of pleasure, since all animals seem to pursue pleasure for its own sake, or else happiness is found in some kind of reason, since the activity of reason seems to be pursued for its own sake as the specifically human function.[26]

The choice is purely dialectical, and no direct justification can be given for either definition of the highest human good. If, on the one hand, we decide to adopt as a first principle the proposition that the highest good is pleasure, then we shall regard our activities of reason as desirable for the sake of their pleasure. If, on the other hand, we adopt as a first principle the proposition that the highest good is reason, then we shall regard our

25. Aristotle, *Nicomachean Ethics*, 1094a13–26, 1095a14–28, 1097a25–32.

26. Aristotle, *Nicomachean Ethics*, 1097b22–1098a20, 1153b7–34.

pleasures as desirable insofar as they attend activities pursued for the sake of their intellectual virtue. We can assume either that reasonable activities are desirable ultimately because they are pleasurable, or instead that pleasurable activities are desirable ultimately because they are reasonable. These two conflicting assumptions represent two fundamental ways to understand our moral knowledge, and we can dialectically examine them by means of reductions to the absurd.

Aristotle hopes that he can make it evident to us that it is self-evident in itself that the highest human good is the activity of reason, and he uses dialectical reasoning accordingly to eliminate anything that might prevent us from seeing this truth, which is taken to be already obscurely known in itself. Thus, Aristotle overcomes our impediments to recognizing as the supremely happy people those who live the life of reason rather than pleasure. By clarifying what we ordinarily say about pleasure, Aristotle makes apparent to us that pleasure does not seem to be the sort of unconditional good that we seek. This insight helps us to recognize and appreciate the various puzzles, problems, and paradoxes that we would commit ourselves to solving or tolerating, along with the common beliefs that we would commit to rejecting or accepting, if we were to decide after all that the highest good is pleasure and we were to assume this definition as a first principle.[27]

Aristotle thus attempts through dialectical recollection to bring us to a point where we are perplexed about the highest human good, and dissatisfied and uncomfortable with the proposal that it is pleasure, but disposed to search along with him in an entirely different direction among the things that we spontaneously know by abstractive induction. Aristotle cannot demonstrate from any supposedly neutral point of view that the highest human good is the activity of reason, but he can dialectically describe for us what happens when this alternative proposal is awarded the status of a first principle, and since he takes the activities of reason to be those in accordance with the highest virtue, he accordingly proceeds to make a case for his proposal indirectly by organizing and clarifying our implicit knowledge of the virtues, first those of character, then those of thought.

At the end of the dialectical analysis, having described and made apparent to us a significant portion of what is involved in the fundamental decision about the highest human good, Aristotle is in a position to place the two opposing definitions side by side, drawing attention one last time to what they each entail, and asking us to judge for ourselves which most clearly represents the truth about happiness.[28] If Aristotle's definition of

27. Aristotle, *Nicomachean Ethics*, 1172b9–1176a30.

28. Aristotle, *Nicomachean Ethics*, 1176a30–1179a33.

happiness satisfies us, then the suggestion that happiness is pleasure will appear absurd. If neither of these definitions satisfies us, then we should either dialectically attempt to formulate a better one, or else dialectically attempt to show that the question concerning the nature of the highest human good is based on some fundamental confusion. The same can be said of the definitions of all the other human goods as well.

Aristotle teaches and employs this dialectical method in all the philosophical sciences that are attempting to arrive at first principles already implicitly known in themselves by abstractive induction. He is the philosopher of common sense because he regards the basic cognitive content of natural human intellection as true but unclear. He is thus the herald of the common knowledge of all mankind, not of his own personal truth or theoretical speculations. His dialectical method is intrinsically sound and is useful for removing conceptual confusions and false assumptions not only from the natural sciences but also from the divine sciences.

THE MINISTRY OF THE BISHOP AND THE ART OF DIALECTIC

The teaching ministry (*munus docendi*) of the diocesan bishop is analogous to that of the Aristotelian philosopher insofar as he must dialectically clarify and defend what the church already spontaneously and implicitly knows, including fundamental truths about happiness and virtue. He must also dialectically make apparent the intellectual errors and inconsistencies in popular opinions that are contrary to such fundamental truths, calling everyone to choose wisely and to live virtuously. In accord with his ecclesial role as a bishop, he is primarily concerned with the cognitive content that is implicitly known by divine revelation and the grace of faith. However, he must also be concerned with that which human reason and abstractive induction implicitly make known. Like the Person of Christ himself, the bishop must prophetically integrate divine knowledge with human knowledge. The content of the science of the faith contains first principles just as the content of natural science does, but it is implicitly known by a supernatural participation of the church in the mind and heart of Christ, not merely by a natural human power.

The episcopate has objective primacy in this supernatural participation in divine wisdom, even though a particular priest, deacon, theologian, or lay person might subjectively happen to have more divine wisdom than his or her bishop. The fundamental teaching duty of the diocesan bishop is formally similar to the Aristotelian dialectician, but the content being organized, taught, and defended is materially more extensive than that which can be known and understood by human reason alone. Informed by the mind and heart of Christ supernaturally through faith, and by the natural powers of his own human intellect and will through reason, the diocesan bishop governs his diocese with wisdom and thus fulfills the human desire for a community ruled by a good shepherd and philosopher king.[29]

This goal may seem like an ideal that can never be realized, but accepting goals that are humanly impossible is fundamental to Christian discipleship and to the perfection of happiness as such. Through Christ, such goals are well-grounded in faith and hope and are possible to attain by charity and grace. Christ and his church fulfill the fundamental aspirations of the human heart for natural and supernatural common goods. The dialectical challenge is to make the divine agency and wisdom of the church apparent in the context of the massive human weaknesses and inconsistencies and moral and intellectual failings of her members. This task is analogous as well to Aristotle's defense of scientific truth and the power of the agent intellect in opposition to the various skeptical philosophies of his own time and culture.

It is important to understand clearly what this classical ideal for the diocesan bishop does and does not entail. As Benedict XVI pointed out in 2010, we are currently in the midst of an "educational emergency"[30] with regard to teaching, explaining, clarifying, and assenting to the basic doctrinal content of the Catholic faith, and thus authentic magisterial interpretations and the proper and convincing exercise of the *munus docendi* of the diocesan bishop are particularly important for the common good of the faithful. Much of contemporary philosophical confusion is the same as it was in Aristotle's day. The very reason why Christ founded the church and initiated its hierarchical teaching ministry through apostolic succession was to remedy the human misery produced by perennial confusions and philosophical mistakes. While the chief shepherd and primary educator of a diocese need not have the personal vocation of a professional philosopher or logician, any more than he needs to have the personal vocation of a professional scientist or mathematician, still he must appreciate and respect all intellectual, moral, and theological virtues as ends in themselves and sources of unity, truth, goodness, and beauty. He must be a personal source of wisdom for others and exemplify in his mind and heart the integration of all the sciences into one harmonious symphony of truth. He must also provide for the examination of the textbooks and other forms of communication to be used

29. Plato, *Republic*, bk. 5.

30. Benedict XVI, "General Audience," para. 4.

in his diocese and regulate their content according to what is consistent with the original apostolic deposit of faith and morals and its authentic Catholic interpretation down through the ages.

Thus, the bishop is a person of authority who prescribes norms and ideals and imposes objective intellectual and doctrinal standards on a comprehensive educational curriculum and praxis. He should aspire to embody a fully human, intellectual, moral, and spiritual life habituated and dedicated to the pursuit of perfective goods such as science, wisdom, understanding, art, prudence, temperance, fortitude, justice, and union with God above all. If he does not personally value and promote such goods over those which are merely utilitarian or delectable, or if he is personally incompetent or uninspiring as an educator and communicator of truth and wisdom, he will have little to no credibility in his own community of educators.

Just as a good diocesan bishop must personally be an educator, he must also—as the one in charge of religious education in all its forms within his diocese—personally have a philosophy of education and a working theory of knowledge that is consistent with the apostolic deposit of faith and morals. One of the main reasons why the philosophies of Plato and Aristotle have traditionally been employed with great success in Christian education can be found in their intrinsic openness to that which is transcendent in the human person and universal in human knowledge. Part of the reason why we are currently in an "educational emergency" with regard to teaching, explaining, clarifying, and assenting to the basic doctrinal content of the Catholic faith can be found in the shift within the philosophy of education away from foundationalism and essentialism toward pragmatism and relativism. Foundationalism and essentialism are capable of preserving a hermeneutic of continuity within the development of science, while pragmatism and relativism are not.

As one who seeks to conserve and transmit the deposit of faith in a manner that is analogous to the efforts of conscientious philosophers to conserve and transmit the deposit of reason, the diocesan bishop must remain committed in principle and in practice to at least a moderate foundationalism and essentialism. He must maintain and utilize a hermeneutic of continuity for the development of Catholic doctrine while encouraging and facilitating progress in understanding the deposit of faith and reason more clearly. Part of his task is to bear witness to the fact that a solid foundation exists for faith and reason in real essences and first principles that are spontaneously understood by the human intellect prior to the theorizing that takes place in the human imagination.

Human knowledge and divine faith are not ultimately subject to the whims of incommensurable theoretical paradigms. The danger of pragmatism is that it turns all natural norms and necessities into human theories and social constructs. Thus, the diocesan bishop must be an epistemological realist who is confident and optimistic that all truth is consistent and commensurable and that not everything is relative or revisable. Such an intellectual commitment does not require him to ignore or suppress the pragmatic and subjective dimensions of the human person, but it does require him not to subjectivize or relativize human nature, scientific knowledge, and the deposit of faith. Either consciously or unconsciously, that which most influences a diocesan bishop's understanding, implementation, and regulation of the *munus docendi* is his antecedent epistemology.

Two distinct paradigms that are foundational and coessential to natural human understanding are (first) the dogmatic order of first principles and scientific demonstration, and (second) the hermeneutic order of phenomenology and existentialism. Aristotelian scholasticism sometimes attempts to suppress all forms of phenomenological existentialism, and phenomenological existentialism sometimes attempts to suppress all forms of Aristotelian scholasticism. The truth is that these two basic paradigms are not totally incommensurable, and an adequate epistemology must include both by holding them in continuity. The antagonism is unnecessary, unfortunate, and counterproductive, especially when directed at those having pastoral authority. The modern existentialist opposition to medieval faculty psychology is just as problematic as the Aristotelian opposition to modern existential psychology. Whenever the phenomenological sciences oppose and attempt to replace traditional Aristotelian metaphysics and epistemology, they saw off the branch on which they are sitting, so to speak. The Aristotelian metaphysics of being as such does not onto-theologically presuppose what it attempts to prove; rather, it ascends to contemplating analogical truths about the transcendent essence of God as pure act through the first principles of being as such, which are known through themselves by abstractive induction.

Aristotle defended the ontology of hylomorphic realism and the objectivity of ordinary human cognition. The Aristotelian philosophical framework is not merely one scientific paradigm among many; rather, it is the prerequisite of ordinary common-sense reasoning and scientific understanding itself. Even St. Bonaventure understood its perennial value and did not intend to condemn it as such in his polemics against those who were putting it to heretical purposes.[31] Those who abandon Aristotelian philosophy of science inevitably fall into positivism, pragmatism, or relativism. It is therefore imperative that the diocesan bishop believe that

31. Benedict XVI, *Theology of History*, 111–50.

the various relevant paradigms of explanation employed by the Catholic Church's magisterium down through the ages are fundamentally commensurable. The hermeneutic of continuity is a realist hermeneutic of integration, not a pragmatist or relativist hermeneutic of disintegration. It is long past time for us to set aside our differences and to attend to what we have in common.

CONCLUSION

The two most fundamental deposits given to the human intellect consist of the basic truths of human reason and of divine revelation, and the *munus docendi* of the diocesan bishop requires him to be diligent in recollecting them, integrating them, explaining them, and defending them. The diocesan bishop is thus called to make the first principles of reason and faith explicit and to demonstrate what they entail for belief and the pursuit of natural and supernatural happiness, and he is also called to clarify and defend the pragmatic relevance of such principles to the fundamental noble aspirations of the human heart toward natural and supernatural common goods. He is not called to theologize or philosophize at will or to promote his own personal opinions and theoretical speculations. He is placed at the service of a truth that is not his own.[32] He is a philosopher of common sense because he regards the basic cognitive content of natural human intellection and supernatural divine faith as true but unclear.

The bishop is thus the supreme herald and the chief prophet of the fundamental knowledge that Christ freely pours into the human heart through the light of reason and the light of faith. The bishop employs a tried-and-true dialectical method of recollection and common-sense reasoning that is reflexively sound and is useful for removing conceptual confusions and false assumptions not only from the natural sciences but also from the divine sciences. He teaches "with the humble, glad certainty of someone who has encountered the Truth, who has been grasped and transformed by it, hence cannot but proclaim it."[33] By virtue of the sacramental character of episcopal ordination, Christ teaches the faithful through him and carries on the mission of the church in the world. As directed by St. Ignatius of Antioch from the very infancy of the church, the Catholic faithful gladly assent with religious submission of mind and heart to the teaching of their local diocesan bishop. In union with the bishop of Rome, he is the one who speaks with the highest authority of Christ and says, "My teaching is not

32. Benedict XVI, "General Audience," para. 5.

33. Benedict XVI, "General Audience," para. 8.

mine. I do not spread my own ideas or what I like, but I am the mouthpiece and heart of Christ, and I make present this one, shared teaching that has created the universal Church and creates eternal life."[34]

BIBLIOGRAPHY

Aquinas, Thomas. *Quaestiones Disputatae de Potentia*. Latin/English ed. Edited by the Aquinas Institute. Translated by Laurence Shapcote. The Works of St. Thomas Aquinas 25. Lander, WY: Aquinas Institute for the Study of Sacred Doctrine, 2024.

———. *Quaestiones Disputatae de Veritate*. Vols. 1–3. Translated by Robert Mulligan et al. Chicago: Henry Regnery, 1954.

———. *Summa Theologiae*. Latin/English ed. Edited by J. Mortensen and Enrique Alarcón. Translated by Laurence Shapcote. The Works of St. Thomas Aquinas 13–22. Lander, WY: Aquinas Institute for the Study of Sacred Doctrine, 2012.

Aristotle. *Athenian Constitution, Eudemian Ethics, On Virtues and Vices*. Translated by H. Rackham. Loeb Classical Library 285. Cambridge, MA: Harvard University Press, 1935.

———. *Nicomachean Ethics*. Translated by H. Rackham. Loeb Classical Library 73. Cambridge, MA: Harvard University Press, 1926.

———. *Physics*. Vol. 1, *Books 1–4*, translated by P. H. Wicksteed and F. M. Cornford. Loeb Classical Library 228. Cambridge, MA: Harvard University Press, 1957.

Benedict XVI. "General Audience." The Holy See, Apr 14, 2010. https://www.vatican.va/content/benedict-xvi/en/audiences/2010/documents/hf_ben-xvi_aud_20100414.html.

———. *The Theology of History in Saint Bonaventure*. Translated by Z. Hayes. Providence, RI: Cluny Media, 2020.

Congregation for Bishops. *Apostolorum Successores*. The Holy See, Feb 22, 2004. https://www.vatican.va/roman_curia/congregations/cbishops/documents/rc_con_cbishops_doc_20040222_apostolorum-successores_en.html.

Dulles, Avery. *The Priestly Office: A Theological Reflection*. New York: Paulist, 1997.

Duns Scotus, John. *Ordinatio IV: 1–7*. Critical ed. of the Latin text. Vol. 11. Edited by the Scotus Commission in Rome. Rome: Frati Quaracci, 2008. Translated by Peter L. P. Simpson. https://www.aristotelophile.com/current.htm.

Francis. "Angelus." The Holy See, Jan 20, 2019. https://www.vatican.va/content/francesco/en/angelus/2019/documents/papa-francesco_angelus_20190120.html.

Ignatius of Antioch. "Letter to the Philadelphians." In *The Apostolic Fathers*, vol. 1, *I Clement, II Clement, Ignatius, Polycarp, Didache*, edited and translated by Bart D. Ehrman. Loeb Classical Library 24. Cambridge, MA: Harvard University Press, 2003.

International Theological Commission. *From the Diakonia of Christ to the Diakonia of the Apostles*. The Holy See, Sep 30, 2002. https://www.vatican.va/roman_curia/congregations/cfaith/cti_documents/rc_con_cfaith_pro_05072004_diaconate_en.html.

Jamison, Tracy. "Wittgenstein and the Dialectical Representation of Concepts." PhD diss., University of Cincinnati, 1999.

34. Benedict XVI, "General Audience," para. 4.

Journet, Charles. *The Church of the Word Incarnate*. Translated by A. H. C. Downes. London: Sheed and Ward, 1955.

Legge, Dominic. *The Trinitarian Christology of St. Thomas Aquinas*. New York: Oxford University Press, 2017.

Newman, John Henry. "The Theology of St. Ignatius." In *Essays Critical and Historical*, 1:222–61. London: Longmans, Green, 1907.

Plato. *Republic*. Vol. 1, *Books 1–5*, translated by Christopher Emlyn-Jones and William Preddy. Loeb Classical Library 237. Cambridge, MA: Harvard University Press, 2013.

Second Vatican Council. *Christus Dominus*. The Holy See, Oct 28, 1965. https://www.vatican.va/archive/hist_councils/ii_vatican_council/documents/vat-ii_decree_19651028_christus-dominus_en.html.

———. *Lumen Gentium*. The Holy See, Nov 21, 1964. https://www.vatican.va/archive/hist_councils/ii_vatican_council/documents/vat-ii_const_19641121_lumen-gentium_en.html.

White, Thomas Joseph. *Principles of Catholic Theology*. Bk. 1. Washington, DC: Catholic University of America Press, 2023.

Sharing the Messianic Throne in Early Judaism and the New Testament

—Samuel B. Johnson

"In him I saw the entire multitude of you."[1] I can think of no more fitting occasion than this Festschrift to reconsider an undervalued theme in contemporary biblical studies, perfectly encapsulated by the preceding quote. In this brief phrase, written to the church(es) of the city of Tralles with reference to their Bishop Polybius, Ignatius of Antioch offers his most distilled expression of a dynamic that runs throughout his letters: namely, that in a single figure he came to see the life of a whole people.[2]

There are intriguing echoes here with a distinct literary patterning at the heart of the Jewish scriptures that depicts individual figures embodying the life and fate of a whole people. In this brief study, I am proposing that a similar patterning appears in various forms throughout the New Testament, also depicting the story of an individual—Jesus of Nazareth—as the story of an entire people living one and the same life and drawn into one and the same fate. This trajectory finally culminates, in a way directly analogous to

1. Ignatius, *To the Trallians*, 1.1 (translations throughout are my own). Translations of Old Testament texts are based on Elliger and Rudolph, *Biblia Hebraica Stuttgartensia*, and New Testament texts are from Aland et al., *Novum Testamentum Graece*.

2. Particularly with reference to bishops, but also occasionally including his company of presbyters and deacons; cf. Ignatius, *To the Trallians* 3.2; Ignatius, *To the Ephesians* 1.3, 2.1, 5.1; Ignatius, *To the Magnesians* 2, 6.1. Allen Brent has written extensively on this theme in Ignatius (which will not be the focus here), frequently employing the language of "corporate personality," a concept that first emerged vis-à-vis the Hebrew Bible in the work of H. Wheeler Robinson (see Robinson, *Corporate Personality in Ancient Israel*, though Robinson's construal of the notion has since been widely critiqued and redirected). See Brent, *Martyr Bishop*, esp. 89–91 and 154; cf. Brent, *Second Sophistic*, esp. 176–78; and Brent, *Imperial Cult*, esp. 218–19.

early Jewish tradition, with a vision of Christ's enthronement "at the right hand" of God as, ultimately, a sort of corporate figure or communal sign. That is, in the early Christian imagination (inclusive of the apostle Paul, the Gospel writers, and those inheriting their writings in subsequent generations), Jesus's exaltation to "the right hand" of God was understood to represent and embody the mystery of a whole people, brought to the same perfection at the end of the ages: a vindicated and exalted humanity, whose archetype and forerunner is the Christ.

PREENACTMENT: THE ONE AND THE MANY IN JEWISH BIBLICAL NARRATIVE

Hebrew Bible scholar Jon Levenson has described in vivid detail how each crucial turn in the story of Abraham has been shaped to depict him as "the man whose life in some mysterious ways preenacts the experience of the Jewish people."[3] Consider, for instance, the "compressed and cryptic" narrative directly following the call of Abram: with blink-and-you'll-miss-it rapidity, readers find Abram and his household sojourning in Egypt following a severe famine, a (perceived) threat of death that drives Sarai into Pharaoh's household in order to preserve Abram's life, the consequent affliction of Pharaoh's household with plagues, and final departure from Egypt with great wealth (Gen 12:10–20). In other words, this micro-narrative "sees in Abram and Sarai's experience a preenactment of the fate of their descendants undergoing the foundational experience of the people Israel that was the Exodus from Egypt."[4] Similarly, Levenson recalls "the eerie little interruption of the covenant-making ceremony" in Gen 15, where Abram receives a kind of prophetic vision (or audition, at least) of the whole story of the exodus in miniature, its first explicit appearance in the Bible. We find in Gen 15:13–16 an "exquisitely artful interlacing of the story of Abram with that of his Israelite descendants," which simultaneously provides the patriarch with an "interpretation of his own life" precisely inasmuch as everything predicted of his descendants has already happened to him.[5] Abram has not only been "living in anticipation of his unconceived and inconceivable progeny; he has also been proleptically living their life in his."[6] The patriarch once again "becomes involved in the suffering of the nation he will eventually father," with the promise of his own death "in peace" at a

3. Levenson, *Inheriting Abraham*, 3.

4. See Levenson, *Inheriting Abraham*, 37, 40.

5. Levenson, *Death and Resurrection*, 88.

6. Levenson, *Death and Resurrection*, 88.

"ripe old age" mirroring his offspring's promised return and restoration to freedom and prosperity.[7] "Abram has, in other words, become a symbol of God's fulfillment of his irrevocable promise despite the horrific and seemingly interminable parenthesis in history that is the oppression and enslavement in Egypt."[8] His life has been carefully shaped, that is, to recapitulate the life of the whole people of Israel.

Variations on the same patterning become constitutive of the remainder of the Genesis cycles. As his very name makes clear, Jacob/Israel is "both a person and a people, both eponymous ancestor of the promised nation and an individual who preenacts the destiny of his descendants."[9] Joseph, similarly, is betrayed by his brothers, threatened with murder, thrown into a pit, rescued only to be enslaved in a land not his, imprisoned again in Egypt under false pretenses, then finally freed, exalted, and vindicated in a way that simultaneously delivers his family and the rest of the inhabited world (Gen 37–50). Joseph, once more with even greater definition and detail, preenacts the experience of the people Israel, also enslaved, threatened with death, and triumphantly delivered—by a figure, one might add, whose own life also preenacts their deliverance through water, journey into the wilderness, and encounter with the Lord at Sinai: Moses. He too "proleptically lives their life in his."[10] In every individual narrative we find the same story reflected.

> The striking parallels between the stories of Jacob and Joseph are thus, at the profound level, owing to their common refraction of the foundational story of the people Israel. Like much in Genesis, these two narrative cycles adumbrate the great national epic in which the people of God, "Israel . . . My first-born son" (Exod 4:22), leaves the promised land in extremis, endures enslavement and attempted genocide in Egypt, and yet, because of the mysterious grace of God, marches out triumphantly. The story of the humiliation and exaltation of the beloved son reverberates throughout the Bible because it is the story of the people about whom and to whom it is told. It is the story of Israel the beloved son, the first-born of God.[11]

7. Levenson, *Inheriting Abraham*, 45.

8. Levenson, *Inheriting Abraham*, 45.

9. Levenson, *Resurrection and the Restoration*, 29. Cf. Levenson, *Death and Resurrection*, 65–68.

10. Reapplying Levenson's comment on Abram to Moses (cf. Levenson, *Death and Resurrection*, 88).

11. Levenson, *Death and Resurrection*, 67; ellipsis in original.

What we find here, then, is a defining characteristic of Jewish biblical narrative. In these stories, it is nearly impossible to discern where the lines of biography end and the lines of national history begin; the story of one is cast and recast in view of the other.[12] Moreover, in subsequent Jewish literature, this play between individual and collective continues to proliferate in an immense variety of ways and invites an equally diverse number of ways of receiving and interpreting it. And through all, it becomes clear that the dynamic works bidirectionally: one can just as easily speak of "reenacting" as "preenacting." In the exodus, the whole people of Israel "reenact" the life of Abraham and the other patriarchs, and, as borne out by later Jewish interpretive traditions, can even be thought to participate in that life.[13] The figural symmetries portray individual figures anticipating the future life of a whole people, and even proleptically living that future, just as much as they invite a people in the present to see their own lives as a reliving or re-presentation of the life of an individual figure from the past.

This dynamism also appears repeatedly in the prophetic tradition, as the lives of individual prophets become cast (and even cast themselves) as symbols of the fate of the whole people, and the fate of the whole people becomes bound to the individual prophet's life.[14] The most well-known and

12. Further examples beyond the patriarchs and Moses could be drawn from Judges (Samson in particular), Samuel (David preeminently), and Kings (Elijah and Elisha especially). One should also note the collectively representative role the Levitical priesthood, especially the high priest, plays in the Priestly tradition (preeminently signified by the high priest's breastplate, which bears twelve stones engraved with the names of the twelve tribes). See Rooke, *Zadok's Heirs*, 22–24. Cf. Palmer, "Embodied Remembrance," 411–46. Cf. Philo, *On Dreams* 2.28.188: when the high priest "stands alone he becomes many; a [whole] tribunal, a whole council, a whole people, a whole multitude, this entire race of human beings collectively."

13. The elaboration and expansion of these correspondences becomes a distinctive mark of a variety of early Jewish interpretive traditions. For instance, vis-à-vis the story of the Binding of Isaac in Gen 22 (the "Aqedah"), Levenson cites *Genesis Rabbah*'s depiction of God showing Abraham the temple "built, destroyed, and rebuilt" in a vision, a midrash which "makes Abraham a sign of eventual Jewish restoration but only after unspeakable travail—travail that he already preenacted" (Levenson, *Inheriting Abraham*, 10, citing *Gen. Rab.* 56:10, which develops "a late biblical identification of the mountain in the land of Moriah, on which the Binding took place, with the Temple Mount in Jerusalem" [2 Chr 3:1]). For numerous and diverse other examples of seeing the Aqedah as a preenactment of the life of Israel (or the life and worship of Israel as a reenactment of the Aqedah) in Jubilees, the Targums, rabbinic traditions, and more, see Levenson, "Rewritten Aqedah of Jewish Tradition," in *Death and Resurrection*, 173–99.

14. On the variety of ways the prophetic tradition appropriates and recasts (and perhaps even influences the final shaping of) some of the patriarchal traditions noted above, see Fishbane, *Biblical Interpretation in Ancient Israel*, 372–79. More particularly, one might recall certain well-known passages where individual prophets embody and enact the life of the nation: Isa 20:1–5; Hos 1:2–8; Ezek 4. On this form of symbolic

illustrative exemplar may be found in the Servant Songs of Second Isaiah (Isa 40–55). Are these passages describing a particular individual? (A royal Davidic or even messianic figure? Moses or an idealized prophet like him, even Isaiah himself?) Or is this "servant" a collective figure, representative of Israel as a whole?[15] In light of the preceding pages, I believe the most coherent answer remains "both": the servant morphs between an individual and a collective figure.[16] Isaiah 42 appears to evoke an individual, "my servant," "my chosen," distinct from the people: "I have given you as a covenant for the people" (cf. 42:1–7). Yet the preceding chapter has already spoken of the whole people of Jacob/Israel, all the "offspring of Abraham," in the same terms ("my servant," my "chosen"; 41:8–9) and continues to do so repeatedly in subsequent chapters (e.g., 44:21, 45:4, 48:20). Most strikingly of all, Isaiah 49 portrays the servant speaking in terms redolent of an individual call narrative (v. 1: "From the womb the Lord called me"), only for the Lord to name this figure as "my servant *Israel*, in whom I will be glorified" (49:3), and then, in the same oracle, to return to addressing a distinctly individual figure who is called to raise up, regather, and restore the tribes of Israel (49:5–6).[17]

The same logic and trajectory of thought appears, and in a sense perfects its arc, in the last book of the Hebrew Bible: Daniel. Numerous scholars have argued that the visionary figure of "one like a human being" (כבר אנש: literally "like a son of man") in Dan 7 appears as a collective representative of the whole people of Israel.[18] Recall that this figure appears within a series of visions: first a vision of four great beasts emerging from the sea, followed

---

action in the prophets, see von Rad, *Old Testament Theology*, 95–98, and Stacey, *Prophetic Drama*. Cf. Levenson, *Death and Resurrection*, 88: "Abram's experience is shown to have been itself akin to a prophetic sign-act. It is a biographical preenactment of the providential design for the whole people Israel."

15. For a helpful summary and representative bibliography, see Childs, *Introduction to the Old Testament*, 314–16, 334–36.

16. Cf. Ibn Ezra's commentary on Isa 53:2–3 where the servant is either "that Israelite who is a servant of the Lord [i.e., the prophet] or the whole [of] Israel" (והנה הוא עבד השם מישראל, או כל ישראל); so too the "man of sorrows" is "the servant of the Lord, or the whole people" (עבד השם, ואם על הכל), as noted by Knohl, *Messiah Confrontation*, 117. Cf. Levenson, *Resurrection and the Restoration*, 176.

17. Cf. Seitz, "How is the Prophet Isaiah," 219–40. In a different but complementary way, the lattermost portion of Isaiah also transposes prophetic expectations for a royal Davidic (even messianic) figure outlined so famously in First Isaiah (especially 9:6–7, echoing 2 Sam 7:12–13) and reapplies the promises of the Davidic covenant to the people of Israel as a whole: "I will make with you all an everlasting covenant, my steadfast love for David" (Isa 55:3; cf. Knohl, *Messiah Confrontation*, 45).

18. For bibliography, see Collins, "Son of Man," 50–66, at 50n2, and Collins, *Daniel*, 30n285.

by a vision of thrones being set up in heaven along with an "Ancient of Days" presiding over the heavenly court, then a vision of the beast(s) being overcome, and finally:

> I saw one like a human being coming with the clouds of heaven, and he reached the Ancient of Days and was presented before him. To him was given dominion, glory, and kingship; and all peoples, nations, and tongues shall serve him. His dominion is an everlasting dominion that shall not pass away, and his kingship one that shall not be destroyed. (Dan 7:13–14)

Immediately following this culminating scene, Daniel asks one of the attending angels to interpret the visions for him. Daniel, the dream interpreter from the first half of the book, becomes the dreamer, whose own dreams now require interpretation (פשר). The *angelus interpres* obliges: the four beasts are four kingdoms, the last of which oppresses the "holy ones of the Most High" (ostensibly representing the reign of Antiochus IV Epiphanes; Dan 7:25). Readers should expect, then, that the "one like a human being" also functions figurally or symbolically—which is exactly what one finds in the direct correspondence that appears between the visionary Son of Man figure being given everlasting "dominion, glory, and kingship" and the interpreting angel's culminating prophecy regarding "the *people* [עם] of the holy ones of the Most High" being given "the kingship, dominion, and majesty of all kingdoms under the heavens; their kingdom shall be an everlasting kingdom, and all dominions shall serve and obey them" (Dan 7:27; Cf. Dan 7:13–14, 18, 22).[19] Just as each of the beasts represents a kingdom,

19. John Collins has argued that the Son of Man figure should rather be identified with the archangel Michael, who acts as the angelic representative of Israel (see *Daniel: A Commentary*, 304–10); while possible, I agree with Israel Knohl that whether, in the first instance, the vision is meant to depict an angelic, human, or purely symbolic figure (or some combination thereof), it still ultimately "refers to a collective representative of the people of Israel" (Knohl, *Messiah Confrontation*, 95). Complementarily, cf. Schäfer, *Two Gods in Heaven*, 144n6; and Rillera, "A Call to Resistance," 757–76, at 771–74. Though in later Jewish reflection the language and imagery of the "Son of Man" appears to develop into a more distinctly individualized "messianic" redeemer figure (cf. Juel, *Messianic Exegesis*, 162–64), that does not mean this figure does not still possess deeply, if not ultimately, corporate dimensions. (If anything, the scholarly disagreement on this question only further underscores the fruitful fluidities inherent to the way corporate figures become individualized and individual figures become collectivized in this literature.) Cf. Schäfer on Qumran's "Daniel Apocryphon" (4Q246): "Just as the Son of Man in Daniel 7 represents the people of Israel in heaven, the Son of God / Son of the Most High in the Daniel Apocryphon is the representative of the people of God on earth" (Schäfer, *Two Gods in Heaven*, 44). On a similar dynamism in 1 Enoch, see Collins, "Heavenly Representative," 111–33. Cf. Collins, *Scepter and the Star*, 181–82. See also Russell, *Method and Message*, 344–45, 350–52. M. Black similarly connects the

the one "in human likeness" represents the victorious reign of the righteous remnant of Israel.

Daniel is, moreover, the Hebrew Bible's first and only clear witness to an idea of postmortem vindication and exaltation that is irreducibly both individual and communal: in a word, to "resurrection."

> And there shall be a time of tribulation, unsurpassed since the nation began until that time; and at that time your people shall be delivered, all who are found written in the book. And many of those who sleep in the dust of the earth shall awake, some to everlasting life, others to shame and everlasting disgrace. And the wise shall shine like the splendor of the firmament; and those who lead many to righteousness, as the stars for ever and ever. (Dan 12:1–3)

In sum, this culminating prophecy, along with Daniel's enigmatic vision of "thrones" being set up and "one like a human being" rising to the Ancient of Days to receive an everlasting reign, ostensibly as a representative figure of the "holy ones of the Most High" and the "wise" who "lead many to righteousness" exalted to heavenly glory, all together project a vast and luminous horizon of hope. As Israel Knohl suggests, it appears that the author took hold of earlier promises of divine splendor and eternal rule, associated especially with the royal enthronement of David and his line, and transferred them to "the whole people of Israel, represented by the 'son of man.'"[20] Though individual strains of such promises can be heard echoing across the corpus of the Hebrew Bible in part, their intensified and expansive sum in Daniel amounts to an unanticipated whole. "Here the divine splendor and

---

"deification" of the "saints of the most high" in Daniel with the vision of the heavenly exaltation of all Israel in the *Testament of Moses* 10 (Black, "Throne-Theophany Prophetic Commission," 57–73, at 61–63).

20. Knohl, *Messiah Confrontation*, 96 (cf. 99); see Pss 2:7 ("You are my son; today I have begotten you . . ."), 45:6–7 ("Your throne, O God, endures forever and ever . . ."), and especially 110:1, where the Lord invites the king to share his throne ("Sit at my right hand . . ."). On the internal ties between Dan 7 and 12, see Rillera, "Call to Resistance," 774: In addition to Dan 7's repeated emphasis on the pattern of suffering and vindication (vv. 14, 18, 21–22, 25, 27), the "association of the 'holy ones' and the persecuted Jews is strengthened when we observe the connection between the length of time the 'holy ones' (קדישי) are 'worn down' by the last horn of the fourth beast in 7:25 and the length of time the 'holy people' (עם־קדש) are being 'shattered' in 12:7—'for a time, times, and half a time' for both. This association between 7:25 with 12:7 and the notion of resurrection highlighted in 12:2–3 suggest that suffering to the point of martyrdom is likely what is envisioned in Dan 7."

star-like radiance and rule and dominion, the very throne of heaven, are given to a whole group."[21]

By all appearances, then, Daniel's vision of the entrance of the "one like a son of man" (Dan 7:13) into kingly glory symbolically preenacts, or recapitulates in heaven, the enthronement of a whole people following great tribulation, and so becomes a corporate figure of the vindication and exaltation of all those whom the promises of righteousness seemed to have failed: those during the Maccabean crisis who suffered oppression, torture, and death under the disenfranchising persecutions of the Seleucid colonization. One need not strain to hear how such a vision could find itself reechoing with even profounder resonances in first-century Roman Judea.

REENACTMENT: THE ONE AND THE MANY IN THE NEW TESTAMENT

Here I am suggesting that a similar patterning appears throughout the varied strata of early Christian literature, and that the Jesus tradition develops in much the same way according to much the same logic. Throughout the New Testament, one also finds Jesus depicted as one "whose life in some mysterious way preenacts the experience" of his followers, and that the story of his humiliation and exaltation is also the "story of a people about whom and to whom it is told."[22] His story becomes their story and their story his, as a figure, embodiment, and (pre)enactment of both tribulation and restoration held out to a whole people that found itself bound to his life.

Perhaps the most convenient and succinct expression of this shared patterning is found in the Apocalypse of John, where the vision of "one like a son of man" reappears.[23] In the last word of the last letter to the seven churches (to Laodicea), just prior to John's own throne vision, the Son of

21. Knohl, *Messiah Confrontation*, 98.

22. Reapplying Levenson's comments on Genesis to the Jesus tradition (Levenson, *Inheriting Abraham*, 3, and Levenson, *Death and Resurrection*, 67). As Levenson notes (Levenson, *Resurrection and the Restoration*, 176), this patterning in the Hebrew Bible has tended to go under appreciated by many scholars, and so (to my knowledge) has also yet to be sufficiently appreciated as precedent for the nature and development of the New Testament tradition.

23. Note how the Apocalypse of John's phrasing "one like a son of man" (Rev 1:13: ὅμοιον υἱὸν ἀνθρώπου; cf. Rev 14:14) offers a more direct translation of Daniel's Aramaic (כבר אנש) than the Gospels' "*the* son of man" (ὁ υἱὸς τοῦ ἀνθρώπου). In the inaugural vision of this figure (Rev 1:13–16), the author weaves together imagery drawn not only from Daniel's Son of Man (Dan 7:13–14) but also his descriptions of the Ancient of Days (Dan 7:9) and of Gabriel (Dan 10:4–9). On the widespread influence of Daniel on the New Testament as a whole, see Evans, "Daniel in the New Testament," 490–527.

Man declares: "To the one who conquers I will grant to sit *with me on my throne, just as I myself conquered and sat down with my Father on his throne*" (Rev 3:21). In a manner directly analogous to Daniel's reapplication of certain messianic ideals to a whole people, we find a similar set of messianic qualities—including sharing the very throne of God—applied both to the individual Son of Man and to the ecclesial community: "To the one who conquers and continues my works to the end, I will give dominion over the nations; to shepherd them with an iron rod, as when clay vessels are shattered—*just as I also* received dominion from my Father" (Rev 2:26–28).[24]

The Olivet discourse, which also foregrounds a vision of the Son of Man (Mark 13:26–27), provides a fitting point of entry for discerning a similar individual and collective dynamism in the Gospels, a literary patterning which only increases in definition and detail as the Gospel tradition develops.[25] Numerous scholars have pointed out the deeply suggestive parallels between Jesus's prophecies concerning the turning of the ages and the immediately subsequent events of the passion narrative in Mark.[26] Jesus tells Peter, James, John, and Andrew "in private" (though in the end, what he says to them he says "to all"; Mark 13:27) that they will be betrayed by their brothers, "handed over" to the Sanhedrin, made to stand trial before governors, beaten, and put to death—though the one "who endures to the end will be delivered" (Mark 13:9–13). There is hardly any detail of Jesus's own passion, that is, that does not belong to what, by his own witness, all the faithful are to suffer at the turning of the ages.[27]

24. Directly alluding to Ps 2:8–9 (cf. Rev 12:5; 19:15) and likely evoking Dan 7:14, 27 as well. Note how scholarly disagreements over the figures of the heavenly woman in Rev 12 (whose child is "caught up [ἡρπάσθη] to God and to his throne"; Rev 12:5) or of the two witnesses in Rev 11:3–12 (who "ascend into heaven in a cloud"; Rev 11:12) echo scholarly disagreements regarding Isaiah's servant and Daniel's *bar enash*: Are they figures of the past, present, or future? Are they individual or collective? (For summary and bibliography, see Aune, *Revelation 6–16*, 599–603, 680, 712.)

25. On the way the "Son of Man" in Mark both "prefigures and embodies" Israel's destiny and also retains an authoritative and "distinct individual identity," see Hays, *Echoes of Scripture*, 59. For a compelling argument that the language and imagery of the "Son of Man" retains collective or corporate dimensions in the teaching of Jesus, cf. Kazen, "Son of Man," 87–108; Kazen, "Coming Son of Man Revisited," 157–76. Cf. Gaston, *No Stone on Another*, 370–409.

26. See especially Lightfoot, *Gospel Message of St. Mark*, 49–58; followed by Gaston, *No Stone on Another*, 478–79; Geddert, *Watchwords*, 89–111; Bolt, "Mark 13," 10–30; Gray, *Temple*, esp. 165–97. For the broader apocalyptic dimensions of Mark's passion narrative, cf. Popkes, *Christus Traditus*, 230–32; Schreiber, *Theologie des Vertrauens*, 33–40.

27. See Hays, *Echoes of Scripture*, 91: the crucifixion of Jesus in Mark is the "embodiment of the agony of God's people in the last days."

The Gospel of Matthew's passion narrative follows Mark's quite closely and so the same patterning appears. Moreover, Matthew's occasional divergences often only serve to make the connection between individual passion and collective tribulation even more explicit: Matthew retains Mark's darkening of the sun in both passion and apocalypse (Mark 13:24 and 15:33 par.) and adds an earthquake (cf. Mark 13:8 par.)—two in fact (Matt 27:51, 54; 28:2; with a playful parallel in 28:4). *A fortiori*, at the moment of Jesus's death, Matthew (uniquely) adds a kind of collective prolepsis of the general resurrection: where *many* bodies of the holy ones of old are raised and then, after Jesus's resurrection, "appear to many" in Jerusalem (27:52–53).[28]

Matthew's Gospel as a whole unfolds an even more explicit and thoroughgoing envisioning of Christ as a corporate figure,[29] a dynamic that reaches a kind of apogee in Luke-Acts, where the individual/collective doubling becomes constitutive of the entire two-volume work. Once again, the Gospel of Luke's passion narrative shares Mark's reduplication of individual and national tribulation and, like Matthew, appears to enhance it: in Mark, Jesus predicts that his followers will be arrested and brought before "governors and kings" (Mark 13:9; cf. Matt 10:18); Luke retains the prophecy (21:12; in reverse order: "kings and governors") but here alone Jesus appears before Herod Antipas during his trial, only to be sent back

28. On the raising of the holy ones as a figure of national restoration in this passage (which appears to draw on Ezek 37:7–14, Zech 14:4–5, and perhaps Dan 12:2), see Archer, "Saints of Matthew 27," 477–95. Cf. Allison, "Scriptural Background," 153–88.

29. Numerous examples could be cited, summarized exceptionally well in Hays, *Echoes of Scripture*, 113–20, 139–43. On the death of the Holy Innocents and subsequent flight to and return from Egypt, see also Eubank, *Wages of Cross-Bearing*, 116 (emphasis added): "The calling of Jesus out of Egypt 'fulfills' [Matt 2:15] God's redemption of Israel from Egypt as well as his promises of faithfulness to Israel in Hosea [11]. Matthew thereby introduces an Israel typology in which *Jesus embodies the role and fate of the entire people*" (cf. 117–18; 130–31). In Matthew's infancy narrative, Jesus (like Moses) relives the life of Israel in Exodus (see Allison, *New Moses*). Similarly, Matthew introduces two corporately inflected sayings about the all-important Son of Man figure not found in Mark: Firstly, the prophecy that the twelve disciples will "also sit on twelve thrones judging the twelve tribes of Israel" at "the regeneration of all things, when the Son of Man is seated on his throne of glory" (Matt 19:28), which aligns with early Jewish speculation on the "thrones" of Dan 7:9 sometimes including the righteous elect participating in the eschatological judgment (cf. Grappe, "Le logion des douze trônes," 204–12); for Luke's version of this saying (22:30), see Matthew Genung's contribution to this volume. Secondly, in Jesus's saying about the Son of Man coming and sitting on "the throne of his glory" and judging "all the nations gathered before him," the righteous "sheep" are invited to "*inherit the reign* prepared for [them] from the foundation of the world" precisely inasmuch as whatever was done for "the least of my brothers" was done "for me" (Matt 25:31–40).

to the governor, Pontius Pilate.[30] Even more strongly, Luke alone has Jesus saying on the *via dolorosa*, "daughters of Jerusalem, weep not for me; weep rather *for yourselves and for your children*"—an especially poignant word for Luke's audience who, a generation or so following the Judean War, had known many more thousands of crucifixions.[31] Though further examples of uniquely Lukan material could be offered in this vein (the expanded narrative of the two revolutionaries crucified with Christ, for instance), far more important is recalling that the end of Luke's Gospel is only the end of the first half of the story.

As Michael Goulder puts it, "The story of Acts is a re-enactment of the story of the Gospel. It consists of a catena of parallels covering all the major incidents of Jesus' incarnate life."[32] Bound by the "hinge" of the doubled ascension narrative (told both in Luke 24 and Acts 1), a carefully wrought diptych begins to form between the life of Jesus and the life of the early church, centered around individual figures who are themselves iconic of the emerging communities as a whole.[33] The apostles' various trials, imprisonments, and persecutions are all narrated with paschal overtones, a patterning most clearly represented in the passion of Stephen, whose death reenacts Christ's—and, as his own directly preceding discourse before the Sanhedrin makes clear, simultaneously reenacts the pattern of affliction and restoration that runs through the lives of the patriarchs (Abram, Joseph, and Moses especially) and prophets, and through them, the life of the whole people of Israel.[34]

30. Luke 22:6–12 (an appearance that preenacts the fates of James and Peter before Herod "the king" in Acts 12 during Passover, and of Paul before Herod Agrippa II in Acts 25–26). The prophecy in Luke 21:12 also adds, uniquely, that his followers will be thrown into "prisons," a detail fulfilled repeatedly throughout Acts (note, *a fortiori*, how Peter swears that he will "die with" Jesus in Mark 14:31 and Matt 26:35, but in Luke 22:33, he says he is prepared for "*prison and* death").

31. See Josephus, *Jewish War*, 5.450.

32. Goulder, *Type and History in Acts*, 52 (almost as if Luke writes an entire volume within the boundless horizon of Matthew 28:20's culminating narrative ellipsis; cf. Peterson, "Matthew's Ending," 140–59).

33. Though susceptible to critiques of "parallelomania" at times, Goulder, *Type and History in Acts*, 52–64, still provides a helpful summary; cf. Talbert, *Reading Acts*, xxiv–xxv. For the broader history of research on literary parallelism between Luke and Acts, see Cole, "Paul as Jesus," 10–30. Note that the effect of the patterning is not just to draw individual and individual together (Jesus and Paul or Peter and Paul, etc.), but also to bind the stories of Israel, Jesus, and church (both Jewish and gentile, through the interwoven types of Peter and Paul) into a single whole (cf. Rothschild, *Luke-Acts*, 129).

34. Cf. Goulder, *Type and History in Acts*, 34–51; Trompf, *Idea of Historical Recurrence*, 122–24. Stephen's "Lord Jesus, receive my spirit" and "Lord, do not hold this sin against them" (Acts 7:59–60) correspond to the words of Jesus unique to Luke's passion

The rest of Acts is consumed with the story of another figure, whose shadowy presence the killing of Stephen first intimates: the apostle Paul (Acts 8:1). Here the ascended Lord's visionary appearance becomes programmatic for the vision of Luke-Acts as a whole: "Saul, Saul why do you persecute *me*?" (Acts 9:4; cf. 22:7 and 26:14). In a way reminiscent also of Matthew's "whatever you did to the least of these, you did to me" (Matt 25:40), one sees the shared life of individual and collective become the defining characteristic of the entire work.[35] Like Jesus's final journey to Jerusalem, Paul's final journey to Rome (via Jerusalem) is overshadowed by multiple predictions of suffering (cf. Acts 20:23), the last of which echoes Gethsemane: "the Lord's will be done" (Acts 21:14; cf. Luke 22:42). Paul too hears an angry mob shout "away with this fellow!" (Acts 21:36, 22:22; Luke 23:18, 21); he too is brought before the Sanhedrin and then sent to the Roman governor of Judaea, who—just as in Luke's Gospel—looks to confirm what province (and thus under whose jurisdiction) this highly politically charged figure is from, and promptly sends him to (another) Herod (Agrippa II), who also had been wanting to see this notorious figure himself. This Herodian, once more in agreement with the Roman governor, finally concludes that this man also had done "nothing worthy of death," yet Paul remains imprisoned (and is finally killed) due to political expediency.[36] In sum, Paul the persecutor becomes Paul the persecuted, and so his own life becomes caught up into the martyred, risen, and ascended Son of Man's mysterious "me."[37]

---

narrative ("Father, forgive them, for they know not what they do" and "Father, into your hands I commit my spirit"; Luke 23:34, 46); the deaths of Stephen and Jesus (which take place just outside of Jerusalem alike) are also both preceded by invocations of the figure of the vindicated and exalted Son of Man (Luke 22:69 and Acts 7:56; the Son of Man's only explicit appearance outside of the Gospels and Revelation in the New Testament).

35. Cf. Luke 10:16 (cf. 9:48 and 6:40): "Whoever listens to you listens to me, whoever rejects you rejects me, and whoever rejects me rejects the one who sent me."

36. Luke 23:10/Acts 25:7, Luke 23:8/Acts 25:22, Luke 23:12/Acts 26.31, etc. See Mattill, "Jesus-Paul Parallels," 15–46, esp. 30–37. Cf. Radl, *Paulus und Jesus*. Cf. Cole, "Paul as Jesus."

37. Notice again that the principle of literary "reenactment" works bidirectionally, as the reader of Acts finds that, in hindsight, the shape of Jesus's life in Luke itself becomes corporately inflected. (On the redactional shaping of the Gospel account in light of Acts, see Mattill, "Jesus-Paul Parallels," 37–40.) Once one discerns this bidirectional patterning, a further door opens for reconsidering certain intriguing correspondences between Luke-Acts and the Gospel of John. John presents its own version of the Jesus-Peter parallel, most strikingly in the risen Jesus's final prophecy over Peter in John 21:18, which is said "to signify the kind of death by which [Peter] would glorify God" (21:19), a phrase that directly reechoes John 12:33 vis-à-vis Jesus's own death and/as glorification. More broadly, the unique lineaments of John's Gospel as a whole appear to have formed around a similar kind of "doubling" of Jesus's life with the life of the

One could say then that Acts develops, in long-form narrative, an intriguing parallel to Paul's own sense of participation "in Christ" outlined in his letters, where, perhaps above all, the story of Jesus's tribulation and exaltation becomes envisioned as a communal mystery.[38] First Thessalonians is our earliest Christian witness to the idea of postmortem vindication and exaltation. When Paul turns to console the community in Thessalonica about "those who are asleep, that you may not grieve as others, who have no hope," he specifically orders belief in Jesus's death and rising toward belief that thus, "in this way also, through Jesus, God will lead forth *with him* those who have fallen asleep" (1 Thess 4:13–14). For all of the difficulties Paul's language and imagery present in this passage,[39] one can at least say that here, at the bedrock of the Jesus tradition, the individual/collective dynamism is already the constitutive heart of the vision: "The dead in Christ will rise first; then *we* who are alive, who are left, shall be rapt up *together with them* in the clouds to come before the Lord in the air; and thus *we* will be with the Lord always" (1 Thess 4:16–17).

This twofold vision of Christ's "end" as figure or preenactment of the eschatological transfiguration of a whole people is nowhere more fully developed than near the end of Paul's first letter to the church in Corinth. Here "Christ" becomes no less a corporate or collective figure than the progenitor of the entire human race: "Adam." We all, as this "Adam," have become living and animate creatures, and we all, as this Adam, likewise find ourselves given over to decay and death (1 Cor 15:21–22, 45).[40] Christ's exaltation,

emerging Christian community. Even if one does not accept the speculative details of J. Louis Martyn's reconstruction of experiences within the "Johannine community" that inspired this doubling, I find it impossible to deny the explanatory power of his basic literary insight into John's "two-level drama": that the text bears witness both to "*einmalig* event[s] in Jesus's lifetime" and simultaneously to Jesus's "powerful presence" in "events experienced by the Johannine church" (Martyn, *History and Theology*, 40). This doubling of individual and collective, bound together by the Paraclete, is nowhere more clearly present than in Jesus's final discourse, where (just like the Olivet discourse in the Synoptic Gospels) Jesus's passion and glorification is explicitly tied to the subsequent tribulation and exaltation of his followers (cf. John 15:18, 20 and 16:2 followed by 17:10, 21–22; cf. Martyn, *History and Theology*, 140–43).

38. In fact, outside of confessional summaries, Paul rarely (if ever) refers to Jesus's resurrection without evoking it as a kind of prolepsis of the general resurrection (cf. Fredriksen, *Paul the Pagans' Apostle*, 6, 132).

39. For a critical overview, see Luckensmeyer, *Eschatology of First Thessalonians*, 173–273. The cloud imagery in particular likely recalls the Son of Man figure from Daniel 7 (cf. Gaston, *No Stone on Another*, 407–8), but may also draw on broader Sinai traditions.

40. On Adam as corporate figure in early Jewish thought (including Paul), see Kaminsky, "Paradise Regained," 15–43, esp. 40–41.

then, offers a vision of animate life lifted into a new reality, "vivifying spirit," that transcends corruption and death (cf. 1 Cor 15:42–55). His exaltation, in other words, becomes the vernal first flowering of the eschatological age of spirit—its "firstfruits" (1 Cor 15:20, 23), language that denotes not only what is "first" temporally or qualitatively but also the offering lifted before God to re-present the whole harvest.[41] In Paul's vision then, Christ was raised, *pars pro toto*, to an incorruptible state (1 Cor 15:42, 52); he himself was "changed" (1 Cor 15:51–52): whatever in his life was subject to decay and loss was plunged into incorruptibility; all the marks of mortal life plunged into immortality (1 Cor 15:53–54); and so, we too, who belong to Christ (1 Cor 15:23), will become as he is, a celestial humanity (1 Cor 15:44–49).[42]

Of course, there is perhaps no more distilled expression of this patterning in the Pauline corpus than the series of passages oriented around a diverse and developing set of collective verbs directly related to the tribulation and exaltation of Jesus.[43] The first is Paul's enigmatic language of having been "co-crucified" (συνεσταύρωμαι) with Christ, understood so intimately that he can say Christ's own life is being re-lived in his (Gal 2:19–20). Turning to Romans, one finds Paul's use of collectively inflected language further dilated: talk of being "co-crucified" reappears, but now he also speaks of being "co-buried" and "co-enlivened" with him.[44] Colossians follows a similar pattern by assuming the language in Romans of being "co-buried" and adding a new event: being "co-raised."[45] Ephesians then completes the thought by introducing the final and ultimate event in the life of Christ: just as the hope held out to all the "holy ones" was "enacted in Christ" when God "raised him from the dead and seated him at his right hand in the heavens,"

41. See Fitzmyer, *First Corinthians*, 569.

42. On Dan 7 providing decisive precedent for Paul's sense of participation and collective exaltation here, I follow Hewitt and Novenson, "Participationism and Messiah Christology," 393–415, esp. 406–9. The argument is further expanded in Hewitt, *Messiah and Scripture*, 119–55.

43. The most thorough treatment of this motif in recent years is Feník, "Enthroned with Christ," 212–63.

44. Rom 6:4–8: "We have been buried with [συνετάφημεν] him by baptism into death, so that, just as Christ was raised from the dead by the glory of the Father, so we too might walk in newness of life. . . . We know that our old self was crucified with him [συνεσταυρώθη] so that the body of sin might be destroyed. . . . But if we have died with [ἀπεθάνομεν σὺν] Christ, we believe that we will also live with [συζήσομεν] him."

45. Col 2:12–13: "When you were buried with [συνταφέντες] him in baptism, you were also raised with [συνηγέρθητε] him through faith in the power of God, who raised him from the dead. And when you were dead in trespasses and the uncircumcision of your flesh, God made you alive together [συνεζωοποίησεν] with him, when he forgave us all our trespasses." See also Col 2:20, which also takes up the "died-with" language from Rom 6:8.

so also did God, "in Christ Jesus, co-raise us up with him and co-seat us with him [συνήγειρεν καὶ συνεκάθισεν] in the celestial places" (Eph 1:20; 2:6). In short, one finds in the Pauline corpus a distinct passage through the whole mystery of the affliction and exaltation of Christ by a tightly concatenating series of verbal developments, culminating finally in a vision of a shared throne: a vision of Christ's ascension to the right hand of God as a sign and preenactment of a hope held out to all who belong to him.[46]

CONCLUSION

Returning, finally, to the occasion of this Festschrift and our opening quotation ("in him I saw the entire multitude of you"[47]), one cannot help but wonder whether this vision of the throne of God, shared first with the anointed one of Israel, who in turn shares it with all those who share in his life, might also offer a certain new (or rather, very old) perspective into the throne—or *cathedra*—that stands at the heart of every diocese to this day.[48] In this throne too, perhaps, we may come to see gifts of authority, of teaching, and of sanctification all together ordered to this same hope, held out to the suffering faithful of every age: in the individual, the mystery of a whole people, vindicated, exalted, and seated at the right hand of the majesty on high.

BIBLIOGRAPHY

Aland, Barbara, et al., eds. *Novum Testamentum Graece*. 28th rev. ed. Stuttgart: Deutsche Bibelgesellschaft, 2012.

Allison, Dale C. *The New Moses: A Matthean Typology*. New York: Wipf & Stock, 2013.

———. "The Scriptural Background of a Matthean Legend: Ezekiel 37, Zechariah 14, and Matthew 27." In *Life beyond Death in Matthew's Gospel: Religious Metaphor or Bodily Reality?*, edited by W. Weren et al., 153–88. Leuven: Peeters, 2011.

46. Cf. 2 Tim 2:11–12: "This saying is trustworthy: If we have died with him [συναπεθάνομεν], we will also live with him [συζήσομεν]; if we endure, we will also reign with him [συμβασιλεύσομεν]." A similar argument has been made that the ultimate aim of Heb 1–2 is to present Jesus's exaltation to the right hand "of the majesty on high" as a prefigurement and preenactment of a promise held out to all the faithful, to whom, as a collective whole, the "coming age" is to be subjected (Heb 2:5–10; see Hurst, "Christology of Hebrews," 151–64).

47. Ignatius, *To the Trallians* 1.1.

48. Note how Ignatius speaks of the lives of the local faithful becoming indissolubly intermixed (ἐνκεράννυμι) with the life of the bishop "as the church is with Jesus Christ and as Jesus Christ is with the Father" (Ignatius, *To the Ephesians* 5.1; cf. Ignatius, *To the Magnesians* 13.1, which Allen Brent takes to be a reference to the episcopal throne surrounded by the presbyterate: Brent, *Imperial Cult*, 216–18).

Archer, Joel. "The Saints of Matthew 27: Why Do They Linger in Their Tombs?" *Journal for the Study of the New Testament* 44.4 (2022) 477–95.

Aune, David E. *Revelation 6–16*. Word Biblical Commentary 52. Grand Rapids: Zondervan, 2017.

Black, Matthew. "The Throne-Theophany Prophetic Commission and the 'Son of Man': A Study in Tradition-History." In *Jews, Greeks and Christians: Religious Cultures in Late Antiquity: Essays in Honor of William David Davies*, edited by Robert Hamerton-Kelly and Robin Scroggs, 57–73. Leiden: Brill, 1976.

Bolt, Peter G. "Mark 13: An Apocalyptic Precursor to the Passion Narrative." *The Reformed Theological Review* 54 (1995) 10–30.

Brent, Allen. *Ignatius of Antioch: A Martyr Bishop and the Origin of Episcopacy*. New York: T&T Clark, 2007.

———. *Ignatius of Antioch and the Second Sophistic: A Study of an Early Christian Transformation of Pagan Culture*. Tübingen: Mohr Siebeck, 2006.

———. *The Imperial Cult and the Development of Church Order: Concepts and Images of Authority in Paganism and Early Christianity before the Age of Cyprian*. Leiden: Brill, 1999.

Childs, Brevard S. *Introduction to the Old Testament as Scripture*. Philadelphia: Fortress, 1979.

Cole, Timothy J. "Paul as Jesus: Luke's Use of Recursion in Luke-Acts." PhD diss., University of Chester, 2021.

Collins, John J. *Daniel: A Commentary on the Book of Daniel*. Minneapolis: Fortress, 1993.

———. "The Heavenly Representative: The 'Son of Man' in the Similitudes of Enoch." In *Ideal Figures in Ancient Judaism: Profiles and Paradigms*, edited by George W. E. Nickelsburg and John J. Collins, 111–33. Chico: Scholars, 1980.

———. *The Scepter and the Star: The Messiahs of the Dead Sea Scrolls and Other Ancient Literature*. New York: Doubleday, 1995.

———. "The Son of Man and the Saints of the Most High in the Book of Daniel." *Journal of Biblical Literature* 93.1 (March 1974) 50–66.

Elliger, Karl, and Wilhelm Rudolph, eds. *Biblia Hebraica Stuttgartensia*. 4th ed. Stuttgart: Deutsche Bibelgesellschaft, 1997.

Eubank, Nathan. *Wages of Cross-Bearing and Debt of Sin: The Economy of Heaven in Matthew's Gospel*. Berlin: De Gruyter, 2013.

Evans, Craig A. "Daniel in the New Testament: Visions of God's Kingdom." In *Formation and Interpretation of Old Testament Literature*, vol. 2, *The Book of Daniel: Composition and Reception*, edited by J. Collins and P. Flint, 490–527. Leiden: Brill, 2001.

Feník, Juraj. "Enthroned with Christ: An Exegetical and Theological Study of Eph 1:20–23 and 2:5–6." STD diss., Catholic University of America, 2008.

Fishbane, Michael. *Biblical Interpretation in Ancient Israel*. New York: Oxford University Press, 1985.

Fitzmyer, Joseph A. *First Corinthians: A New Translation with Introduction and Commentary*. The Anchor Yale Bible 32. New Haven: Yale University Press, 2008.

Fredriksen, Paula. *Paul the Pagans' Apostle*. New Haven: Yale University Press, 2017.

Gaston, Lloyd. *No Stone on Another: Studies in the Significance of the Fall of Jerusalem in the Synoptic Gospels*. Leiden: Brill, 1970.

Geddert, Timothy J. *Watchwords: Mark 13 in Markan Eschatology*. Sheffield, UK: Sheffield Academic, 1989.

Goulder, M. D. *Type and History in Acts*. London: SPCK, 1964.

Grappe, Christian. "Le logion des douze trônes." In *Le Trône de Dieu*, edited by Marc Philonenko, 204–12. Tübingen: Mohr Siebeck, 1993.

Gray, Timothy C. *The Temple in the Gospel of Mark: A Study in Its Narrative Role*. Tübingen: Mohr Siebeck, 2008.

Hays, Richard B. *Echoes of Scripture in the Gospels*. Waco, TX: Baylor University Press, 2017.

Hewitt, J. Thomas. *Messiah and Scripture: Paul's "In Christ" Idiom in Its Ancient Jewish Context*. Tübingen: Mohr Siebeck, 2020.

Hewitt, J. Thomas, and Matthew V. Novenson. "Participationism and Messiah Christology in Paul." In *God and the Faithfulness of Paul: A Critical Examination of the Pauline Theology of N. T. Wright*, edited by Christoph Heilig et al., 393–415. Minneapolis: Fortress, 2017.

Hurst, L. "The Christology of Hebrews 1–2." In *The Glory of Christ in the New Testament: Studies in Christology in Memory of George Bradford Caird*, edited by L. D. Hurst and N. T. Wright, 151–64. Oxford: Clarendon, 1987.

Ignatius of Antioch. "To the Ephesians." In *The Apostolic Fathers: Greek Texts and English Translations*, 3rd ed., edited and translated by Michael W. Holmes, 182–201. Grand Rapids: Baker Academic, 2007.

———. "To the Magnesians." In *The Apostolic Fathers: Greek Texts and English Translations*, 3rd ed., edited and translated by Michael W. Holmes, 202–213. Grand Rapids: Baker Academic, 2007.

———. "To the Trallians." In *The Apostolic Fathers: Greek Texts and English Translations*, 3rd ed., edited and translated by Michael W. Holmes, 214–23. Grand Rapids: Baker Academic, 2007.

Juel, Donald. *Messianic Exegesis: Christological Interpretation of the Old Testament in Early Christianity*. Philadelphia: Fortress, 1988.

Kaminsky, Joel S. "Paradise Regained: Rabbinic Reflections on Israel at Sinai." In *Jews, Christians, and the Theology of the Hebrew Scriptures*, edited by Alice Ogden Bellis and Joel S. Kaminsky, 15–43. Atlanta: Society of Biblical Literature, 2000.

Kazen, Thomas. "The Coming Son of Man Revisited." *Journal for the Study of the Historical Jesus* 5.2 (2007) 157–76.

———. "Son of Man as Kingdom Imagery: Jesus between Corporate Symbol and Individual Redeemer Figure." In *Jesus from Judaism to Christianity: Continuum Approaches to the Historical Jesus*, edited by Tom Holmén, 87–108. London: T&T Clark, 2007.

Knohl, Israel. *The Messiah Confrontation: Pharisees versus Sadducees and the Death of Jesus*. Philadelphia: Jewish Publication Society, 2022.

Levenson, Jon D. *The Death and Resurrection of the Beloved Son: The Transformation of Child Sacrifice in Judaism and Christianity*. New Haven: Yale University Press, 1993.

———. *Inheriting Abraham: The Legacy of the Patriarch in Judaism, Christianity, and Islam*. Princeton: Princeton University Press, 2012.

———. *Resurrection and the Restoration of Israel: The Ultimate Victory of the God of Life*. New Haven: Yale University Press, 2006.

Lightfoot, R. H. *The Gospel Message of St. Mark*. Oxford: Clarendon, 1950.

Luckensmeyer, David. *The Eschatology of First Thessalonians*. Göttingen: Vandenhoeck & Ruprecht, 2009.

Martyn, J. Louis. *History and Theology in the Fourth Gospel*. Louisville: Westminster John Knox, 2003.

Mattill, A. J. "The Jesus-Paul Parallels and the Purpose of Luke-Acts: H. H. Evans Reconsidered." *Novum Testamentum* 17 (1975) 15–46.

Palmer, Christine Elizabeth. "Embodied Remembrance: The Inscribed Priestly Seals in Israel's Worship." In *The Body Lived, Cultured, Adorned: Essays on Dress and the Body in the Bible and Ancient Near East in Honor of Nili S. Fox*, edited by Kristine H. Garroway et al., 411–46. Cincinnati: Hebrew Union College Press, 2022.

Peterson, Jeff. "Matthew's Ending and the Genesis of Luke-Acts: The Farrer Hypothesis and the Birth of Christian History." In *Marcan Priority Without Q: Explorations in the Farrer Hypothesis*, edited by John. C. Poirier and Jeffrey Peterson, 140–59. New York: T&T Clark, 2015.

Philo. *On Flight and Finding. On the Change of Names. On Dreams*. Translated by F. H. Colson and G. H. Whitaker. Loeb Classical Library 275. Cambridge, MA: Harvard University Press, 1934.

Popkes, Wiard. *Christus Traditus: Eine Untersuchung zum Begriff der Dahingabe im Neuen Testament*. Zürich: Zwingli, 1967.

Radl, Walter. *Paulus und Jesus im lukanischen Doppelwerk: Untersuchungen zu Parallelmotiven im Lukasevangelium und in der Apostelgeschichte*. Frankfurt: Peter Lang, 1975.

Rillera, Andrew Remington. "A Call to Resistance: The Exhortative Function of Daniel 7." *Journal of Biblical Literature* 138.4 (2019) 757–76.

Robinson, H. Wheeler. *Corporate Personality in Ancient Israel*. Minneapolis: Fortress, 1964.

Rooke, Deborah W. *Zadok's Heirs: The Role and Development of the High Priesthood in Ancient Israel*. New York: Oxford University Press, 2000.

Rothschild, Clare K. *Luke-Acts and the Rhetoric of History: An Investigation of Early Christian Historiography*. Tübingen: Mohr Siebeck, 2004.

Russell, D. S. *The Method and Message of Jewish Apocalyptic: 200 BC–AD 100*. London: SCM, 1964.

Schäfer, Peter. *Two Gods in Heaven: Jewish Concepts of God in Antiquity*. Princeton: Princeton University Press, 2020.

Schreiber, Johannes. *Theologie des Vertrauens: Eine redaktionsgeschichtliche Untersuchung des Markusevangeliums*. Hamburg: Furche, 1967.

Seitz, Christopher R. "How Is the Prophet Isaiah Present in the Latter Half of the Book? The Logic of Chapters 40–66 within the Book of Isaiah." *Journal of Biblical Literature* 115.2 (1996) 219–40.

Stacey, David. *Prophetic Drama in the Old Testament*. London: Epworth, 1990.

Talbert, Charles H. *Reading Acts: A Literary and Theological Commentary on the Acts of the Apostles*. Macon: Smyth & Helwys, 2005.

Trompf, G. W. *The Idea of Historical Recurrence in Western Thought: From Antiquity to the Reformation*. Berkeley: University of California Press, 1979.

Von Rad, Gerhard. *Old Testament Theology*. Vol. 2, *The Theology of Israel's Prophetic Traditions*. Edinburgh: Oliver and Boyd, 1965.

Part III—*Munus Regendi*

The Restoration of a Diocese

Archbishop William Henry Elder of Cincinnati, 1880–1904

—David J. Endres

INTRODUCTION

AMONG THE SURVIVING PAPERS of Archbishop William Henry Elder (1819–1904) are sixteen pages of sermon notes for a bishop's consecration. Whether Elder ever delivered this sermon is unknown, but the document helps illumine Elder's understanding of the episcopacy.[1] The text begins, "Dearly beloved . . . today you have witnessed one of the spectacles which most forcibly brings home to our hearts the infinite love of God to men: the consecration of a bishop in God's Holy Catholic Church."[2]

The text provides no clues as to the time or place it was written. Was it when Elder was a young bishop in Natchez, Mississippi, shepherding a small but growing flock? Was it when he endured the horrors of the Civil War under federal occupation and briefly suffered house arrest? Was it when he was called to Cincinnati in the aftermath of a severe financial scandal? The sermon does not indicate Elder's personal appropriation of the episcopacy, but it speaks to an elevated understanding of his office—that may have been tempered by his experiences of turmoil and trial.

1. Elder was the principal consecrator of eight bishops between 1880 and 1900. See Lonsway and Pembleton, *Episcopal Lineage*, 9.

2. William Henry Elder, "Sermon on Consecration of Bishop," undated, Sermon on Consecration of Bishop file, box 2, RG 1.3, Archbishop William H. Elder Papers, ser. 1.3–12, Sermons and Notes, Archives of the Archdiocese of Cincinnati (hereafter AAC).

This study of Elder's years as archbishop of Cincinnati (1880–1904) draws on a range of sources, including Elder's voluminous correspondence, to offer a detailed account of his leadership and impact on the church in Cincinnati. Through an examination of his reform initiatives, this research provides insights into the role of a bishop and the challenges of leading during a period of turmoil. Though a historical case study, it may offer some guidance for leadership in our contemporary milieux, especially in the case of intra-diocesan controversies, financial stresses, and priest shortages.

Elder, the third bishop and second archbishop of Cincinnati, was named coadjutor with the right of succession to Archbishop John Baptist Purcell (1800–1883) in 1880. When Elder was appointed, his fellow bishops were reluctant to congratulate him. The archdiocese was in the midst of litigation, weighed down by a potential debt of nearly $4 million (approximately $120 million today), resulting from a bank failure. While the extent of the archdiocese's indebtedness was battled out in the courts, the seminary was closed and assets were frozen, endangering the work of parishes, schools, and diocesan initiatives. Due to the bankruptcy's cause, the laity were angry and anxious, and the clergy were suspicious and disheartened.

In the face of this daunting challenge, Elder was not paralyzed. The then sixty-year-old prelate had already been a bishop for two decades and had faced many challenges. He did not claim exceptional financial or organizational acumen, but the seasoned shepherd set about reorganizing diocesan structures, promoting accountability, and regaining trust. Elder's reforms included refounding the seminary, correcting unsound practices, easing ethnic discord, and systematizing diocesan structures—accomplishing all of it with humility, charity, and zeal. Archbishop Elder was a wise and prudent administrator who utilized legislative, parochial, educational, and curial reforms to transform his diocese from the brink of financial ruin to a model of centralization and growth.[3]

A SCANDAL ABATED

It is impossible to overstate the impact of the financial scandal on the Catholic laity and clergy of the Archdiocese of Cincinnati. In 1878, the bank controlled by Father Edward Purcell, the brother of Archbishop Purcell,

3. Elder was a forerunner in the updating of diocesan structures and practices, narrowly predating big city "consolidating bishops" like Archbishops George Mundelein of Chicago, William O'Connell of Boston, Dennis Dougherty of Philadelphia, and John Glennon of St. Louis, who "brought order, centralization, and businesslike management to their previously chaotic dioceses." See Kantowicz, *Corporation Sole*, 2.

failed. While the archdiocese did not sponsor the bank, the Purcell brothers' finances were practically inseparable, and the bank's deposits were routinely used for various church projects, including building St. Peter in Chains Cathedral. Father Purcell's poor recordkeeping practices prevented any certainty about the actual amount deposited, but it likely exceeded $25 million over the bank's forty years. When the bank failed, due to unfortunate investments rather than malfeasance, the liabilities totaled $3.87 million—a staggering sum.[4]

Angry creditors demanded repayment and litigation quickly ensued. In January 1880, the same month of Elder's appointment to Cincinnati, the legal assignee of the Purcell brothers petitioned in court to sell 211 churches, convents, schools, and orphanages—leading to great fear and confusion among clergy and laity. Attorneys for the archdiocese sought to defend the church's interests but acknowledged it might be impossible to prove bank funds had not been used for church properties' acquisition and improvement.[5]

Elder arrived in Cincinnati on April 18, 1880, and soon became acquainted with both the gravity and complexity of the situation. While his instinct was to pay the debt to the last dollar—if such were even possible—his fellow bishops cautioned him from accepting liability. He privately agonized whether justice might demand assuming the entire debt. However, Philadelphia Archbishop James F. Wood joined other bishops in warning him, "By no means" acknowledge the debt, "don't think of such a thing."[6] Elder understood the implications and always referred to it as "the Purcell debt"—not the archdiocese's or his own.

While the so-called "Church Case" played out in court, Elder attempted to collect funds for Purcell's creditors and, depending on the legal outcome, to repurchase parishes and schools. His fellow bishops organized a drive, which was moderately successful, but the funds remained unassigned, waiting for the trial's outcome. Soon the creditors, and even non-creditors, began criticizing Elder for his supposed inaction. An open letter in the *Cincinnati Commercial* from non-creditor Catholics charged the coadjutor with "inexplicable silence" and "premeditated inaction." They blamed him in part for the "protracted litigation" in which the church found itself. Twice they petitioned the pope for his removal.[7]

4. Hussey, *1878 Financial Failure*, 8–10.

5. Hussey, *1878 Financial Failure*, 21.

6. Hussey, *1878 Financial Failure*, 25.

7. "An Open Letter," *Cincinnati Commercial*, Aug 13, 1882; "Petitioning the Pope," *Cincinnati Commercial Gazette*, Aug 3, 1886.

Elder's published rebuttal reminded his readers that the bank failure and ensuing legal case occurred before he arrived in Cincinnati: "The lawsuit being already in progress when I came, I was no party to it, and I have had no power to control it, in one way or another." Elder, not being named in the proceedings, said he was powerless to disrupt the suit's progress. However, he would continue to assist the "most distressed" creditors as he was able. "Whether I shall be able to do more," he said, "I do not know, but if anything more shall be in my power, I shall do it cheerfully and devotedly."[8]

Beggars came to Elder's door nearly every day. At first, he refrained from handouts, worrying that it would lead to a dangerous frenzy. Then he began giving out a few dollars at a time from his personal funds and friends' contributions, but it did little to satisfy the need. Elder sympathized with those whose savings had vanished, acknowledging that many could not afford basic necessities: rent, food, or clothing. He understood that the bank failure disproportionately impacted the impoverished, the immigrant, and the elderly. Many, who had trusted the church with what little they had, lost everything.

Elder felt tremendous pressure to resolve the debt, but he eschewed any of the schemes proposed to him, including an out-of-state lottery which, though technically prohibited by Ohio law, promised to raise $3 million in a single year. The plan, fortunately, never got off the ground.[9] Elder maintained hope that the entire debt could be repaid, praying for a large and unexpected act of charity or perhaps even the direct intervention of the Holy See, but this never occurred.

On December 1, 1883, the court ruling was announced: Archbishop Purcell had held church properties "in trust." They had been primarily paid for by the congregations themselves—not the Purcell bank. Such properties were protected and could not be sold to erase the bank debt, but where it was probable that monies had been used to buy or build churches or other religious institutions, "such amount with interest" could be recovered. The court found that several parishes and institutions, including the cathedral and seminary, were obligated to repay $143,000. The plaintiffs were outraged, calling it a "barren victory [for the Church] over the desolate poor of Cincinnati."[10]

The plaintiffs appealed the ruling, and, due to Archbishop Purcell's death on July 4, 1883, Elder became the case's defendant. Elder pleaded with

8. "A Letter from Bishop Elder," *Cincinnati Commercial*, Aug 19, 1882.

9. Hussey, *1878 Financial Failure*, 19. The local Catholic newspaper, the *Catholic Telegraph*, even pushed for the lottery scheme; see "Our Great Catholic Debt," *Catholic Telegraph*, Nov 23, 1882, 4.

10. Hussey, *1878 Financial Failure*, 27–28, 35.

the creditors' lawyer to let the case rest, offering to do all he could to repay them, but they pressed on with the appeal.[11] The Ohio Supreme Court upheld the earlier decision in the case (by this time known as *Miller and Tafel v. Elder*), announcing its judgment on December 21, 1888. According to the decision, the archdiocese repaid what bank funds the court decided were spent on Catholic projects, and the Purcell brothers' assets were converted into cash. Dividends were then provided to the creditors, totaling 7.125 percent of the deposits.[12]

Elder, now free to make goodwill payments to the creditors, organized a fundraising committee. Elder proposed that he would begin to pay off the debts of any creditor willing to accept one-fourth of the principal owed. By asking the clergy and laity to offer what they could for the "honor of religion," subscriptions steadily increased.[13] Nearly twenty years after the financial collapse, Elder explained, "Many of them still come to us and we help them as we can."[14] The affair would not be closed until the final payment was made half a year after Elder's death in 1904, but the scandal by this time had largely been abated.[15]

For the local church, recovery was slow but consistent. The court's decision that parish and school properties could not be sold set off a flurry of building and enhancements of existing churches, schools, rectories, and convents. Funds diverted to the attorneys and for fundraising for the creditors were freed up for parishes, schools, and diocesan institutions. Elder's steady leadership helped in the recovery, and the charitable assistance the church offered, even if it was insufficient to satisfy the magnitude of the need, helped those most afflicted by the unfortunate financial failure of Elder's predecessor.

11. Elder to John B. Mannix, Letter Book 3, Nov 17, 1883, 288–91, box 1, RG 1.3, Archbishop William H. Elder Papers, ser. 1.3-04-05, Outgoing Correspondence (hereafter Outgoing Correspondence), AAC; Elder to T. D. Lincoln, Esq., Letter Book 3, Nov 24, 1883, 303, box 1, Outgoing Correspondence, AAC.

12. Hussey, *1878 Financial Failure*, 31–32.

13. "Hallelujah: Relief for the Creditors," *Catholic Telegraph*, Apr 14, 1887; "Archdiocese of Cincinnati: To the Friends of the Late Most Rev. Archbishop Purcell," *Catholic Telegraph*, Jun 14, 1888; "Subscriptions," *Catholic Telegraph*, Nov 29, 1888.

14. Elder to Father John Kreckel, Feb 10, 1896, Letter Book 10, 484, box 2, Outgoing Correspondence, AAC.

15. Hussey, *1878 Financial Failure*, 32.

A SEMINARY REBORN

Mount St. Mary's of the West, Cincinnati's diocesan-run seminary, was one of the casualties of the Purcell bank failure. The seminary—then in its fiftieth year—was forced to close in 1879 due to the uncertainty surrounding the archdiocese's financial condition. At the time of its closure, the school had nearly one hundred seminarians, two-thirds of whom were minor seminarians (not yet students of theology). The preparatory program was discontinued, and the archdiocese's major seminarians were sent to St. Mary's Seminary in Baltimore, while the future of the seminary property depended on the litigation's outcome.[16]

Elder's concern for the lack of clergy was a frequent theme in his correspondence. Many priests did not live past their fifties, and by the late nineteenth century, an older generation of mainly European-born priests needed to be replaced. Depending on the rates of death or sickness, Elder often found himself desperate. The archbishop, for instance, wrote to the Baltimore seminary rector in 1884, asking if any of his seminarians were so advanced as to be ordained: "We are very much in need now. . . . Three very active priests have died in the last four months and some others have lost their health—all in different ways, so that now I have need of six priests."[17]

Without sufficient priests for all of his parishes, Elder encouraged flexibility. Since he could not assign a pastor to the church in the sparsely populated town of Newport, for instance, he asked three neighboring pastors to take turns offering the sacraments. Each could say Mass there "if not on Sundays, then at least, perhaps a weekday visit would suffice."[18] Some pastors with large congregations were alone, without other priests assisting them. Elder apologized to the pastor of St. Mary's, a large German parish in Cincinnati's Over-the-Rhine neighborhood, for requiring the parish's assisting priest to make monthly visits to a Brown County congregation—thirty-five miles to the east.[19]

Though the archdiocese had fewer than ten seminarians in the early 1880s, Elder regretted that there were not more funds available to assist with the education of future priests. He could pay the "pensions" of some (usually after philosophy studies were completed) but not all. To seminarian F. X.

16. Kelly and Kirwin, *History of Mt. St. Mary's*, 302.

17. Elder to Father A.[lphonse] L. Magnien, Apr 17, 1884, Letter Book 3, 487, box 1, Outgoing Correspondence, AAC.

18. Elder to Father Mathias Kenk, CPPS, Jan 6, 1885, Letter Book 4, 33, box 1, Outgoing Correspondence, AAC.

19. Elder to Father Bernard Menge, May 14, 1890, Letter Book 7, 135, box 1, Outgoing Correspondence, AAC.

Lasance (who would become a nationally known author of prayer books and spiritual guides), he wrote that only those from poor families could be helped. He asked Lasance to discern whether he truly required assistance from the sacrifices of the faithful, reminding him that if ordained, he would have a steady source of income.[20]

Dissatisfied that the archdiocese's seminarians were trained far from home, Elder expressed the desire to reopen the seminary in Cincinnati as soon as possible, but he lacked the financial means. The vacant Mount St. Mary's Seminary property was briefly entertained as the location of a national Catholic seminary. Bishop John Lancaster Spalding (a distant cousin of Elder's) of Peoria, Illinois, inquired about the seminary's status in the summer of 1880. He reasoned that if it were for sale, the US bishops could perhaps purchase it. Founding a national seminary in Cincinnati, he wrote to Elder, "would add dignity to the See [of Cincinnati], inspire courage in the people . . . and help in some slight measure to lighten your financial burden." Elder agreed to sell the property for $125,000, yet the plan failed to gain support from other bishops—most of whom were set on Washington, DC, for the location of the proposed Catholic University of America.[21]

Knowing that a robust local seminary system could help answer the need for more clergy, Elder began taking steps to restart Mount St. Mary's. The opportunity presented itself when a local Catholic philanthropist, Reuben R. Springer, died, willing $100,000 to the archdiocese to educate priests. In the spring of 1887, Elder recruited several priests to teach. Elder recognized that the work would not be easy. To the new rector, Father Thomas Byrne, who had been unenthusiastically pulled from his role at the cathedral, Elder reminded, "It will be an additional means for you to give glory to God." Soon other priests were recruited for the faculty.[22]

Having sat vacant for eight years, the seminary building was in poor condition. Vandalism and neglect left the building open to the elements, ruining everything inside. Desks, chairs, tables, and beds were "destroyed or damaged to such an extent as to be useless." Officials assembled an army of carpenters, plumbers, and painters. Repairs totaling $18,000 were

20. Elder to Mr. F. X. Lasance, Nov 20, 1880, Letter Book 1, 269–70, box 1, Outgoing Correspondence, AAC.

21. Elder, for his part, thought that the nation's capital was a poor choice for the Catholic University of America as it was filled with "unscrupulous men" who would lead astray young and impressionable theology students. Elder to Bishop J. L. Spalding, Sep 12, 1880, Letter Book 1, 188–89, box 1, Outgoing Correspondence, AAC; see also Ellis, *Formative Years*, 68–75, 134–35; Ellis, *Life of James Cardinal Gibbons*, 391.

22. Elder to Father Thomas Byrne, Feb 13, 1888, Letter Book 5, box 1, Outgoing Correspondence, AAC.

completed in the spring and summer of 1887, and the school reopened that fall. The first year began with only twenty-seven seminarians (two-thirds from the archdiocese), but enrollment increased to one hundred within five years.[23]

To support seminary education, Elder organized an annual collection to be taken up in each parish on Pentecost. The seminary, he explained, is the "nursery" for all other "institutions of religion," including churches, schools, and hospitals. Educating the seminarians locally would bring about a "brotherly spirit" and help them become more aware of "local wants."[24] The archbishop exhorted the people to greater generosity, which he believed could assist in calling forth religious vocations.[25] Elder's dream of a comprehensive seminary system was furthered with the founding of a stand-alone minor seminary. Elder founded St. Gregory's Preparatory Seminary in 1890 in Mount Washington, to the east of the city.

Elder was concerned with the quality, not just the quantity of priests. He required priests to pass junior clergy exams and address any deficiencies if they were to continue to possess the faculties to preach and hear confessions.[26] Beginning in 1887, based on the Second Plenary Council of Baltimore's legislation, he initiated quarterly ecclesiastical conferences. All priests of the archdiocese were required to attend. These conferences considered questions of dogma, morality, and Scripture, with a case or question selected in advance and then presented by one of the priests. These study days formed the basis for the clergy's continuing education.[27]

During Elder's tenure, the number of diocesan clergy grew from 134 to 174, and the size of ordination classes increased from an average of three to nine. Under his leadership, Mount St. Mary's Seminary was reopened, and St. Gregory's Preparatory Seminary was founded. The number of seminarians studying for the archdiocese increased from a handful to over one hundred.[28] By this time, he felt there was a reasonable prospect that "our

23. Kelly and Kirwin, *History of Mt. St. Mary's*, 366, 368.

24. Kelly and Kirwin, *History of Mt. St. Mary's*, 367–68.

25. "Archdiocese of Cincinnati," *Catholic Telegraph*, Jun 6, 1889; "[Official] Archdiocese of Cincinnati," *Catholic Telegraph*, May 15, 1890.

26. "The Diocesan Synod of the Archdiocese of Cincinnati," *Catholic Telegraph*, Oct 28, 1886

27. "Ecclesiastical Conferences," *Catholic Telegraph*, Mar 3, 1887.

28. For the number of priests and seminarians, see *Sadliers' Catholic Directory*, 105; and *Catholic Directory, Almanac, and Clergy*, 64. In 1904, Cincinnati's two seminaries had over two hundred students, but not all were affiliated with the Archdiocese of Cincinnati, though it is likely a significant number were from the archdiocese. Annual ordinations were deduced from clergy lists: Lamott, *History of the Archdiocese*, 355–76.

own diocese will supply vocations enough to meet the spiritual demands of our people . . . and may in time send out apostolic missionaries to other dioceses and even to pagan countries."[29] Elder's dream of a well-formed, local presbyterate with sufficient priests was closer to realization.

ORDER RESTORED

Clerical misconduct and disputes among clergy and laity were frequent concerns for Elder. Upon his arrival, he discovered that some of his priests could be uncouth, disobedient, or ill-tempered. One pastor shot off a pistol in a crowd, apparently to disperse his critics and assert his authority. Another refused to say Mass on Easter Sunday but took up a collection anyway. A third lit up a cigar during a graveside service—while still wearing cassock, surplice, and biretta.[30] In response to such conduct, Elder did not shy away from discipline, considering it a paternal duty: "Even when a priest makes a mistake, the bishop is his father and desires to help him."[31] For instance, when Elder discovered a pastor had attended a performance of *Romeo and Juliet* (contrary to a diocesan statute that forbade clergy from attending the theater), he reproved him mildly. But when the priest tried to justify himself, Elder responded strongly: synodal law could not be violated for one's "musical advancement."[32]

Elder could be direct with disobedient priests. He wrote to a pastor in Wyoming, a community just outside of Cincinnati: "I do not want to be harsh: but really you try my patience a good deal. . . . More than once I had to complain of your not attending to my letters. I hope there will be a thorough change in you in this regard."[33] When a survey to pastors on church music went unanswered, he reminded three priests of their

29. Elder to Father John Mackey, Dec 21, 1897, Letter Book 11, 583–87, box 2, Outgoing Correspondence, AAC.

30. Elder to Father James O'Donnell, May 31, 1882, Letter Book 2, 50, box 1, Outgoing Correspondence, AAC; Elder to Father William H. Sidley, Apr 8, 1896, Letter Book 10, 547–48, box 2, Outgoing Correspondence, AAC; Elder to Father Francis J. Goetz, Feb 9, 1899, Letter Book 13, 75–76, box 2, Outgoing Correspondence, AAC.

31. Elder to Father Denis Mackey, Sep 5, 1885, Letter Book 4, 353, box 1, Outgoing Correspondence, AAC.

32. Elder to Father Andrew Hemmersbach, Mar 7, 1899, Letter Book 13, 118, box 2, Outgoing Correspondence, AAC; Elder to Father Andrew Hemmersbach, Mar 12, 1899, Letter Book 13, 126, box 2, Outgoing Correspondence, AAC.

33. Elder to Father J.[ohn] S. Singleton, Mar 27, 1890, Letter Book 7, 91, box 1, Outgoing Correspondence, AAC.

obligation—under obedience—to reply to him.[34] When he learned that a pastor had taken up a second collection for himself, he wrote to him: "The practice of taking up a collection in church on Christmas, Easter, and other feasts for the additional benefit of the pastor is forbidden in this diocese. Please do not do it again."[35] When a pastor kicked his assisting priest out of the rectory and left his belongings in the front yard, Elder chided the pastor: "If this is true, it is a direct violation of the bishop's administration. The bishop only can appoint and renew assistants. You must return his property and place them where they had been before."[36] But Elder kept in mind that those priests needing correction were relatively few: "Instead of worrying at the bad examples of some few unworthy priests, how joyfully we ought to entertain ourselves at the sight of the great army of faithful and hard-working priests."[37]

Elder did not shy away from asserting the proper authority of the clergy in disputes with their congregations, but he was often deferential to lay church wardens, especially in their oversight of temporal matters. However, in writing to Father Francis Quatman about a group of church wardens attempting to control their pastor, he asked the priest to remind them of the "great difference between Catholics and Protestants."

> Catholics know that their Church is established by Our Lord Himself and He has appointed that it must be taught and governed by the Apostles and their successors, the Bishops and Priests of the Church. If the laymen were to rule in any congregation, then that congregation would not be a part of the Catholic Church. It would be a protestant church governed by men and not by God.[38]

Sometimes Elder waded into protracted disputes between clergy and laity, often involving the management of temporal affairs. An element of the German congregation in the town of Maria Stein revolted, with the church wardens claiming the right to parish property. Elder first advised the pastor to respond with a light touch: "Speak as gently as possible to soothe their

34. For instance, Elder to Father William D. Hickey, May 21, 1898, Letter Book 12, 116, box 2, Outgoing Correspondence, AAC.

35. Elder to Father John J. Kennedy, Mar 5, 1885, Letter Book 4, 126, box 1, Outgoing Correspondence, AAC.

36. Elder to Father John J. Kennedy, Sep 16, 1897, Letter Book 11, 452, box 2, Outgoing Correspondence, AAC.

37. Elder to unknown, May 10, 1895, cited in Elder, *Character Glimpses*, 103.

38. Elder to Father Francis Quatman, Jun 3, 1898, Letter Book 12, 147–49, box 2, Outgoing Correspondence, AAC.

minds. Do not call them a *rebel party*, nor use any other words that will offend them. We must make a great deal of allowance for human nature."[39] But when the wardens refused, Elder sent a letter of excommunication to be circulated among the dissidents and their supporters.[40] To restore their access to the sacraments, Elder had each sign a statement that read: "We the undersigned . . . acknowledge ourselves bound to accept and obey all the laws and regulations of the Church, as given by our lawful rulers in the Church: the pastor, the Archbishop, and the sovereign pontiff, and by those acting under their authority." Furthermore, they were to promise to obey the archbishop "in deed and word . . . without any qualification or mental reservation."[41] The efforts at reconciliation were successful; there was no lasting schism in the parish, though the pastor had to meet personally with some parish members to coax their assent.[42]

For Elder, rules were important but not sacrosanct. Each situation needed to be judged with prudence and charity. When it came to the question of a parishioner who could not afford pew rent, Elder explained to the pastor that "no one may exclude him from hearing Mass." He advised the pastor to make some places in his church available to anyone—regardless of ability to pay.[43] However, for the person who could pay, it was a grave injustice to withhold support. To one closefisted parishioner, Elder admonished, "How can you claim to have the spirit of a good Catholic when out of all the means which God has given you, you will not offer back to God $12 a year?"[44]

When it came to mixing religion and recreational alcohol use, however, Elder was uncompromising. He frequently reminded pastors of the diocesan policy that forbade alcohol consumption at parish events, including picnics and fairs. Elder considered a violation of this rule grounds for the priest's suspension or removal or even placing the entire congregation

39. Elder to Father B.[ernard] Austermann, CPPS, Jun 9, 1880, Letter Book 1, n.p, box 1, Outgoing Correspondence, AAC (emphasis original).

40. Elder to Father Thomas Eisenring, CPPS, Mar 21, 1885, Letter Book 4, 159–63, box 1, Outgoing Correspondence, AAC; Elder to Father Thomas Eisenring, CPPS, Apr 30, 1885, Letter Book 4, 230, box 1, Outgoing Correspondence, AAC.

41. Appendix to Elder to Father Thomas Eisenring, CPPS, Apr 16, 1885, Letter Book 4, 189, box 1, Outgoing Correspondence, AAC.

42. Elder to Father Thomas Eisenring, CPPS, Jan 21, 1889, Letter Book 6, 225–26, box 1, Outgoing Correspondence, AAC. For more on this dispute, see Mizer, *St. John the Baptist*, 67–69; Leugers, *St. John Church*, 32–34.

43. Elder to Father Andreas Fabian, Jan 31, 1885, Letter Book 4, 68–71, box 1, Outgoing Correspondence, AAC.

44. Elder to Miss Sophie Kearney, Feb 13, 1885, Letter Book 4, 95–96, box 1, Outgoing Correspondence, AAC.

on interdict (excluding them from the sacraments).[45] The policy was tested in 1889 when beer—perhaps as much as 150 kegs' worth—was consumed at the dedication of Sacred Heart Church in Camp Washington (Cincinnati). The beer was served apparently without the pastor's consent or knowledge, but Elder placed him on a week's leave and said he was responsible for "having failed in the care and vigilance which a pastor is bound to exercise."[46]

Elder was a prudent and fair administrator: he was patient with the weak but did not avoid offering correction and challenge. He promoted harmony within congregations, made clergy accountable, and was vigilant to avoid scandal. His shepherding of clergy and laity showed a desire to prevent human foibles, as much as possible, from impeding the ministry of the church.

AN ETHNIC CHURCH UNITED

In becoming Cincinnati's archbishop, Elder found himself shepherding a multi-ethnic local church. In many areas of the archdiocese, congregations were formed according to ethnicity and language. This meant a German-speaking Catholic congregation could be found near an English-speaking one. Later, additional parishes were created for other groups, whether Italian, Eastern European, or African American. As he was of "American" stock, Elder did not identify with any single ethnic group. While this might have led him to pursue an assimilationist agenda, he determined that national churches—with one dominant ethnic group—were a temporary necessity.

Elder sought as much as possible to provide priests who spoke the language of the majority of the congregation. For general parish meetings, he advised a vote should be taken to determine the language used, but "whenever necessary all matters must be explained in the other language." He concluded that if English were chosen, "everyone shall have the right of expressing himself in German." For parish societies, each should determine the official language of its meetings and records.[47]

45. *Synodus Dioecesana Cincinnatensis*, 130–31; Elder, "To the Clergy and Laity of the Archdiocese," Jul 6, 1889, Letter Book 6, 400–401, box 1, Outgoing Correspondence, AAC.

46. Elder, "To the Clergy and Laity of the Archdiocese," Jul 6, 1889, Letter Book 6, 400–401, box 1, Outgoing Correspondence, AAC; "A Pastor's Punishment," *Cincinnati Commercial Gazette*, Jul 7, 1889. The church wardens denied such a large quantity of beer was sold and affirmed that the pastor knew nothing of the intent to serve it. See "Sacred Heart Church: Wardens Set Themselves Right on the Recent Sale of Beer," *Cincinnati Commercial Gazette*, Jul 14, 1889.

47. Elder to Father John Schoenhoeft, Apr 2, 1886, Letter Book 4, 424, box 1,

Divisions along ethnic and linguistic lines had been essential for the growth of the US church, but by the 1890s, Elder envisioned a church less influenced by "nationalism" and one that embraced a pan-ethnic consciousness—where parish boundaries dictated parish membership, not ethnic background. Elder was concerned about the ill effects of nationalism. Such divisions "crippled the Church in many places." He admitted, for instance, that German traditions could "bring up children in piety and in the family spirit," but "after they get out into the world, they are in many ways a hindrance."[48] As populations shifted and communities became more diverse, in some locales strict ethnic separation was impossible. He reminded a German audience that the church in the United States had no "Irish parishes" but only parishes in which English was primarily spoken. He argued that, even in so-called "German parishes," English should be used whenever possible to care for the spiritual needs of non-German speakers in the church's vicinity.[49]

Elder, however, did not support non-Germans attending German churches. When he became aware that an Irish pastor in Hamilton was so unpopular that English-only speakers were attending the German parish, he forbade the German pastor from accepting their pew rent, stating that they should go where they can "hear and understand the instructions of His Sacred Word."[50] Parochial divisions by ethnic and language groups often created complexities. In cases where the mother and father were of different ethnicities, he advised the mother to go to her church with her children until they reached the age of seven and thereafter with the father—who should be viewed as "head of the family." The children, consequently, should be baptized only in his church.[51] But as the German language became less understood—even among those of German ancestry—Elder realized that many would choose to attend English-speaking churches. When a German pastor asked Elder in 1898 to intervene to prevent this exodus, he replied that he could not forbid the English-speaking children of German parents from attending an English-speaking church.[52] By the turn of the century,

Outgoing Correspondence, AAC.

48. Elder to Cardinal James Gibbons, Dec 16, 1886, Letter Book 5, 34–36, box 1, Outgoing Correspondence, AAC.

49. Elder to Father Joseph Stoeppelmann, Dec 15, 1898, Letter Book 12, 425, box 2, Outgoing Correspondence, AAC.

50. Elder to Father Raphael Hesse, OSF, Oct 2, 1896, Letter Book 10, 672, box 2, Outgoing Correspondence, AAC.

51. Elder to Father Raphael Hesse, OSF, Oct 14, 1896, Letter Book 10, 685, box 2, Outgoing Correspondence, AAC.

52. Elder to Father Jos. A. Meyer, May 13, 1898, Letter Book 12, 99, box 2, Outgoing

ethnic distinctions in parochial life were becoming less significant, leading to his desire to form territorial parishes irrespective of ethnicity.[53]

Elder's promotion of nonethnic parishes was prescient, foreseeing the weakening of ethnic neighborhoods and tribal loyalties. He explained to a group of priests in 1891 that the faith would ultimately be sustained through English: "A great many [German-Americans] in fact have little or no opportunity of going to a German church or even seeing a German priest" and "if they exercise their religion at all, will have to do it in the English language." For this reason, he pressed for bilingual catechesis: "Let him learn his Catechism in German—but also in English."[54] Noting the number of young people in German parishes who could not understand the language, Elder also encouraged German pastors to preach in English. Aware that it was a sensitive issue, he did not promulgate such a policy but encouraged pastors privately to make greater use of English for instruction.[55]

Elder viewed ethnic and linguistic identities as important but saw the downside of exaggerated nationalism. While respecting the traditions brought from the Old World, he was able to look toward a future in which race and nation would be less important than the church's unitive "catholicity."

A CURIA REFORMED

Elder's experience as a bishop convinced him of the need for collaboration in governing. His curial reforms included the addition of several vicarious and consultative offices. He first established the position of chancellor, appointing Father Henry Moeller (his secretary and eventual coadjutor and successor) in the fall of 1886. Elder sought the assistance of a six-person college of consultors, a matrimonial tribunal, a court for disciplining clergy, an archdiocesan building committee, and a system of geographically based deaneries.[56]

Correspondence, AAC.

53. Elder to Archbishop Sebastian Martinelli, Mar 28, 1898, Outgoing Correspondence (Typed), Dec 21, 1897–Oct 2, 1903, 62, box 3, Outgoing Correspondence, AAC.

54. Elder to Father Charles Hahne, Sep 21, 1891, in "Bericht über die Verhandlungen der fünften General-Versammlung Deutsch-Amerikanischen Priester-Vereins in Buffalo, N.Y.," (St. Louis) *Pastoral-Blatt* 26.1 (January 1892), supplement, 3.

55. Elder to Bishop Thomas S. Byrne, Sep 12, 1897, Letter Book 11, 445, box 2, Outgoing Correspondence, AAC.

56. Elder to Father Henry Moeller, Oct 11, 1886, Letter Book 4, 644, box 1, Outgoing Correspondence, AAC; *Synodus Dioecesana Cincinnatensis*, xix–xx, 64–66.

Elder believed in the power of legislation to shape the priorities and practices of the archdiocese. In reforming the diocesan curia and legislating for the broader local church, Elder harnessed the force of the national meetings of the US bishops: the Second and Third Plenary Councils of Baltimore (1866 and 1884). Additionally, he oversaw two provincial councils (1882 and 1889) and two diocesan synods (1886 and 1898), which drew from the decisions of the Baltimore councils and combined to unify and systematize diocesan organization.

Elder's reworking of the diocesan statutes included the division of the archdiocese according to three deaneries (Cincinnati, Springfield, and Sidney) and insistence upon territorial boundaries for congregations. To end "parish raiding," neighboring pastors were to agree on the boundaries between their parishes and, in case of a dispute, request the archdiocese appoint a panel of arbiters.[57] The archbishop relied closely on the priests appointed as deans, who often were tasked with investigating conflicts such as boundary disputes and, at times, disciplining clergy. Deans were expected to conduct annual visitations of parishes and schools and examine teachers. This was especially important in the northern reaches of the archdiocese, far removed from the see city.[58]

As populations shifted and new congregations were created, Elder worked to redistribute personnel, which required reassigning many priests (over forty new assignments occurred in 1887 alone). He attempted to match priests' interests and capacities with their assignments.[59] Elder admitted using reassignments as an opportunity to correct priests and offer them a "fatherly admonition." While he expected priests to be obedient, he acknowledged that their input in the assignment process could be helpful. In writing to one Dayton pastor whom he wished to reassign to Cincinnati, he stated that he would not move him without consultation in case of some objection. The priest's concerns were apparently compelling; Elder decided to keep him in Dayton.[60] Another pastor was asked to resign his appointment to teach in the seminary. Elder asked for his consent, explaining, "I do not like to have anyone teach unless he can take pleasure in it and give his

57. "The Diocesan Synod of the Archdiocese of Cincinnati," *Catholic Telegraph*, Oct 28, 1886; *Synodus Dioecesana Cincinnatensis*, 56–57.

58. *Synodus Dioecesana Cincinnatensis*, 5, 61–62.

59. Gilmartin, "Partial Appraisal," 56.

60. Elder to Cardinal James Gibbons, Jan 27, 1882, Letter Book 1, 746, box 1, Outgoing Correspondence, AAC; Elder to Father James O'Donoghue, Jan 11, 1882, Letter Book 1, 707–8, box 1, Outgoing Correspondence, AAC.

heart to it." The priest must have demurred; he retained his pastorate for the next decade.[61]

In line with the legislation of the Third Plenary Council of Baltimore, which mandated a school for each parish, Elder remained convinced of the absolute necessity of a separate Catholic school system. Elder instructed that where Catholic schools were established, sending Catholic children to other schools could be sinful. He retained permission to exempt parents from the obligation to enroll their children in Catholic schools, and if parents confessed the sin of not sending their children to a parochial school, only their pastor could absolve them.[62] However, Elder was not unbending on the school question. Elder equivocated when a pastor explained that one family lived too distant from the parish school to attend in the winter months. The archbishop judged that the children's mother should be free to send them to another school, but he refrained from consenting: "Do not say that the bishop gives permission—just say that in the circumstances, you will not blame her."[63]

Seeking to expand Catholic education to every parish, Elder surveyed the congregations to determine the status of their educational efforts. Elder informed pastors that each was expected to begin a school unless he granted explicit permission to defer its establishment "for good cause."[64] For instance, he wrote to one Cincinnati pastor, informing him that his parish was one of the largest, if not the largest, congregation with no school. He noted that it had been twelve years since the Baltimore Council had required that all parishes establish schools within ten years: "I have been indulgent with you for two years longer. My conscience is already reproaching me severely. . . . Your school must be put in operation in September of next year."[65] The pressure placed on pastors yielded some results. When Elder assumed the role of archbishop, the archdiocese educated 20,000 students in 88 elementary schools. Twenty years later, the number of students had grown to 26,000 among 103 schools. Parish-based schools were formed in

61. Elder to Father Francis Messmer, Oct 1, 1896, Letter Book 10, 669, box 2, Outgoing Correspondence, AAC.

62. "The Diocesan Synod of the Archdiocese of Cincinnati," *Catholic Telegraph*, Oct 28, 1886; "New Rules Are Made Which Will Govern Catholics of This Diocese in the Future," *Cincinnati Commercial Tribune*, Dec 31, 1898.

63. Elder to Father J. N. Schoenfeld, Dec 1, 1882, Letter Book 2, 310, box 1, Outgoing Correspondence, AAC.

64. "The Diocesan Synod of the Archdiocese of Cincinnati," *Catholic Telegraph*, Oct 28, 1886.

65. Elder to Father John J. Kennedy, May 6, 1898, Letter Book 12, 76, box 2, Outgoing Correspondence, AAC.

90 percent of urban congregations and grew to reach 70 percent of rural localities within the archdiocese.[66]

Among his various reform efforts, Elder took a particular interest in regulating liturgical music, establishing a commission on church music composed of priests and church organists. The Cincinnati provincial council of 1882 supplied the rationale: "There is grave cause for dissatisfaction with much of the music now in use in the services of the Church. Much of it is profane; much of it so undevotional and secularized that often, if the sacred words were withdrawn, one would fancy he was in the concert-room, or listening to the sensuous strains of the opera."[67] Recognizing that sacred music should raise the heart and soul to God, the commission developed a list of approved music. No other music was to be played in any of the churches, and new musical compositions were to be submitted to the commission for a decision. Within a few years, the commission's music catalog became a "fixed institution" of the archdiocese, ensuring the propriety of all musical selections used in worship.[68]

Elder strengthened the system of pastors regularly reporting to curial officials. Annual financial reports were to be submitted to the chancellor as well as statistical and demographic data, which, if inadequate or concerning, could result in a summons to the chancery.[69] Elder asked a pastor to speak with him about "some irregularities" in his last financial report, which the archbishop used as an opportunity to offer "some special cautions and directions concerning the administration of [his] congregation."[70] Through this reporting, the archbishop became aware of the strengths and weaknesses of his congregations (and pastors). Such data helped address the need for specialized ministries. Among the institutions Elder helped found was a short-lived school for the deaf located at the cathedral and boys' and girls' homes to protect young people from the dangers of urban life.[71]

66. Fortin, "Queen City Catholicism," 131.

67. "Concilium Cincinnatense Provinciale," 250.

68. Elder, "To the Clergy Diocesan and Regular of the Diocese of Cincinnati," Jul 26, 1899, Outgoing Correspondence (Typed), Dec 21, 1897–Oct 2, 1903, 186–87, box 3, Outgoing Correspondence, AAC; Elder, "To the Revd. Clergy," Mar 12, 1902, Outgoing Correspondence (Typed), Dec 21, 1897–Oct 2, 1903, 374, box 3, Outgoing Correspondence, AAC.

69. See Parish Statistical Reports, RG 4.9, Finance Office Records, AAC. Compare, for instance, 1880 to 1881, when additional data on sacramental reception, parish membership, and school enrollment began to be collected.

70. Elder to Father John Cusack, Aug 24, 1896, Letter Book 10, 632, box 2, Outgoing Correspondence, AAC.

71. *Synodus Dioecesana Cincinnatensis*, 66. For more on these institutions that Elder helped found, see Endres, *Bicentennial History*, 114–15, 134–36.

Through Elder's curial reforms, the clergy was called to greater accountability. Pastors were obligated to submit detailed annual reports; deans were tasked with visiting parishes and schools annually; and diocesan consultors advised the archbishop on important questions. In the wake of two provincial councils and two diocesan synods, Elder had promulgated a clear, uniform set of laws for the local church. The archdiocese became a model for curial oversight and centralization, holding priests (and their parishes and schools) to professional standards.

CONCLUSION

As Elder approached fifty years as a priest and forty years as a bishop, his episcopal confreres were amazed by the archdiocese's revitalization. Most remembered the bank failure, the Purcell brothers' fate, and the former humbled state of the church in Cincinnati. Given the challenges, the growth of Catholic institutions was surprising. On the occasion of Elder's golden jubilee of priestly ordination in 1896, Cardinal James Gibbons praised Elder for "the number of churches, schools, hospitals, and asylums that have been added to the list during his administration."[72] Under Elder's leadership, the local church benefited from thirty-two additional parishes or missions, and the archdiocese grew to 200,000 Catholics, nearly 300 priests, 180 churches, and over 100 Catholic schools.[73]

Institutional growth was only part of the story. Elder's legacy was not primarily bricks-and-mortar but reforming and centralizing. His revamping of the curia included structures of accountability and additional levels of collaboration. Known for his magnanimity, humility, and prayerfulness, Elder inspired others as he successfully surmounted the challenges of financial turmoil, disorganization, a priest shortage, and ethnic disunity. During his twenty-four years of shepherding the church in Cincinnati, Elder presided over the archdiocese's restoration. He witnessed to the bishop's calling—as he himself once wrote—to show "the infinite love of God to men."[74]

BIBLIOGRAPHY

Archives of the Archdiocese of Cincinnati (AAC). Archbishop William H. Elder Papers. RG 1.3; Finance Office Records, RG 4.9, Cincinnati.

72. Elder, *Character Glimpses*, 99.
73. *Catholic Directory, Almanac, and Clergy*, 64.
74. Elder, "Sermon on Consecration of Bishop," AAC.

Catholic Directory, Almanac, and Clergy List for the Year of Our Lord 1904. Milwaukee: M. H. Wiltzius, 1904.

"Concilium Cincinnatense Provinciale IV: Habitum Anno 1882." In *Acta et decreta quatuor conciliorum provincialium Cincinnatensium, 1855–1882*, 157–262. Cincinnati: Benziger Brothers, 1886.

Elder, Susan B., ed. *Character Glimpses of Most Reverend William Henry Elder, D.D.: Second Archbishop of Cincinnati*. Cincinnati: Frederick Pustet, 1911.

Ellis, John Tracy. *The Formative Years of the Catholic University of America*. Washington, DC: Catholic University of America Press, 1946.

———. *The Life of James Cardinal Gibbons, Archbishop of Baltimore, 1834–1921*. Vol. 1. Milwaukee: Bruce, 1952.

Endres, David J. *A Bicentennial History of the Archdiocese of Cincinnati: The Catholic Church in Southwest Ohio, 1821–2021*. Milford, OH: Little Miami, 2021.

Fortin, Roger A. "Queen City Catholicism: Catholic Education in Cincinnati." In *Urban Catholic Education: Tales of Twelve American Cities*, edited by Thomas C. Hunt and Timothy Walch, 121–45. Notre Dame, IN: Alliance for Catholic Education, 2010.

Gilmartin, Thomas V. "A Partial Appraisal of the Character and Works of Archbishop William Henry Elder from His Letters of 1887–1888." *St. Meinrad Essays* 12.2 (December 1959) 53–63.

Hussey, M. Edmund. *The 1878 Financial Failure of Archbishop Purcell*. Cincinnati: Cincinnati Historical Society, 1978.

Kantowicz, Edward R. *Corporation Sole: Cardinal Mundelein and Chicago Catholicism*. Notre Dame, IN: University of Notre Dame Press, 1983.

Kelly, Michael J., and James M. Kirwin. *History of Mt. St. Mary's Seminary of the West, Cincinnati, Ohio*. Cincinnati: Keating, 1894.

Lamott, John H. *History of the Archdiocese of Cincinnati, 1821–1921*. New York: Frederick Pustet, 1921.

Leugers, Henry J. *St. John Church, Maria Stein, Ohio, 1836–1986*. Maria Stein, OH: n.p., 1986.

Lonsway, Jesse W., and Aaron Pembleton. *The Episcopal Lineage of the Hierarchy in the United States, Revised 1790–1963*. Cincinnati: Charger, 1963.

Mizer, Paul. *St. John the Baptist Catholic Church, Maria Stein, Ohio: The 175th Anniversary, 1836–2011*. Celina: Messenger, 2011.

Sadliers' Catholic Directory, Almanac and Ordo for the Year of Our Lord 1881. New York: D. and J. Sadlier, 1881.

Synodus Dioecesana Cincinnatensis Tertia: Habita die 9[a] Novembris, 1898. Cincinnati: J. Berning, 1899.

Bishop as Chairman of the Board

Practical Aspects of the Governing Mission of the Episcopacy

—Anthony J. Stoeppel

The church has long used advisory and consultative groups of people as a tool to assist bishops in the governance, supervision, and oversight of dioceses. From the apostolic age, we see examples of bishops functioning as the chair of a council that advises him on important decisions. Even to the present, the local ordinary is required by canon law to form and use councils prior to making and executing certain decisions. The essential nature of councils in the ordinary's exercise of his governing mission warrants a study of certain principles a bishop might use in his capacity as chair of those bodies and other institutional boards. We propose an application of select best practices for chairs of nonprofit boards to bishops who fulfill a similar leadership role. Admittedly, ecclesial councils at the diocesan level differ from nonprofit boards in terms of their structure, authority, and scope. Nonetheless, we propose that the valuable leadership lessons learned from the nonprofit world pertain to a bishop who chairs canonically mandated councils and the other boards in his diocese.

We present here a brief review of the church's use of councils and boards throughout her history and a survey of the applicable canons. The church's social doctrine along with academic literature from the business sector provides guiding principles for bishops in their capacity as chairmen of these various councils and boards. We conclude by synthesizing the various sections into practical considerations for bishops in maximizing the effectiveness of their role as chairman of the board.

BRIEF REVIEW OF THE CHURCH'S HISTORICAL USE OF BOARDS

The early Christians' use of councils for religious governance and judicial matters grew out of their Jewish heritage. The Jewish people looked to the Sanhedrin as their supreme council of notable leaders who carried out their self-government.[1] While tracing a history back to the time of Moses (Num 11:16), the Sanhedrin exerted significant influence during the time of Jesus Christ and the apostles (see Matt 26:57; Mark 14:55, 15:1; Luke 22:66; John 11:47; and Acts 4:15, 5:21, 6:12, 22:30, 23:1, 24:20). Therefore, not surprisingly, the apostles also turned to a conciliar model for resolution and decision-making as important issues arose. The Council of Jerusalem, as recorded in Acts of the Apostles chapters 15–16, depicts many others surrounding St. Peter and freely giving their opinion on the matter at hand, but the first pope clearly has the central role and makes the final decision.

After the apostles, the early church fathers gave evidence that the use of councils and boards played an important role in the governance of the local churches. St. Ignatius of Antioch speaks of the entire presbyterate as a council or senate for the local bishop when he says, "I exhort you to strive to do all things in harmony with God: the bishop is to preside in the place of God, while the presbyters are to function as the council of the Apostles."[2]

St. Cyprian, in a letter to the priests of Carthage, clearly stated the use he made of the presbyterate as a council that guided him in exercise of his ministry: "From the beginning of my episcopacy, I made up my mind to do nothing of my own private opinion without your advice and without the consent of the people."[3]

St. Benedict in his *Rule*, immediately after delineating the qualities of a good abbot, dedicated an entire chapter to commanding the abbot to seek the counsel of all members of the community whenever special business arises.[4] He continued by noting that younger members often give the best counsel, so they should not be excluded based upon their lack of age or experience. Nonetheless, as less important business arises, it suffices for the abbot to seek counsel from the senior members. The Father of Western Monasticism concludes this chapter by quoting Sir 32:24 on the value and necessity of seeking counsel prior to making a decision: "Do everything with counsel and having so done thou wilt not repent."

1. Souvay, "Sanhedrin."
2. Ignatius, *To the Magnesians*, 69–74.
3. "To the Presbyters and Deacons" in Cyprian, *Letters of St. Cyprian*, 89.
4. Benedict, *RB 1980*, 178–81.

This model of the entire presbyterate functioning as a council depends upon all the priests living with or near the bishop. While this arrangement held for the first several centuries, as Christianity gained freedom and expanded beyond cities, the need grew to serve the baptized in rural areas. Therefore, as more and more priests served in parishes far away from the cathedral, these same priests could no longer assist the local bishop in a conciliar role as before. Bishops continued to seek counsel from priests, but they tended to do so from the priests stationed at the cathedral.[5] This shift on the bishop's part of seeking counsel from the entire presbyterate to a select group of priests near him led to the development of cathedral chapters. For more important issues that required the counsel of a greater number of priests or even the entire presbyterate, bishops would convoke diocesan synods.[6]

The use of cathedral chapters prevailed for the centuries to follow. However, the church's missionary efforts from the sixteenth century onwards meant that newly created dioceses often did not have sufficient priests to constitute and maintain a cathedral chapter. By the nineteenth century, bishops in missionary lands devised an arrangement of priests living near, but not necessarily in, the city of the episcopal see serving as diocesan consultors on matters about which the bishop could seek advice.[7] This structure of diocesan consultors gained universal recognition as an alternative to cathedral chapters in the 1917 *Code of Canon Law*.[8] Nonetheless, the 1917 code obliges bishops to form and use one group or the other as advisors on matters regarding the governance of his diocese.

Nearly fifty years later, the Second Vatican Council reinforced the need of bishops to seek counsel from the presbyterate and people in the exercise of the governing mission of their episcopacy. *Christus Dominus* makes clear that the local bishop shepherds his diocese, but he does so with the assistance of his priests by regularly meeting with them as his council.[9] The document *Presbyterorum Ordinis* goes as far as to call for a "priest senate" that advises the bishop in the management and governance of the diocese.[10] Even *Sacrosanctum Concilium* called for the bishop to create pastoral-liturgical commissions to advise him in the regulation of the sacred liturgy,

5. Purcell, "Institute of the Senate," 136–37.

6. Coulter, "Presbyterium of the Diocese," 8–12.

7. Klekotka, "Diocesan Consultors," 17; Ayrinhac, *Constitution of the Church*, 257–59.

8. Gasparri, *Codex Iuris Canonici*, c. 423 (hereafter cited in text as *CIC/1917*).

9. Second Vatican Council, *Christus Dominus*, 283–316.

10. Second Vatican Council, *Presbyterorum Ordinis*, 317–64.

music, and art.[11] Subsequent to the Second Vatican Council, Pope St. Paul VI promulgated a *motu proprio* in 1966 entitled *Ecclesiae Sanctae*, which called generally for a new canon law code and specifically for canons on the establishment of a presbyteral council in each diocese.[12] The Sacred Congregation for the Clergy's *Presbyteri Sacra*,[13] the 1971 Synod of Bishops' *Ultimis Temporibus*,[14] and the 1973 *Directory for the Pastoral Ministry of Bishops*[15] further defined the presbyteral council as a consultative aid to governance in the diocese while making clear that the bishop makes the final decision.

Bishops today continue to use councils and boards of clergy and lay people quite extensively, even in some instances when they are not canonically or legally required to do so. Even a quick search of diocesan websites lists several councils and boards that assist the local ordinary in the varied ministries as part of the governance of his diocese. For the assignments of clergy, many bishops depend upon a personnel board to advise them. In addition to a presbyteral council, some bishops have added a deacon council. Ministries such as Catholic Charities often have a governing board consisting of clergy and laity. As part of every diocese's approach to protect young people, a confidential and consultative review board advises bishops on the "assessment of allegations" and the "determination of a cleric's suitability for ministry."[16]

CODE OF CANON LAW ON BISHOPS AND BOARDS

As mentioned above, the 1917 *Code of Canon Law* required bishops to establish either a cathedral chapter or a board of diocesan consultors over whom he would preside and seek advice. The 1917 code affirmed that the local ordinary had the final say, but it also specified topics about which the bishop had to hear from the cathedral chapter or the diocesan consultors prior to making a decision. The topics include the support of cathedral canons (*CIC/1917*, cc. 394, 403), removable and irremovable pastors (c. 454), appointment of quasi-pastors (c. 457), reserving sins to himself (c. 895), ordering extraordinary processions (c. 1292), defining stipends (c. 1303), appointment of deputies at seminaries (c. 1359), handling of endowment

11. Second Vatican Council, *Sacrosanctum Concilium*, 117–162.
12. Second Vatican Council, *Ecclesiae Sanctae*, 624–33.
13. Sacred Congregation for the Clergy, "Presbyteri Sacra," 459–65.
14. Synod of Bishops, "Ultimis Temporibus," 897–922.
15. Congregation for Bishops, *Directory for the Pastoral Ministry*, 198–201.
16. United States Conference of Catholic Bishops, *Promise to Protect*, 8–10.

funds (c. 1415), dismemberment of benefices (c. 1428), execution of wills (c. 1517), function of an administrative council (c. 1520), and safeguarding money and moveable goods (c. 1547). In addition to presiding over meetings of the cathedral chapter or diocesan consultors, the 1917 code required bishops to preside over meetings of a diocesan synod (c. 357), elections of superioresses of religious communities (c. 506), and the administrative council of the diocese (c. 1520).

In comparison to the 1917 code, the 1983 *Code of Canon Law* increases the number of councils or boards that a bishop chairs. The local bishop presides over the presbyteral council (*CIC/1983*, c. 500, sec. 1),[17] the finance council (c. 492, sec. 1), the college of consultors (c. 502, sec. 2), the diocesan pastoral council (c. 514, sec. 1), a diocesan synod (c. 462), and elections of superiors of autonomous monasteries and supreme moderators of institutes of diocesan right (c. 625). The diocesan curia may have groups over which the bishop is the chairman, such as the episcopal council (c. 473, sec. 4). In those dioceses with Catholic schools, the canons foresee the bishop exercising his watchful care of those institutes by organizing and presiding at meetings of the schools' board of directors (cc. 806, sec. 2; 810 sec. 2). Where ecclesiastical universities and faculties exist, the local bishop may go about fulfilling his oversight responsibilities in an official capacity by serving as chairman of the board (c. 818).

Of all the councils and boards that a bishop chairs, the presbyteral council, composed exclusively of priests, functions as a senate that advises the local ordinary in the governance of the diocese (*CIC/1983*, c. 495). The finance council, which may include lay people, has several duties including, but not limited to, the preparation of an annual budget and review of receipts and expenditures (c. 493). The college of consultors is comprised of six to twelve priests from the presbyteral council chosen by the bishop to fulfill a number of tasks as specified in the law (c. 502). The roles of the other councils and boards over which a bishop chairs are self-explanatory given the name and statutes or bylaws of the group.[18]

In addition to requiring the bishop to constitute certain councils and boards, the 1983 *Code of Canon Law* continues the 1917 code's practice of obliging the local bishop to hear, listen to, or consult councils or boards regarding certain issues, but it changes the topics. The bishop must hear, listen to, or consult the presbyteral council regarding the erection or closing of parishes (*CIC/1983*, c. 515, sec. 2), relegation of a church to profane use

17. Catholic Church, *Code of Canon Law*, (hereafter cited in text as *CIC/1983*).

18. Examples include the Catholic Charities board, the episcopal council, and the clergy personnel board.

(c. 1222, sec. 2), imposition of a diocesan tax (c. 1263), and the calling of a diocesan synod (c. 461, sec. 1). The ordinary must hear, listen, or consult the finance council regarding the imposition of a diocesan tax (c. 1263), performance of important acts of administration (c. 1277), naming or removal of the finance officer (c. 494, secs. 1–2), investment of money and moveable goods assigned to an endowment (c. 1305), and commuting of wills (c. 1310, sec. 2). The bishop must hear, listen to, or consult the college of consultors regarding the performance of important acts of administration (c. 1277) and the naming or removal of the finance officer (c. 494, secs. 1–2). New to the 1983 code are decisions regarding temporal matters about which a bishop must receive the consent of particular councils and boards prior to acting. He must receive the consent of the finance council and the college of consultors prior to the performance of extraordinary acts of administration (c. 1277) and the alienation of goods within the competency of the bishop (c. 1292, sec. 1).

SOCIAL DOCTRINE PRINCIPLES FOR CHAIRMAN OF BOARDS

Boards are composed of people, and the advice that episcopal councils give to bishops concerns decisions that impact large numbers of families and individuals. Therefore, there exist social consequences, both in the composition and in the advice outcomes, that these councils and boards offer to the local bishop in his decision-making process. To ensure, then, that these councils and boards function in a truly Catholic manner, they have the foundational principles of the church's social doctrine as a guide. While here is not the place for a thorough analysis of the Catholic social doctrine in the context of our topic, we can at least derive from the concepts a few applications for a bishop as chairman of these councils and boards. By moving from the theory of Catholic social doctrine to its practical application, a bishop as chairman of the board illustrates how the church is not just a thought leader but provides a concrete example for others in the world to follow regarding governance of organizations. Here we take the conceptual principles from chapter 4 of the *Compendium of the Social Doctrine of the Church*.[19] While that chapter lists several topics, the relationship among each of them means that one principle cannot stand alone or without the others.

19. Catholic Church, *Compendium of the Social Doctrine*, paras. 160–208 (hereafter cited in text as *CSDC* and by paragraph number).

This chapter of the *Compendium* begins by quoting *Gaudium et Spes* 26 that defines the first principle of the common good as "the sum total of social conditions which allow people, either as groups or as individuals, to reach their fulfillment more fully and more easily" (*CSDC*, 164). The common good is not the simple sum of the particular goods of each subject of a social entity, but rather "the effort to seek the good of others as though it were one's own good" (*CSDC*, 167). The common good is not purely material, nor is it an end in itself. Rather, we seek the common good to attain the ultimate end of our lives: God (*CSDC*, 170). Given the communal nature of striving for the common good, everyone has a responsibility to achieve it (*CSDC*, 166), and "no one is exempt from cooperating, according to each one's possibilities, in attaining it and developing it" (*CSDC*, 167). Nonetheless, the bishop has a particular responsibility of guaranteeing the common good as part of his governing *munera* (*CSDC*, 168), so he depends upon his councils and boards to advise him in this difficult task of maximizing the common good given the scarce resources of the diocese.

A part of enhancing the common good includes a recognition that all goods come from God and are given for our use to help us return to him. This principle of the universal destination of goods "requires a common effort to obtain for every person and for all peoples the conditions necessary for integral development" (*CSDC*, 175). Therefore, the bishop and his boards do well to ask with each decision if anyone is being left out by the approach in question. Further, given that "the right to private property is subordinated to the right to common use" (*CSDC*, 177), the church must lead in the use of private property, most especially land, for the common good (*CSDC*, 180). To carry out these assessments toward maximizing the common good, bishops and their councils and boards need a clear idea of the private property holdings of the diocese and how they are used. Inherent within the question for bishops and boards regarding the use of diocesan resources is taking time to consider the consequences those decisions have so that the diocese benefits and the common good is enhanced (*CSDC*, 178), but that others, most especially the poor and marginalized, are not harmed (*CSDC*, 182).

These deliberations regarding the resources of the diocese may lead to questions of subsidiarity concerning support given to subordinate organizations like deaneries, parishes, and nuclear families in the fulfillment of their duties. The broad authority given to bishops in the governance of the diocese makes centralized and bureaucratic solutions appear noteworthy and feasible, but such ideas often contradict the principle of subsidiarity. The principle of subsidiarity, applied here, requires the bishop and his boards to exercise restraint when an issue does not apply to them, or ask how diocesan resources might be used to help the local-level community in their achievement of the common good and taking proper responsibility for their own reality (*CSDC*, 187). Sometimes the broader-level institution must temporarily substitute itself in the place of the local-level institution in an effort to establish equality, justice, and peace, but such interventions should not last longer than necessary (*CSDC*, 188).

When the bishop and his councils and boards practice subsidiarity, it implies real participation on the part of everyone toward the common good (*CSDC*, 189). The bishop ought to expect, and at times insist upon, the participation of the representative members of the councils and boards. At the same time, while participation often takes place through representation found on councils and boards, modern technology allows for greater participation beyond the representatives to include each individual of the whole.

The true and authentic participation of everyone, either as a whole or through representatives on councils and boards, builds solidarity. Solidarity is a social principle and a moral virtue that determines the order of institutions and how the individuals and people at the various levels depend upon one another (*CSDC*, 193). This interdependence of all relationships between the bishop and the people entrusted to his care heightens the roles of councils and boards that strive for unity, such that bishops and the members of the various councils and boards might give of themselves, not for a personal special interest, but for the greater common good (*CSDC*, 194).

To live these goals of common good, universal destination of goods, subsidiarity, participation, and solidarity requires open, honest, and engaging dialogue between the bishop and those who serve on boards, and then communication of the results of those conversations, where applicable, to the wider public. Those who serve on boards help the bishop discover the truth of the situation at hand and what is necessary for resolution (*CSDC*, 198). Whether the issue be a change in the diocesan tax considered by the presbyteral council and its effects on large and small parishes, suspicion of professional misconduct by a pastor investigated by a review board, or the sale of a parish building deliberated by the college of consultors, to arrive at the truth demands that bishops and board members are dutifully bonded together in solidarity in the free pursuit of truth and justice by expressing freely at board meetings what is upright and just while refusing anything immoral (*CSDC*, 199, 200). The bishop and his councils and boards' search for commutative, distributive, and legal justice should not take a reductionist vision of merely fulfilling a contract, but a wider horizon that includes solidarity and love (*CSDC*, 203). Love becomes the governing principle for bishops and boards, for "it is from the inner wellspring of love that the values of truth, freedom and justice are born and grow" (*CSDC*, 205).

BOARDSOURCE ON CHAIRMAN OF NONPROFIT BOARDS

The National Center for Nonprofit Boards, now known as BoardSource, has over thirty-five years of nonprofit governance experience by way of consultations, products, and services. Among their many publications is a book by Mindy R. Wertheimer that suggests best practices for nonprofit board chairs in fulfilling their role of service for the organization.[20] The fulfillment of the responsibilities and the effectiveness of a board ultimately falls upon the chairman. Therefore, Wertheimer developed her applicable points for board chairmen specifically based upon the duties of a board generally as described in Richard Ingram's book *Ten Basic Responsibilities of Nonprofit Boards*.[21] To one extent or another, every board determines the mission and purposes of the organization, selects the chief executive, supports and evaluates the chief executive, ensures effective planning, monitors and strengthens programs and services, ensures adequate financial resources, protects assets and provides financial oversight, builds a competent board, ensures legal and ethical integrity, and enhances the organization's public standing.

Wertheimer divides the qualities of a board chair into two broad categories of the *how* of exhibiting leadership and the *what* of executing governance duties (*BCH*, 12–15). The *how* of exhibiting leadership consists of personal qualities of being genuine, approachable, and humble. The chair encourages open communication within the group by his own example of first being a good listener and skilled communicator who sees himself as a student and a teacher. The chair seeks to learn as much as he can from the board during their discussions. Nonetheless, the chair also guides the board in its deliberations and instructs it when he believes its members have veered off the course of the mission. The leadership of the chair means that he develops and engages board members in best governance practices. When the board experiences success, the chair leads in celebrating their achievements. Along with all the board members, the chair demonstrates a true passion for the mission, values, and service of the organization. The chair also upholds legal and ethical standards of conduct, ensures that board members and management speak with one voice in the community, and

20. Wertheimer, *Board Chair Handbook* (hereafter cited in text as *BCH*).

21. Ingram, *Ten Basic Responsibilities*.

champions adequate transparency, compliance, and accountability for the organization's operations.

The *what* of executing governance duties for the board chair begins with the hiring, monitoring, and evaluation of the chief executive. The chair functions as the primary contact for board members and ensures that they fulfill their governance duties of care, loyalty, and obedience. The chair presides at all meetings, develops meeting agendas, and assures a working communication structure among the board, committees, and task forces. The chair keeps the board focused on its primary governance work of assessing organizational alignment with its mission, crafting a strategic plan, evaluating programs within the context of the strategic plan, overseeing the fiscal operation, ensuring legal and ethical compliance, and safeguarding against risk. As the community ambassador for the organization, the chair cultivates relationships with community stakeholders and donors in personal and group settings.

The best board chairs combine all of the leadership qualities listed above for the good of the organization (*BCH*, 17). Nonetheless, no board chair has the fullness of all of these leadership qualities. Therefore, the board chair may opt to seek out training to improve in certain areas or delegate certain tasks to other board members who are more suited for that work. Recognizing that every organization has its challenges, the board chair identifies and embraces whatever arises without micromanaging the management team.

As far as his interactions with board members, the board chair sets the standard of engagement in terms of duty of care, loyalty to the organization, and obedience to the mission. A board chair must care about the organization by staying informed, asking questions, reading all meeting materials ahead of time, exercising judgment, and participating in board discussions. The board chair serves in the interest and loyalty of the organization, not himself. Finally, the board chair obeys the organization's mission by safeguarding contributions from extraneous expenses or waste and verifying regulatory and reporting compliance standards (*BCH*, 20). The formal orientation of new board members provides a forum during which the chair can establish these clear expectations (*BCH*, 22).

In addition to the interactions with the board, the board chair maintains a healthy relationship with the chief executive by seeing their collaboration through the lens of good governance practices (*BCH*, 27–28, 33). Good governance means that, from the beginning, explicit expectations for the mutual roles and responsibilities along with regular meetings of clear communication take place. To ensure a productive partnership for the long term, the relationship needs to be assessed with a willingness to have the courage to make changes where necessary (*BCH*, 33).

In his interactions with the board and management, the board chair listens effectively by giving his full attention to the person speaking and then asking open-ended questions that begin with "*what*" or "*how*" to find shared meaning (*BCH*, 35–37). Such questions elicit expansive answers that give more details to the questions and issues at hand. Empathy functions as a useful tool for the board chair to encourage more participation and open dialogue with everyone (*BCH*, 40–41). By demonstrating that he understands the points raised by board members, the chair shows that he listens attentively to everything being said. To resolve misperceptions, divergent opinions, points not addressed, or to challenge someone who is not listening effectively, the board chair has the power to use confrontation to bring about a healthy, generative conversation (*BCH*, 41–42). Examples of using confrontation for a generative conversation would be to define the opposing opinions and seek to understand how those different ideas arose, call upon someone who is not paying attention in a meeting to stay focused, and ask silent board members what issues have not yet been addressed.

The board chair takes responsibility for the ongoing development of the board and board members. Specifically, this duty means that the board chair takes an active involvement in identifying potential board members, orientating new board members, sustaining ongoing board members in their roles, and preserving a relationship with outgoing board members (*BCH*, 48). Each of these tasks requires extensive cultivation of personal relationships with each board member, which may come about through individual meetings, training sessions, board retreats, board self-assessment exercises, and delegation (*BCH*, 53–54). Board chairs must also address individual or group issues that arise from time to time (*BCH*, 55–59).

To ensure that boards and the organizations they govern do not become stagnant, Wertheimer recommends using the generative thinking model of Richard Chait, William P. Ryan, and Barbara E. Taylor.[22] This structure begins by pinpointing signals that indicate a need for change, analyzes those issues from a variety of organizational perspectives, and uses past experience to predict the future.[23] The following questions are suggested to initiate generative discussions: What keeps you awake at night about the organization? What are we missing in this discussion? How can we frame this situation differently? What best explains our recent successes? Our setbacks? What headline would we most/least like to see about the

22. Chait et al., *Governance as Leadership*.

23. Chait et al., *Governance as Leadership*, 85–88.

organization? What is the biggest gap between what the organization claims it is and what it actually is? How do we incorporate the organization's core values in our work? What is the best possible outcome? The worst-case scenario? How would we operate differently as a for-profit organization? If you were on the board of a competing organization, what would you do to most effectively compete against us?[24]

Whether it is ordinary business or because the discussions from using the generative thinking model bring about issues that require decisions, every board needs to have a clear decision-making process. A common method that allows the use of all the leadership skills presented above is finding the facts about the situation at hand, analyzing the data or information, brainstorming potential options, devising a clear action plan with who is responsible for each part and metrics for desired outcomes of each point, and agreeing on a feedback loop of follow-up and evaluation (*BCH*, 163–66).

To assist the decision-making process, one of the most important roles of the board chair is the crafting and execution of a meeting agenda. Meeting agendas will have information items, discussion items, and action items (*BCH*, 69). To go through agendas more efficiently during the meeting itself, and to avoid wasting time listening to numerous reports and not dedicate sufficient time to quality discussion, one best practice is the use of the consent agenda. The consent agenda combines all of the informational items in a series of written reports and promulgates the contents prior to the meeting. Examples of consent agenda material often include previous board meeting minutes, meeting agenda, report from the chief executive, reports from all committees and task forces, routine correspondence, and information about special events. Board chairs must hold accountable fellow board members and staff for reading the consent agenda prior to the meeting itself.

In addition to the practical tasks described above, the board chair is responsible for organizational issues of a more global nature. Board chairs confirm adequate communication among the board, committees, and staff (*BCH*, 76–78). Board chairs take the lead but also engage fellow board members in resource development, most especially soliciting contributions for the organization (*BCH*, 79–82). While not needing to be an expert in finance, the board chair must verify ample transparency and fiscal oversight of the organization as a whole and its programs by way of the finance committee and the board as a whole (*BCH*, 82–84). The board chair collaborates with the chief executive to initiate, monitor, and evaluate strategic

24. Chait et al., *Governance as Leadership*, 123.

and program plans for the organization (*BCH*, 85–90). At least annually, the board chair should conduct a performance evaluation of the chief executive, the board itself, and perhaps each individual member of the board (*BCH*, 91–96).

PRACTICAL CONSIDERATIONS FOR BISHOPS AS EFFECTIVE CHAIRMEN OF BOARDS

The bishop of any diocese in the United States is the chairman of several diocesan councils and boards. The demands placed on him because of this responsibility require that the bishop know at a high level *how* to exhibit leadership and *what* he does to execute governance. Any shortcoming or weakness of the personal qualities of *how* to be an effective chairman can be overcome through training or coaching. Training may be needed in areas, such as learning *Robert's Rules of Order*, to run meetings well.

As for coaching, the coach attends a few meetings and observes the bishop as chairman. Subsequently, he provides the bishop honest feedback on how to improve in this role of chairman, most especially on matters concerning engagement of board members. Coaching presents an opportunity for a lay person experienced in governance to share his or her talents with the local bishop without making the greater commitment of serving on a council or board. A good coach helps the bishop to recognize that, while he is a shepherd at heart, he also governs a very large organization. While the bishop embodies both roles, they are distinct. Clergy seek to help people have an encounter with Jesus Christ, whereas the chairman strives to move an organization forward in completing its mission. Consequently, there is a difference in the attitudinal approach between serving as a cleric and serving as chairman of the board, and an experienced coach can help the bishop transition from one to the other. Coaching, then, improves the bishop and brings about greater productivity from the councils and boards he chairs toward accomplishing the mission of the organization and enhancing the common good.

After taking time to develop himself, the first relationship that the bishop, as chairman of the council or board, will want to foster is with those he has chosen to fulfill the executive role on behalf of the bishop such as the vicar general, episcopal vicars, or directors of diocesan ministries. The relationship between the bishop and those who hold these episcopal appointments does not hold a perfect analogy to the nonprofit arrangement where the chair and executive are two separate persons with distinct responsibilities. In an ecclesial context, the bishop maintains his executive role while serving as chairman of councils and boards, but the bishop may delegate the actual execution of the decisions he makes to those whom he chooses. Given the fact that the bishop maintains his authority as executive such that the person acting does so in the name of the bishop, regular meetings between the bishop and those he delegates to execute his decisions have an even more indispensable value relative to the nonprofit structure at building solidarity; regular meetings ensure clear communication and unambiguous expectations while respecting subsidiarity. The frequency of those meetings will vary depending upon the role or ministry in question. The bishop may choose to meet weekly, or more frequently, with his vicar general, particularly when the latter executes decisions made in conjunction with the presbyteral council or college of consultors. The canonical finance officer of the diocese, directors of chancery offices, deans of ecclesiastical faculties, presidents or principals of Catholic schools, and other diocesan-level personnel most likely also meet monthly, if not more frequently, with the bishop, depending upon the circumstances. These conversations inevitably include an update of ongoing affairs, recap the previous council or board meeting, run down progress on action items from those previous meetings, and prepare the consent and the discussion agenda for the forthcoming meetings.

An ongoing part of the bishop's evaluation of each of his councils and boards includes consideration of the composition of these bodies. The best councils and boards provide representative advice that achieves solidarity among the different constituencies while maximizing the common good. The absence of someone from a particular culture, expertise, age, or geographical location may merit the bishop seeking out an additional board member. The priests of the diocese and development officer may suggest names to cultivate relationships for this purpose.

As for the composition of the presbyteral council, historically, all the priests of the diocese participated in their regular meetings. While it may not be practical for the entire presbyterate of a diocese to meet regularly for reasons of geography and size of the group, the bishop might use annual convocations or other meetings where the entire presbyterate is present to seek counsel on important decisions. Particularly in light of the recent Catholic Project survey that concludes that most priests do not trust their bishop,[25] the bishop may continue meeting with the presbyteral council but expand the methods of participation so that every priest has a voice regarding certain issues. Digital forms and surveys allow for easy solicitation,

25. Catholic University of America, "Catholic Project."

compilation, and analysis of the entire presbyterate on certain questions along with feedback on the results.

Whether board composition has stayed the same or radically changed from year to year, organizing an annual orientation or retreat provides a forum for the bishop to make certain that every member, especially new ones, understands the expectations of engagement from them. Orientation or retreat encounters also give the bishop the opportunity to teach the members about the mission of the church, his vision for the diocese, and the principles found in Catholic social doctrine. Within this framework, the bishop then assures the board members that he genuinely seeks their advice based upon their experience and expertise. The bishop has appointed these specific people to teach and advise him in the decisions he must make as the chief shepherd of the local flock. The bishop, then, sees these appointed members as part of his governance team. The bishop may wish to say something like the following: "I attend council and board meetings to learn from all of you the best way I might teach, sanctify, and govern this diocese toward the fulfillment of our mission and vision. I may make the final decision, but we are a team." With this level of solidarity coming from the bishop, the members of councils and boards become energized and want to participate in future meetings as they witness their advice, suggestions, and ideas being executed by their ordinary.

As for the *what* of executing governance, everything begins and ends with the council or board meetings themselves. At the center of the immediate preparation prior to council or board meetings is the bishop fulfilling his responsibility for crafting the agendas in conjunction with the executives. As noted above, a good practice is to divide the agenda into information, discussion, and action items. To avoid spending unnecessary time on information items, the bishop, as chairman, should ensure that the members receive the consent agenda no later than one week in advance of the meeting. To achieve this goal, all minutes, reports, and suggested agenda items must be submitted to the bishop between eight and fourteen calendar days prior to the meeting to allow for collation and distribution. For those councils and boards that the bishop chairs which are consultative, an ideal meeting spends the greatest amount of time engaging in generative discussions of the most important topics to help the bishop make the best decision, and the agenda should reflect that priority. For those councils and boards that the bishop chairs which have a fiduciary responsibility, an ideal meeting gives ample time to generative discussions, but first dedicates sufficient time for evaluation and feedback of the issues at hand, diocesan ministries, or specific programs under the purview of that council or board.

At the meetings themselves, the bishop as chairman needs to make sure that someone takes good minutes of the meeting, paying particular attention to action items, who is responsible to complete those action items, and by what date. The bishop also maximizes participation and efficiency as he applies some standard procedure, such as *Robert's Rules of Order*, to run the meeting. The bishop also sticks to the agenda of information, discussion, and action items, and holds to a decision-making process as described in the preceding section treating secular boards. Using *Robert's Rules of Order*, or another practice, keeps meetings on task and saves them from becoming chaotic. Adhering to the agenda means that information and discussion items may lead to action items, but not necessarily at that meeting itself. If time is not pressing, and to give adequate discernment of Catholic social doctrine to each of the steps of the decision-making process, a good custom for councils and boards would be to address at one meeting the information and discussion items and then decide at a future meeting on the action items related to that information and discussion. In other words, information and discussion of a generative nature takes place during one meeting, but no vote on an action item related to that information and discussion takes place until the next meeting. Action items that the council or board votes on should include a clear statement of who is responsible to complete the task and how the council or board will evaluate the progress. If that does not happen, the decision gets easily lost and forgotten. For consultative agenda items, like the ones that dominate the agenda of presbyteral council meetings, the bishop should never feel pressured into making decisions during the meeting. The bishop always has the right to conclude discussion by thanking the participants and then announcing that he will make his final decision in the future.

At the meetings, the most important part for the bishop is the discussion agenda. During this phase, the bishop learns the most about his diocese, priests, and people as he asks generative questions like those listed in the previous section and those that incorporate Catholic social doctrine such as the following: How would Jesus apply Catholic social doctrine to this situation? Given the facts, how do we address this issue by enhancing the common good of the presbyterate or people of the diocese? How can we as a presbyterate live greater solidarity? How can we use diocesan resources to preach the Gospel more effectively and contribute more to the common good? How can we use church property to contribute more to the common good? What do we have that we do not use to preach the Gospel and contribute more to the common good? What do we need to do to make sure that no one is being left out by this approach? How might someone or a group be hurt by this decision? What would the devil like us to do, and how do we keep ourselves from doing that? How might diocesan resources be used to help local-level communities in their achievement of the common good? How in truth, freedom, and justice do we love in this situation?

The bishop as chairman seeks everyone's participation in honest dialogue before the group rather than in private, side conversations outside of the meeting. Therefore, the bishop may need to call upon quiet members or use the speaking limits suggested by *Robert's Rules of Order* to keep talkative members in check.

After a meeting, the bishop as chairman ensures that the minutes are communicated to all the members as soon as possible. It is a small task, but it bolsters solidarity among the members. Also, the minutes become the basis of the next meeting's information, discussion, and action agenda items within the context of the decision-making process. The bishop does well to take a moment to evaluate the meeting and consider the ongoing development of himself and the council or board in terms of effectiveness, efficiency, composition, and engagement. Successes should be applauded at the next meeting, and areas which require improvement ought to be addressed.

Given all the above, the role of chairman demands assistance from more than one person. The best chairman has a highly competent, detail-oriented secretary who orchestrates communication regarding the agenda, reports, and minutes so that the operation of the council or board runs smoothly. In the case of a bishop, he also has at his disposal the vicar general, vicar for clergy, moderator of the curia, and episcopal vicars to help bear the administrative burden on behalf of the bishop. These lieutenants carry the bulk of the load so that the bishop has adequate time to discern the best possible decision that maximizes the common good for the people of his diocese.

CONCLUSION

The church has always recognized that the decisions made by bishops carry such weighty consequences that they should not be made without seeking advice from councils. Canon law now enshrines the use of councils and boards and even mandates bishops to seek consultation prior to making specific decisions. Given the ever more complex world in which we live, a bishop, now more than ever, does well to form competent and expert teams of councils and boards steeped in Catholic social doctrine and then to solicit recommendations and direction from them to help him make good decisions that enhance the common good and ultimately lead to the salvation of souls. As a bishop does that, he fulfills his mission of governing his diocese in the role as chairman of the board.

BIBLIOGRAPHY

Ayrinhac, H. A. *Constitution of the Church in the New Code of Canon Law*. New York: Longmans, Green, 1930.

Benedict. *RB 1980: The Rule of St. Benedict in Latin and English with Notes and Thematic Index*. Abridged edition. Edited by Timothy Fry et al. Collegeville, MN: Liturgical, 1981.

Catholic Church. *Code of Canon Law, Latin-English Edition*. Washington, DC: Canon Law Society of America, 1983.

———. *Compendium of the Social Doctrine of the Church*. Washington, DC: United States Conference of Catholic Bishops, 2004.

Catholic University of America. "The Catholic Project: National Study of Catholic Priests." October 19, 2022. The Catholic Project. https://catholicproject.catholic.edu/national-study-of-catholic-priests/.

Chait, Richard, et al. *Governance as Leadership: Reframing the Work of Nonprofit Boards*. Hoboken, NJ: John Wiley & Sons, 2005.

Congregation for Bishops. *Directory for the Pastoral Ministry of Bishops: Apostolorum Successores*. Vatican City: Libreria Editrice Vaticana, 2004.

Coulter, Gary. "The Presbyterium of the Diocese." *Homiletic & Pastoral Review*, 105 (April 2005) 8–12.

Cyprian. *The Letters of St. Cyprian*. Translated by G. W. Clarke. Ancient Christian Writers 1. New York: Newman, 1984.

Gasparri, Pietro, ed. *Codex Iuris Canonici Pii X Pontificis Maximi Iussu Digestus, Benedicti Papae XV Auctoritate Promulgatus*. Westminster, MD: Newman, 1957.

Ignatius of Antioch. *To the Magnesians*. Edited by J. Quasten and J. C. Plumpe. Translated by James Kleist. Ancient Christian Writers 1. Westminster, MD: Newman Bookshop, 1946.

Ingram, Richard T. *Ten Basic Responsibilities of Nonprofit Boards*. 2nd ed. Governance Series 1. Washington, DC: BoardSource, 2009.

Klekotka, P. J. "Diocesan Consultors." *Canon Law Studies* 8 (1920) 17.

Purcell, J. W. "The Institute of the Senate of Priests." *The Jurist* 38 (1978) 136–37.

Robert, Henry M., et al. *Robert's Rules of Order Newly Revised*. New York: Public Affairs, 2020.

Sacred Congregation for the Clergy. "Presbyteri Sacra." *Acta Apostolicae Sedis* 62 (1970) 459–65.

Second Vatican Council. *Christus Dominus*. In *Vatican Council II: The Basic Sixteen Documents: Constitutions, Decrees, Declarations*, edited by Austin Flannery, 283–316. Northport, NY: Costello, 1996.

———. *Ecclesiae Sanctae*. In *Vatican Council II: The Conciliar and Post Conciliar Documents*, edited by Austin Flannery, 624–33. Northport, NY: Costello, 1984.

———. *Presbyterorum Ordinis*. In *Vatican Council II: The Basic Sixteen Documents: Constitutions, Decrees, Declarations*, edited by Austin Flannery, 317–64. Northport, NY: Costello, 1996.

———. *Sacrosanctum Concilium*. In *Vatican Council II: The Basic Sixteen Documents: Constitutions, Decrees, Declarations*, edited by Austin Flannery, 117–62. Northport, NY: Costello, 1996.

Souvay, Charles. "Sanhedrin." In *The Catholic Encyclopedia*. New York: Robert Appleton, 1912. http://www.newadvent.org/cathen/13444a.htm.

Synod of Bishops. "Ultimis Temporibus." *Acta Apostolicae Sedis* 63 (1971) 897–922.

United States Conference of Catholic Bishops. *Promise to Protect, Pledge to Heal: Charter for the Protection of Children and Young People: Statement of Episcopal Commitment*, rev. ed. Washington, DC: United States Conference of Catholic Bishops, 2018.

Wertheimer, Mindy R. *The Board Chair Handbook*. 3rd ed. Washington, DC: BoardSource, 2013.

Judging the Twelve Tribes of Israel

The Episcopacy and the Kingdom of God

—Matthew C. Genung

In the Gospel according to Luke, during the Last Supper discourse (Luke 22:24–38), Jesus confers a kingdom on the apostles in which they are seated upon thrones judging the twelve tribes of Israel (Luke 22:29–30). In its teaching on the *munera* of the local bishop, *Lumen Gentium* refers to the Lukan Last Supper discourse in order to indicate the way in which he is to exercise his authority, although not drawing on the verses under consideration in this essay. Instead, the council fathers refer to Luke 22:26–27 in which the Lord insists upon table *diakonia* as the model for ecclesial governance.[1] Rather than focusing on the humble service of church leadership, the verses under consideration in this essay highlight the activity of apostolic judgment taking place in the context of eating and drinking at the Lord's table in his kingdom while seated on thrones (v. 30). Perhaps it is not surprising that the council fathers ignored these verses because partaking at table with Jesus and sharing in his regal activity of judgment seem out of step with the previous statements describing the way of the church leader who, rather than reclining at table, is a humble table servant. More surprising, however, may be that these verses are not used in any magisterial documents at least since Vatican I, whether pertaining to the exercise of ecclesial ministry or not.[2] Nonetheless, this dominical teaching as recounted by Luke,[3] and the

1. Second Vatican Council, *Lumen Gentium*, sec. 27.

2. De Mey, "Authority in the Church," 307–23.

3. The "same" dominical teaching is found in Matt 19:28, although in a different literary context and with slight but highly significant formal differences. For form- and literary-critical discussion of these texts, see especially Dupont, "Le logion des douze

way in which he narrates its accomplishment in the early days of the church, should be instructive for the needs of governing the church today.

This essay will study the dominical proclamation in Luke 22:29–30 and the way in which Luke portrays the beginning of its fulfillment in the Acts of the Apostles.[4] Specifically, following the narrative thread in Luke-Acts, we will reflect upon the conditions for the establishment of the apostles in this office, the type of activity constitutive of this judging, the criteria to be used, and its aims. Our objective is to show that the instructions of the resurrected Lord to his apostles during the final commission (Luke 24:44–48) indicate the way in which it is intended to be carried out. Two examples from the Acts of the Apostles will provide evidence of this intention on the part of the evangelist. The conditions for its continuation will be shown in the dominical imitation indicated by the Lord himself in its institution. It is hoped that this reflection will shed some light on the episcopal ministry relevant for the church today.

TABLE SERVICE AS ECCLESIAL AUTHORITY

During the Lukan Last Supper, after the institution of the eucharistic meal and Jesus's announcement that one of the Twelve (at table with him) would betray him, the topic devolved into a contentious dispute about who among them is recognized to be the greatest (22:24).[5] From this rivalry comes the teaching on ecclesial leadership as humble *diakonia* rather than domination as exerted by "the kings of the nations" (22:25–27). The discussion is about the greatest among them *in the kingdom*, based upon the immediate context (vv. 16–18, which refer to the eschatological kingdom; and v. 25, which refers to the kingdoms of the world). On the one hand, as the council fathers affirm, leadership in Jesus's kingdom *must* be humble service, antithetical to the type of rule wielded among the nations.[6] It is also characterized as the way of authority exemplified by and shared with the service of Jesus. The

trônes," 355–92; also Nelson, *Leadership and Discipleship*.

4. For a comprehensive study of the question of the literary relationship of the Gospel of Luke and Acts of the Apostles, see Backhaus, *Das lukanische Doppelwerk*, 240. Whatever its redactional history, we adhere to the judgment that the canonical Gospel of Luke and Acts of the Apostles consist in a redactional composition resulting in a two-volume literary unit intended to be read as such.

5. Φιλονεικία (philoneikia), literally "love of victory," is rivalry or contentiousness. Here it describes the nature of the conversation as intensely competitive in a negative way. On this term's usage in vice lists, see Wolter, *Gospel According to Luke*, 468.

6. Γινέσθω (ginesthō), a present imperative verb, indicates that this is not a suggestion but rather an attitude that must be maintained at all times.

institution of the apostles as judges is built upon this teaching in the verses which follow.

EATING AND DRINKING AS SHARING IN AUTHORITY

In Luke 22:29–30, Jesus establishes the apostles as participants in the exercise of his authority in his kingdom. This thesis seems easy enough to defend based upon the syntax of the verses and the lexicography of thrones and judging. In our view, the English translation that best conveys the linguistic modalities of the Greek is the following:[7] "And I confer a kingship on you, just as my father conferred one on me, such that you eat and drink at my table in my kingdom and sit upon thrones judging the twelve tribes of Israel" (Luke 22:29–30).[8]

Jesus confers a kingship on the apostles *with the purpose that* they eat and drink with him and sit on thrones of judgment in his kingdom.[9] Exegetical questions concerning the meaning of the thrones and judging the twelve tribes are discussed below. The immediate question regards the meaning of the segment of the clause announcing that the apostles will be eating and drinking at the Lord's table. The majority of authors consider this to be a promise for an eschatological reward to be enjoyed only at the consummation of the world and the Last Judgment of the living and the

7. Biblical translations are the author's own. Translations of Old Testament texts are based on Elliger and Rudolph, *Biblia Hebraica Stuttgartensia*, and New Testament texts are from Aland et al., *Novum Testamentum Graece*. References to the Septuagint (hereafter LXX) are from Rahlfs and Hanhart, *Septuaginta*.

8. Some important nuances arising from the tense and mood of the Greek are difficult to convey in a simple English translation. Verse 29 is the main clause while v. 30 is subordinate, and provides the purpose of the main action. Bear in mind that in the main clause, the present indicative διατίθεμαι (diatithemai) "I confer" is an instantaneous present, indicating that the action is effected at the moment the words are spoken; the kingship is conferred when Jesus utters the words rather than at some unspecified future time. See Wallace, *Greek Grammar beyond the Basics*, 517. The purpose of the main action is indicated in the ἵνα (hina) (purpose) clause. See Wallace, *Greek Grammar beyond the Basics*, 473. The verbs ἔσθητε (esthēte) "that you eat" and πίνητε (pinēte) "that you drink" are present subjunctive, while καθήσεσθε (kathēsesthe) "that you sit" is a future subjunctive. These tenses are equivalent in a final clause, such that the future tense does not indicate future time but communicates the purpose of the main action. The present tense of these subjunctives indicates that the action is habitual, so that the eating, drinking, and sitting are not individual, punctiliar events, but are customary. See Wallace, *Greek Grammar beyond the Basics*, 521; Blass and Debrunner, *Greek Grammar*, sec. 369.

9. On βασιλεία (basileia) as "kingship" rather than "kingdom," see Joüon, "Notes philologiques sur les évangiles," 355.

dead at the end of time.[10] But, it will be argued here, the biblical context favors a different interpretation, one which corresponds more closely to the throne theme in the second part of the clause, and coheres more fully with the narrative themes and plot. In short, eating and drinking at the table of the Lord belongs to the institution of the apostles as participants in Jesus's regal authority in the church.

EATING AND DRINKING IN LUKE

First let us consider the theme of eating and drinking in some biblical texts. Luke contains more episodes of Jesus sharing meals with sinners, tax collectors, and leaders of the people than the other Gospels do.[11] These meal scenes, as well as parables utilizing the banquet motif, prefigure and illuminate the eschatological banquet in order to show characteristics of the kingdom and conditions for entering it. These passages do not touch on the theme of leadership in the kingdom of God.[12] As such, they do not shed much light on the interpretation of Luke 22:28–30.

EATING AND DRINKING AT SINAI

A more profitable context, based on formal as well as thematic connections, is the meal shared on Mount Sinai in the sight of God by Moses, Aaron, Nadab, Abihu, and seventy elders of Israel (Exod 24:9–11): "Moses went up, as did Aaron, Nadab, Abihu and seventy elders of Israel, and they saw the God of Israel. Beneath his feet was like sapphire tilework as clear as the heavens. Yet he did not extend his hand against the leaders of the Israelites. They beheld God, and they ate and drank." The theme of establishment of the authority of the elders in Exod 24:9–11 becomes more apparent when it is read in light of Num 11:11–30. Especially relevant are Num 11:17b and 25, where Yhwh commands Moses to gather seventy of the elders at the tent of meeting to put them into prophetic service: "I will take some of the spirit that is on you and confer it on them so that they share in the burden

10. Authors include Marguerat, *Le jugement*, 460–72; Bovon, *Luke 3*, 174–75; Wolter, *Gospel According to Luke*, 473. See Nelson, *Leadership and Discipleship*, 224n21 for an extensive bibliography listing authors of the two positions, as well as his arguments in favor of an end-of-time interpretation.

11. For a list and brief discussion, see Nelson, *Leadership and Discipleship*, 62n56, 62n57.

12. See Heil, *Meal Scenes in Luke-Acts*, esp. 311; Esposito, *Jesus' Meals with Pharisees*, esp. 351–55.

of the people with you. . . . And Yhwh came down in the cloud and spoke to him, he took some of the spirit that was on him and gave it upon seventy of the elders. The spirit rested upon them and they prophesied."[13] In Exod 24, Moses summons Aaron, his sons, and the elders to partake in a divine vision and meal before the Lord in order that they are sanctioned to share in Moses's mediatorial role between Yhwh and his people, an appointment which is confirmed in Num 11, with the intention that the elders share in Moses's burden. His burden is to communicate divine revelation and to adjudicate cases so that the people live in conformity with his teaching or Torah, and thereby enjoy either the covenant blessing or its curses for those who disobey. The most salient point here is that Moses and his auxiliaries share a vision of Yhwh and a meal before him without suffering death or injury, which indicates a close relationship with Yhwh for whom they are entrusted to carry out the most sensitive of charges.[14]

Covenant Authority and the Kingdom

As in Luke, this meal takes place after the establishment of the covenant. At Sinai the covenant was ratified in Exod 24:3–8 with the erection of twelve pillars, the sacrifice, writing and reading the book of the covenant, and the dispersion of blood. Moses "poured the blood of the covenant on the altar and on the people, proclaiming that this is the blood of the covenant which Yhwh has established with you upon all of these words" (Exod 24:8). This formulation is echoed by Jesus in Luke's institution narrative where the covenant established at Sinai is recalled: "This cup is the new covenant in my blood, which will be shed for you" (Luke 22:20b).[15]

In addition, the covenant in both texts pertains to the establishment of the kingdom of God. The Exodus meal scene concludes the covenant pericope that began with the promise of becoming a "kingdom of God"

13. On this text, see Cocco, *Sulla cattedra di Mosè*, 149–203.

14. On this text and support for the thesis of the meal and vision of Exod 24:11, see Ska, "Vision and Meal," 165–83.

15. Exodus 24:8 LXX reads τὸ αἷμα τῆς διαθήκης (to haima tēs diathēkēs), "the blood of the covenant"; Luke 22:20 reads ἡ καινὴ διαθήκη ἐν τῷ αἵματί μου (hē kainē diathēkē en tō haimati mou), "the new covenant in my blood." On the parallels between these texts, see Fitzmyer, *Gospel According to Luke*, 1402. Luke's version also recalls the new covenant of Jer 31:31, which itself refers back to the covenant at Sinai. On the nature of the covenant formula in Exod 19–24, especially on the end of the Sinai pericope, see McCarthy, *Treaty and Covenant*, 243–76; Nicholson, "Covenant Ritual in Exodus 24:3," 874–86.

(Exod 19–24).[16] The covenant formulary begins with an offer: "If you keep my covenant . . . you shall be to me a kingdom of priests" (Exod 19:5–6).[17] The kingdom theme similarly underlies the Lukan narrative.[18] The apostles are to eat and drink with Jesus in his kingdom, the kingdom which he is conferring upon them (v. 29).[19]

A view that includes the Acts of the Apostles shows the fulfillment of this promise beginning within the Lukan narrative: "God raised this one on the third day and made him visible, not to all the people, but to us, the witnesses previously appointed by God, we who ate and drank with him after he rose from the dead" (Acts 10:40–41). This passage discloses details of events that occurred between Easter and Passover, filling in some gaps left open in the narrative exposition related in Acts 1:3: "To them he presented himself alive, after his suffering, by many proofs over forty days, appearing to them and speaking about things pertaining to the kingdom of God." Like Exod 24:11, these texts insist both upon the divine vision and the meal the selected collaborators shared together: "appearing to them" (1:3), "made him visible to us . . . we who ate and drank with him" (10:40–41).

Naturally, the summary account of the resurrection appearances of Jesus to the apostles (Acts 1:2) is laconic. No specifics are provided to the reader about the kingdom of God. This is a narrative exposition, and so only that information needed in order for the plot to be correctly followed is

16. The beginning of the episode in which Yhwh summons Moses with Aaron, his sons, and the elders to the mountain precedes the covenant conclusion ceremony, while the execution of the command and the meal comes after. For an explanation of this complexity, see Ska, "From History Writing," 160–64.

17. The Hebrew construction rendered into English as "you shall be to me" indicates possession. In this context, the kingdom that Israel will become belongs to God. The further sense of the kingdom of God as one which is ruled by God is also clear in the book of Exodus, where the main problem involves the question of whom Israel will serve. Israel is to serve God alone, as he is king. On the meaning of "kingdom of priests," and a concise history of its interpretation with extensive bibliography, see Ska, "Exodus 19:3–6," 147–53.

18. The root βασιλευς (basileus) is repeated five times in this short passage: Luke 22:16, 18, 25, 29, 30.

19. Even here the covenant language is evident because the term translated here as "confer" is from the lemma διατίθημι (diatithēmi), which means to establish a covenant. It is a cognate with διαθήκη (diathēkē), the term for covenant. The LXX has eighty-six instances of the verb, of which all except four or five refer to the establishment of a covenant (διαθήκη [diathēkē]), usually between Yhwh and Israel. The word is rare in the New Testament, occurring seven times including Luke 22:29. In all other instances, it refers to the establishment of a covenant or to a last will and testament.

provided to the reader.[20] In this case, the reader of Acts is directed to search for meaning as it pertains to the kingdom theme.

To highlight its importance, let us note that the final dialogue between the apostles and the resurrected Lord immediately before his ascension is on precisely this same topic. The characters themselves inquire about the restoration of the kingdom: "Lord, are you going to restore the kingdom to Israel at this time?" (Acts 1:6). The term we translate as "restore," ἀποκαθίστημι (apokathistēmi), is uncommon in the New Testament and is a technical term used in prophetic literature in oracles promising the restoration of Israel to the land (cf. Hos 11:11; Jer 15:19, 16:15, 23:8, 24:6, 27:19). Malachi 3:23 uses this term to describe the mission of the coming Elijah, and in reference to this prophecy, it is taken up in Mark 9:12 and Matt 17:11 during the discussion between Jesus and three apostles descending from the Mount of Transfiguration. In Acts it is used in the latter sense of fulfillment. As such, the employment of this term by Luke colors the topic with messianic overtones. This is a strong indication that the fundamental question in Acts pertains to the kingdom and its restoration to Israel as fulfillment of divine promises recounted in the Scriptures.

Although Jesus's response is ambiguous about the timing of this restoration, he is eminently clear about the role of his apostles in its regard: they are to be his "witnesses in Jerusalem, all Judea and Samaria, and to the end of the earth" (Acts 1:8). We will need to determine if the role of witness is linked to their establishment in authority of Luke 24:30, or if it needs to be understood as an independent responsibility, a task undertaken below. However, first let us see how the narrative answers the disciples'—and the readers'—question about the restoration of the kingdom to Israel.

In Acts 10:40–41, when the reader learns that the apostles did in fact already eat and drink with the Lord, some gaps from Acts 1 are correctly filled, and the reader is aware that what was prepared in Luke 22:30—namely, that they will eat and drink with the Lord in his kingdom—had begun to be realized. The reader knows that the restoration of the kingdom is underway. It is reasonable to conclude, based on Luke 22:28, that the apostles should therefore be acting as judges.

In short, these three texts, when read together, show Jesus's institution of the apostles as leaders in his kingdom (Luke 22:28–30), the restoration of which has begun to be carried out in Acts (Acts 1:3; 10:40–41). Comparing these texts with Exodus, where the vision of God and the meal signifies the establishment of Aaron, his sons, and the elders as those who will share

20. On gaps as a narrative technique and their relevance, see Sternberg, *Poetics of Biblical Narrative*, esp. 235–37.

authority with Moses and will continue to exercise authority in Israel after Moses has gone, Luke 22:28–30 similarly recounts Jesus's establishment of the apostles with his authority in his kingdom.

JUDGING THE TWELVE TRIBES OF ISRAEL IN ACTS

If the dominical intention for the apostles eating and drinking at the Lord's table in this kingdom refers to their establishment as participants in his authority, sitting upon thrones judging the twelve tribes of Israel indicates the nature and scope of this office. Nonetheless, some questions remain. What type of judging are the apostles doing, and which Israel is being judged? These questions are treated in order.

The meaning of the verb κρίνειν (krinein) "to judge" can be understood from the milieu of the court, where it indicates the act of rendering a judgment, guilty or innocent, according to the law and the facts of the case. In this setting, the objective is normally to condemn or to acquit. The biblical sense of the term is often more broad, frequently including the act of governing more generally.[21] This does not exclude the juridical sense, but encompasses it.

Most authors interpret Luke 22:30 to signify this latter sense of governing more generally, for a variety of reasons.[22] For one, according to the New Testament texts, the role of judging in the juridical sense of a final judgment remains the responsibility of Jesus. This is clear according to texts which refer to the Last Judgment in Acts (Acts 10:42, 17:31; cf. Matt 25:34). Therefore, it appears less likely that Luke 22:30 intends to confer this specific act of judgment on the apostles. Furthermore, a survey of passages referring to thrones in the New Testament shows that this motif refers to the exercise of power more broadly.[23] This is also the case in some Old Testament texts that show affinity with the Lukan passage. Psalm 122:4–5 is the only Old Testament text that refers both to thrones (plural) and to tribes together: "For there the tribes go up, the tribes of Yhwh; a witness to Israel, to give thanks to the name of Yhwh. For there are seated the thrones of justice, the thrones of the house of David." In this psalm, the tribes go up to Jerusalem, the city

21. Κρίνειν (krinein) in the LXX translates שפט (špṭ), which more often than not has the sense of judging, although it has the sense of governing in approximately 30 percent of the cases. For further analysis, see Büchsel, "κρίνω," 921–41.

22. See, among others, Marguerat, *Le jugement*, 460–72.

23. Regarding the throne of David as metaphor for his rule, see Luke 1:32; Acts 2:30. For divine authority, see Acts 7:29; Col 1:16; Heb 1:8; among others. On the contrary, Dupont sees a strict judicial meaning here. See Dupont, "Le logion des douze trônes," 389. For him, Israel will be judged by the persecuted apostles.

in which Israel can trust due to the righteous ruling which takes place there. The subsequent verses indicate that the thrones of justice of the house of David secure peace and prosperity for Israel. If Luke is recalling this psalm, as is suggested by several authors, the meaning of judgment undertaken by the apostles in the kingdom is broader than a tribunal milieu and would include the concept of beneficent governance in general.[24]

Psalm 132:12 is also instructive in the interpretation of the throne motif. It refers to the Davidic covenantal promises that ensure that, should his sons faithfully observe the covenant stipulations, they shall sit on his throne forever, assuring the Lord's blessings of prosperity, salvation, and security from enemies. Psalm 72, where the king's righteous judgment redounds to prosperity for the people, should be added in this regard. The same is the case for the messianic king of Isa 11:1–5. Each of these texts shows that justice linked to the royal throne in the Bible goes beyond discrete judgments in the tribunal and foresees the goods that result from the righteous royal judgment in the general sense of regal governance. The goods promised in these texts are nothing more than examples of covenant blessings.

A third argument arises from the Gospel context. Jesus had already given the Twelve authority over demons, diseases, and to announce the kingdom of God (see Luke 9:1–6). Although these activities correspond to the powerful works of Jesus carried out throughout the Gospel of Luke, he did not otherwise specify that they are also to participate in his authority as final judge.

One final argument from philology may be added. As was noted above, the subjunctive and future verbs in the final clause of Luke 22:30 indicate habitual, rather than punctiliar, action.[25] The same is true of the term κρίνοντες (krinontes) "judging," a present participle that also indicates habitual action rather than a single, punctiliar act. From this linguistic perspective, it is clear that the judging to be undertaken by the apostles is integral with their authority in the kingdom, not a single act to be undertaken at the end of time.

YOU ARE WITNESSES OF THESE THINGS

If this assessment seems reasonable based on the biblical antecedents, it needs to be shown by the Lukan narrative continuation. Luke 22:30 is the

24. This is the interpretation of Fitzmyer, *Gospel According to Luke*, 1419; followed by Bovon, *Luke* 3, 176n54. Cf. 1 Sam 8:20; Isa 16:5; and Dan 9:12 where this same sense is seen. For more examples, see Büchsel, "κρίνω," 921–41.

25. See note 8 above.

only passage in Luke-Acts where the apostles are said to be seated upon thrones judging.[26] When the resurrected Lord commissions the apostles in Luke-Acts, he does not use the vocabulary of judging, but instead commissions the apostles as witnesses (Luke 24:48; Acts 1:8). Is it enough to indicate that witness terminology is, strictly speaking, one that also belongs to the milieu of the tribunal?[27] It is true that a witness is not the judge; however, the witness is necessary for a juridical procedure that accords with the law and the facts of the case. This is precisely what the apostles are commissioned to do upon receipt of the gift of the Holy Spirit, and which they immediately undertake on Pentecost.[28] Two examples of the speeches in Acts in which the apostles exercise this mission will show that the witness mission is where the apostles fulfill their authoritative roles conferred upon them beginning at the Last Supper.

Peter's Witness on Pentecost

Peter is the first to exercise this ministry. He does so on Pentecost.[29] His speech comes in two parts, each as a reaction to a statement of the Jews gathered together as a crowd. The first part (Acts 2:14–36) is given in response to the inquiry about the meaning of the phenomena experienced by the crowd, namely, hearing Galileans speaking in the diversity of their languages. Peter explains the phenomenon by quoting, alluding to, and interpreting several biblical passages. The first is Joel 3:1–5. From the context, this passage is fulfilled in the Pentecost event of the outpouring of the Spirit. Peter's explanation indicates that the prophecy is also fulfilled in Jesus's passion. His quotation of Pss 16:8–11 and 110:1 and allusion to 2 Sam 7:12 and Ps 132:11 indicate, based on Scripture and the life of Jesus, that God revealed his identity as Lord and Davidic Messiah. This revelation is now known with certainty.

26. Cf. the parallel text in Matt 19:28.

27. On the etymology and use of nominal and verbal forms of μαρτυς (martys) in biblical and non-biblical texts, see Strathmann, "μάρτυς, μαρτυρέω, μαρτυρία, μαρτύριον," 474–504.

28. Nearly 20 percent of New Testament witness terminology is found in Acts. Verbal and nominal forms from the root μαρτυς (martys) number 207 in the Greek New Testament according to the following distribution: Matt 12x; Mark 11x; Luke 9x; John 48x; Acts 39x; Paul 35x; Hebrews 13x; Pastorals 21x; Revelation 19x. Johannine literature contains by far the greatest usage at 84x. The distribution of the term in Luke-Acts (48x) with only 9 in Luke, the fewest occurrences among the Gospels, is thus very significant.

29. In this speech, Peter refers to himself and the other apostles as witnesses in Acts 2:32, and the narrator characterizes his speech with the same term in 2:40.

In the course of his speech, Peter interprets both the events surrounding the life, passion, and resurrection of Jesus by adverting to Scripture, and at the same time, interprets those same Scriptures based on the new revelation in Jesus's paschal mystery. He presents a case showing that despite what God had done—proving who Jesus is by powers, wonders, and signs (repeating vocabulary of Joel)—these men knowingly killed Jesus by having him crucified by lawless men. In his presentation of the facts, both from Scripture and from their experience, he solemnly accuses them of a capital crime, which is not only the unjust death sentence of Jesus but also the rejection of God.

The second part of Peter's speech (Acts 2:38–39) is a response to the positive reception on the part of the crowds to the first part of his speech. It consists in two imperatives: "repent (μετανοήσατε [metanoēsate]) and be baptized," followed by the consequences of the forgiveness of sins and receipt of the gift of the Holy Spirit. This part of his speech is also justified with allusions to Scripture, namely, the same passage of Joel 3:5.[30]

Some takeaways from this speech can now be assessed. First, it is addressed in an explicit manner to Israel as the people of God. The various terminology used throughout the speech indicates this important point: "Judeans, and all Jerusalem residents" (Acts 2:14), "Israelites" (v. 22), "brothers" (v. 29), and finally "the whole house of Israel" (v. 36).[31] The recipients of Peter's teaching and judgment are the people Israel as a totality, with whom Peter and the Eleven are in a covenantal relationship of brotherhood.[32] The addressees of Peter's speech are identical with the twelve tribes of Israel of Luke 22:30.

Second, Peter is exhorting them to open their minds to understand the meaning of what has been revealed in Christ with proofs from the Scriptures. The speech of Peter begins with two imperatives: "Let it be known to

30. Commentators also see Isa 57:19 here.

31. The πᾶς οἶκος Ισραηλ (pas oikos Israēl), *whole house of Israel* is not a common syntagma in the LXX (Septuagint), found only 6x, but *house of Israel*, οἶκος Ισραηλ (oikos Israēl) is much more common: 50x in the LXX. *The whole house of Israel*, כָּל־בֵּית יִשְׂרָאֵל (kol-bêṯ yiśrā'ēl) is a very common designation for Israel in the Hebrew Bible: 112x in MT (Masoretic Text). In most texts, it is a technical term referring to Israel as a people in its entirety. See for example in Exod 40:38, referring to all of Israel arrayed around the Lord in the tabernacle; Ezek 37:11, in the oracle of the dry bones, used to designate all of Israel dispersed in exile, about to be gathered together into the land. For οἶκος Ισραηλ (oikos Israēl), *house of Israel*, in parallel with the *tribes of Israel*, see Amos 3:1 and Ezek 45:8.

32. For the Old Testament usage of "brother" as covenantal terminology, see Priest, "Covenant of Brothers," 400–406. For New Testament usage, see Matt 12:46–50; 1 Cor 5:11; among others. For its use in Acts, see Fitzmyer, *Acts of the Apostles*, 222.

you, listen to what I say" (Acts 2:14). Peter is authoritatively proclaiming something new that does not comport with their understanding: "For it is not as you suppose, that these people are drunk . . . on the contrary this is what was spoken through the prophet" (v. 16). In Luke 24:44–48, Luke recounts the commissioning of the apostles as witnesses, which Jesus does by first opening their minds to understand the Scriptures (v. 45). The fundamental meaning of the Scriptures now given to them becomes the content and the purpose of the witness to be given by the apostles, namely that (1) the Messiah must suffer and rise from the dead; (2) repentance (μετάνοιαν [metanoian]) in his name for the forgiveness of sins is to be proclaimed to all the nations, beginning from Jerusalem; (3) all of which is in fulfillment of the law of Moses, the Prophets, and the Psalms, i.e., the whole of Scripture. Peter is using the Scriptures to show that what has happened to Jesus is both *in* fulfillment of the divine plan and *for* the fulfillment of the divine plan. The authority given to Peter is being utilized and is achieving the ends as intended by Jesus in Luke 24:44–48.

Third, by quoting the text of Joel, the speech exhibits important elements of the prophetic *rîb*, a type of juridical procedure whose aim is reconciliation rather than condemnation.[33] The text cited from Joel follows upon the prophet's call to Israel to repent and return to Yhwh and to the observance of his covenant after having broken it. It includes a warning of judgment, using the language of the Day of Yhwh, on which the judgment of the people will take place, lest the people "rend their hearts" and return to the Lord who will show mercy and forgive them (Joel 2:12–13). The metaphor called for, the rending of hearts, is a gesture symbolic of penitence or sorrow for the committed infraction, which assumes recognition of the truthfulness of the prophetic accusal, and a desire for forgiveness and reconciliation. The positive consequence in Joel 3:1–5a, quoted in Acts, is the result of the people's adherence to the prophetic call, and their "return to the Lord."[34] Peter omits the second part of Joel 3:5 in which it is stated that only a remnant will survive and be summoned to Jerusalem. The reaction of the crowd to Peter's speech—"they were pierced to the heart" (Acts 2:37)—indicates that, having returned to the Lord, they belong to this remnant.[35]

33. On this juridical procedure in general, see Bovati, *Ristabilire la giustizia*. On the formulation "rend your hearts" as a request for pardon in the context of the prophetic *rîb*, see p. 125. For an abridged, English translation of Bovati's work, see *Re-Establishing Justice*.

34. The text is quoted with some adaptations. On the form of Joel 3:1–5 in Acts 2:16–21, see Kilpatrick, "Some Quotations in Acts," 81–83.

35. Based on the context, it seems reasonable that the term κατενύγησαν (katenygēsan) indicates a typological relationship with Joel 2:13, but one cannot be

Further on, Acts 2:40 recounts the closing exhortation of Peter's speech in summary fashion: "Be saved from this crooked generation." "Be saved" once again recalls Joel 3:5. The phrase "crooked generation" alludes to Deut 32:5, where the same term refers to the people of Israel who rebelled against Yhwh in idolatry and were therefore subjected to the covenant curses. A distinction is drawn between those who belong to the community gathered around the Twelve, which, according to what was just said, are like the remnant in Joel, and those who reject the Lord, referred to as "this crooked generation" warned against in Deuteronomy. Peter's speech is a type of judgment pronounced against those of Israel who are rejecting the Lord. The result of Peter's speech is the beginning of the restoration of Israel in which some are saved by the acceptance of the apostles' witness while others are not. This is constitutive of the prophetic *rîb*.

Peter's speech is followed by the first of a series of summary reports recounting the effects of the speeches and narratives in which Peter and the others bear witness to the Lord. These summaries show the development of ecclesial life, focusing on the great fellowship and benefits enjoyed by all those who turn back to the Lord and join the church.[36] This is based on communal dedication to the apostolic teaching, the breaking of the bread, prayer, and radical sharing of property and possessions. Acts 4:34 recounts that "there was no one needy among them," recalling Deut 15:4, which promises the same to Israel in the land, conditioned upon Israel's adherence to the covenant Torah. This promise is fulfilled in the new community of believers, about to be designated "*ekklesia*," church (Acts 5:11).

Peter's witness to Israel in Jerusalem then consists in a typical juridical procedure in which an accusation of covenant violation is made, with the intention that the guilty party concedes and repents, returns to the Lord, and the covenant relationship is reestablished.

sure; it is difficult to interpret because this lemma is a *hapax legomenon* in the New Testament and is not the same term as found in LXX Joel 2:13 (διαρρήξατε [diarrēxate]), nor is it otherwise a translation of MT קרע (qrʿ). In all six instances of the lemma in the LXX, the usage is metaphorical, as here, and often refers to being humbled, rebuked, or silenced. This would comport with the Joel context. For the New Testament usage of related terms, in John 19:34 it refers to the soldiers piercing Jesus's side, and in Romans 11:8 (κατάνυξις [katanyxis], a *hapax legomenon* in the whole Bible) it is a description of the stupefied hardened heart, referring to Deut 29:3; Isa 6:9; 29:10. The reaction is the opposite in Acts, where their hearts were open to the reception of Peter's message.

36. The major summaries are Acts 2:42–47; 4:32–35; and 5:12–16. On these texts, see Noorda, "Scene and Summary," 475–83; Fitzmyer, *Acts of the Apostles*, 97–98.

Paul's Witness to the Synagogue in Antioch

Paul's address in Pisidian Antioch (Acts 13:16–42) exhibits several parallels to Peter's Pentecost speech.[37] First, his addressees are Jews belonging to the local synagogue, whom he refers to as "fellow Israelites and others who are God-fearing" (v. 16), and as "descendants of Abraham, and those God fearers among you" (v. 26). Here we see the similarity to the addressees of Peter's speech, but the audience includes a group of nonethnic Jews who are either proselytes or connected to the synagogue with the Jews in some way.[38]

In his address, Paul presents a synthesis of salvation history beginning with the election of the patriarchs down to John the Baptist, and like Peter, interprets these events by quoting and alluding to the Scriptures, proclaiming Jesus to be the fulfillment of the divine plan and of the promises.[39] Paul refers to this as "the message of salvation" which has been sent to "us," referring to the descendants of Abraham as well as those God-fearers among them (Acts 13:26).

Like Peter, Paul also accuses the inhabitants and leaders of Jerusalem of having unjustly condemned Jesus to death. That they "failed to recognize Jesus" is interpreted and expressed as fulfilling the prophets (v. 27). His account is concluded with a stern warning to his interlocutors. In the final exhortation, Paul admonishes them to remain steadfast in the grace of God which they had begun to accept. Their refusal to believe would fulfill the prophetic threat of Hab 1:5, putting them in the same position as the inhabitants of Jerusalem who, in infidelity to God, condemned Jesus. Acts 13:44–47 recounts the events of the following Sabbath when the synagogue reconvenes. Because "the whole city" gathered to hear "the word of the Lord," the Jews who had previously been receptive to the message return and reject Paul's message they had received the week before, thereby fulfilling the warning from the previous week. Paul and Barnabas interpret this rejection as fulfillment of the divine word, and thereby pronounce a judgment: "You judge yourselves unworthy of eternal life" (v. 46). Like Peter, Paul authoritatively interprets the Scriptures in the light of the revelation of Jesus Christ (Luke 24:44–49) in witnessing to Israel, a witness which, in this

37. Luke-Acts is noted for its employment of the rhetorical figure of comparison, or *synkrisis*. See Aletti, *Il racconto come teologia*, 71–103.

38. God-fearers refers to the Gentiles living in their community and worshiping Yhwh with the Jews, adhering to a portion of the Mosaic law.

39. Paul's speech uses some of the same as well as different biblical texts than are found in Peter's: 1 Sam 13:14; 16:12–13; 2 Sam 7:14; 1 Kgs 2:10; Pss 2:7; 16:10; 89:20–21; Isa 11:1; 55:3; Hab 1:5.

case, highlights the rejection rather than acceptance of the message and its aftereffects.

The consequential move by Paul is to "turn to the Gentiles."[40] This is motivated by the interpretation of Isa 49:6 as a divine command to them: "I have set you as a light to the nations, for you to be for the salvation to the ends of the earth" (v. 47). The summary result of this proclamation consists in (1) the glorification of God on the part of the Gentiles, (2) the reception of their message in faith by an undistinguished group of "all those who have been designated for eternal life," (3) the continuing movement of the "word of the Lord" throughout the whole region, and (4) the persecution and expulsion of Paul and Barnabas from the region (vv. 48–49). The interplay of acceptance and rejection alludes to Jesus's public ministry, but more immediately, moves his program forward: "You will be my witnesses . . . to the ends of the earth" (Acts 1:8). Paul, like Peter, is empowered to interpret the Scriptures and the signs of the times to recognize the divine command given to him, which he faithfully follows.

These two exemplary texts of speeches from Acts of the Apostles show that the witness mission of the resurrected Lord to the apostles is one which belongs to the *rîb*, a particular type of juridical procedure known in Israel especially in the Prophets. The fundamental operations undertaken in these speeches are to testify to the resurrection of Jesus and to proclaim its meaning through an empowered interpretation of the Scriptures. Having established the truth of Jesus, the accusation against Israel for breach of covenant is made, with the hope for repentance and reconciliation, which is referred to as salvation, and comes in the form of integration in the life of the church. Paul's speech highlights the two alternatives: either the message of salvation is accepted, which brings life to those who receive it, or it is rejected, which brings separation to those who reject it.

Certainly there are other examples that show this same pattern in Acts. In fact, the book ends with the Jews rejecting Paul in Rome and the proclamation that the Gentiles will accept his message, which they do (Acts 28:28–31). Further examples of judging undertaken by the apostles in Acts could be added to those considered here. Peter's death sentence to Ananias and Sapphira in Acts 5:1–11, Peter's judgment of the reception of the Holy Spirit by Cornelius and the Gentiles in Acts 10–11, the apostles' judgment about the role of the Law in the church in Acts 15 are some important examples. Regardless of the type of judging these other passages exemplify, it seems clear that the proclamation of Jesus to the apostles about their role

40. The verb is in the present tense, indicating a durative action rather than a one-time event.

sharing in his authority in the kingdom during the Last Supper not only begins to be exercised in Acts but is of the essence of the way that the life and growth of the church is narrated. The way in which it is exercised remains of fundamental importance for the church today.

YOU ARE THE ONES

If we may be permitted one final point, the condition upon which Jesus confers the kingship on the apostles in Luke strikes us as somewhat strange: "You are the ones who have remained with me in my trials" (Luke 22:28). The verb is in the perfect tense. It seems strange because in the immediate context the disciples seem to misunderstand the meaning of discipleship, warranting Jesus's correction (vv. 24–27), and in the immediate situation they are about to be sifted by Satan. This is foreseen by Jesus in the following discourse with Peter, in vv. 31–34. Despite these weaknesses and failures, throughout the Gospel of Luke the apostles are presented in a much more favorable light than they are in Mark.[41] This favorable picture continues during Jesus's arrest and the remainder of the Lukan Passion narrative. For example, whereas Mark recounts that the disciples all fled at the arrest of Jesus (Mark 14:50), Luke omits that detail, and instead, immediately recounts that Peter followed Jesus from a distance to the house of the high priest (Luke 22:54). Mark indicates only that the women from Galilee stood by watching while Jesus is crucified (Mark 14:40–41), while Luke reports the presence of his disciples as well (Luke 24:49).[42] Because of this, despite their present failures, it can be understood that the apostles have indeed remained with Jesus in his trials.

Acts presents an improved picture of the faithful abiding of the apostles. Each of them, in the course of their bearing witness to Jesus, undergoes similar trials to that faced by Jesus during his ministry, and they do not waver in confronting these trials. They remain steadfast in fidelity to God as they proclaim his Gospel. Some bear witness in their death; others, in prisons and in trials, defending themselves against unjust accusations, against various types of violence and general hardships encountered in the course of setting out and proclaiming the truth.

To stand by Jesus in his trials means to enter into the trials faced amidst being his witness and to persevere in them in the course of governing in his

41. For examples of the improved characterization of the apostles vis-à-vis Mark during Jesus's ministry, see Brown, *Apostasy and Perseverance*, esp. 57–62.

42. For further examples and an evaluation, see Brown, *Apostasy and Perseverance*, 68–69.

kingdom. Rather than a reward, the conferral of Jesus's kingship, eating, drinking, and judging with Jesus, comes with a share in the cross. To govern with Jesus means to suffer with Jesus. From this perspective, it seems clear that the table *diakonia* insisted upon by Jesus in Luke 22:25–27 and eating and drinking with Jesus at his table in his kingdom (v. 30) are inverse sides of the same coin.

BIBLIOGRAPHY

Aland, Barbara, et al., eds. *Novum Testamentum Graece*. 28th rev. ed. Stuttgart: Deutsche Bibelgesellschaft, 2012.

Aletti, Jean-Noël. *Il racconto come teologia: Studio narrativo del terzo vangelo e del libro degli Atti Degli Apostoli*, 1st ed. con aggiunte. Bologna: Centro Editoriale Dehoniano, 2009.

Backhaus, Knut. *Das lukanische Doppelwerk: Zur literarischen Basis frühchristlicher Geschichtsdeutung*. Beihefte zur Zeitschrift für die neutestamentliche Wissenschaft. Berlin: De Gruyter, 2022.

Blass, F., and A. Debrunner, eds. *A Greek Grammar of the New Testament and Other Early Christian Literature*. Chicago: University of Chicago Press, 1961.

Bovati, Pietro. *Re-Establishing Justice: Legal Terms, Concepts and Procedures in the Hebrew Bible*. Translated by Michael J. Smith. Journal for the Study of the Old Testament Supplement Series 105. Sheffield, UK: JSOT, 1994.

———. *Ristabilire la giustizia*. 2nd ed. Analecta Biblica 110. Roma: Editrice Pontificio Istituto Biblico, 2005.

Bovon, François. *Luke 3: A Commentary on the Gospel of Luke 19:28—24:53*. Edited by Helmut Koester. Translated by James Crouch. Hermeneia: A Critical and Historical Commentary on the Bible. Minneapolis: Fortress, 2012.

Brown, Schuyler. *Apostasy and Perseverance in the Theology of Luke*. Analecta Biblica 36. Rome: Pontifical Biblical Institute, 1969.

Büchsel, Friedrich. "κρίνω." In *Theological Dictionary of the New Testament*, vol. 3, edited by Gerhard Kittel, translated by Geoffrey W. Bromiley, 921–41. Grand Rapids: Eerdmans, 2006.

Cocco, Francesco. *Sulla cattedra di Mosè: La legittimazione del potere nell'Israele post-esilico (Nm 11; 16)*. Bologna: Centro Editoriale Dehoniano, 2007.

De Mey, Peter. "Authority in the Church: The Appeal to Luke 22,21–34 in Roman Catholic Magisterial Teaching and in the Ecumenical Dialogue." In *Luke and His Readers: Festschrift A. Denaux*, edited by R. Bieringer et al., 307–23. Bibliotheca Ephemeridum Theologicarum Lovaniensium 182. Leuven: Leuven University Press, 2005.

Dupont, Jacques. "Le logion des douze trônes (Mt 19,28; Lc 22,28–30)." *Biblica* 45.3 (1964) 355–92.

Elliger, Karl, and Wilhelm Rudolph, eds. *Biblia Hebraica Stuttgartensia*. 4th ed. Stuttgart: Deutsche Bibelgesellschaft, 1997.

Esposito, Thomas. *Jesus' Meals with Pharisees and Their Liturgical Roots*. Analecta Biblica 209. Rome: Gregorian and Biblical, 2015.

Fitzmyer, Joseph A. *The Acts of the Apostles*. The Anchor Bible 31. New York: Doubleday, 1998.

———. *The Gospel According to Luke: X-XXIV*. The Anchor Bible 28A. New York: Doubleday, 1985.

Heil, John Paul. *The Meal Scenes in Luke-Acts: An Audience-Oriented Approach*. Society of Biblical Literature Monograph Series. Atlanta: Society of Biblical Literature, 1999.

Joüon, Paul. "Notes philologiques sur les évangiles: Luc 2,31." *Recherches de Science Religieuse* 18 (1928) 345–59.

Kilpatrick, G. D. "Some Quotations in Acts." In *Les Actes des Apôtres: Traditions, redaction, théologie*, edited by J. Kremer, 81–97. Bibliotheca Ephemeridum Theologicarum Lovaniensium 48. Leuven: Leuven University Press, 1979.

Marguerat, Daniel. *Le jugement dans l'Évangile de Matthieu*. 2nd ed. Le Monde de la Bible. Genève: Labor et Fides, 1993.

McCarthy, Dennis J. *Treaty and Covenant: A Study in Form in the Ancient Oriental Documents and in the Old Testament*. 2nd ed. Rome: Biblical Institute, 1978.

Moran, William L. "A Kingdom of Priests." In *The Bible in Current Catholic Thought*, edited by John L. McKenzie, 7–20. New York: Herder, 1962.

Nelson, Peter K. *Leadership and Discipleship: A Study of Luke 22:24–30*. SBL Dissertation Series 138. Atlanta: Scholars, 1994.

Nicholson, Earnest W. "The Covenant Ritual in Exodus 24:3–8." *Vetus Testamentum* 32 (1982) 74–86.

Noorda, Sijbolt J. "Scene and Summary: A Proposal for Reading Acts 4,32—5,16." In *Les Actes des Apôtres: Traditions, redaction, théologie*, edited by J. Kremer, 475–583. Bibliotheca Ephemeridum Theologicarum Lovaniensium 48. Leuven: Leuven University Press, 1979.

Priest, John F. "The Covenant of Brothers." *Journal of Biblical Literature* 84 (1965) 400–406.

Rahlfs, Alfred, and Robert Hanhart, eds. *Septuaginta*. Stuttgart: Deutsche Bibelgesellschaft, 2006.

Second Vatican Council. *Lumen Gentium*. *Acta Apostolicae Sedis* 57 (1965) 5–67.

Ska, Jean-Louis. "Exodus 19:3–6 and the Identity of Post-Exilic Israel." In *The Exegesis of the Pentateuch: Exegetical Studies and Basic Questions*, 147–53. Forschungen zum Alten Testament 66. Tübingen: Mohr Siebeck, 2009.

———. "From History Writing to Library Building: The End of History and the Birth of the Book." In *The Pentateuch as Torah: New Models for Understanding its Promulgation and Acceptance*, edited by Gary N. Knoppers and Bernard M. Levinson, 145–70. Winona Lake, IN: Eisenbrauns, 2007.

———. "Vision and Meal in Exodus 24:11." In *The Exegesis of the Pentateuch: Exegetical Studies and Basic Questions*, 165–83. Forschungen zum Alten Testament 66. Tübingen: Mohr Siebeck, 2009.

Sternberg, Meir. *The Poetics of Biblical Narrative: Ideological Literature and the Drama of Reading*. Bloomington, IN: Indiana University Press, 1985.

Strathmann, Hermann. "μάρτυς, μαρτυρέω, μαρτυρία, μαρτύριον." In *Theological Dictionary of the New Testament*, vol. 4., edited by Gerhard Kittel, translated by Geoffrey W. Bromiley, 474–504. Grand Rapids: Eerdmans, 2006.

Wallace, Daniel B. *Greek Grammar beyond the Basics: An Exegetical Syntax of the New Testament*. Grand Rapids: Zondervan, 1996.

Wolter, Michael. *The Gospel According to Luke*. Vol. 2, *(Luke 9:51–24)*, translated by Wayne Coppins and Christoph Heilig. Waco, TX: Baylor University Press, 2016.

Index

www.ingramcontent.com/pod-product-compliance
Lightning Source LLC
Chambersburg PA
CBHW060336100426
42812CB00003B/1018
* 9 7 9 8 3 8 5 2 1 7 6 9 4 *